AQUINAS' SEARCH FOR WISDOM

. . . being that is in created things cannot be understood except as derived from divine being, just as a proper effect cannot be understood except as derived from its proper cause.

— St. Thomas Aquinas, *De Pot.*, III, 5, ad lm.

CHRISTIAN CULTURE AND PHILOSOPHY SERIES

GENERAL EDITOR
DONALD A. GALLAGHER, PH.D.
PROFESSOR OF PHILOSOPHY
BOSTON COLLEGE

The colophon for the CHRISTIAN CULTURE AND PHILOSOPHY SERIES consists of the Greek letters X and P, symbolizing Christianity, embraced by C, a variant of Σ, representing the Greek word *sophia*.

Aquinas'
SEARCH FOR WISDOM

VERNON J. BOURKE, Ph.D.
Professor of Philosophy
St. Louis University

THE BRUCE PUBLISHING COMPANY
MILWAUKEE

NIHIL OBSTAT:

JOHN E. TWOMEY, S.T.L., PH.D.
Censor deputatus

IMPRIMATUR:

✠ WILLIAM E. COUSINS
Archbishop of Milwaukee
August 10, 1964

Library of Congress Catalog Card Number: 65–12046

MADE IN THE UNITED STATES OF AMERICA

To the memory of the
VERY REVEREND HENRY CARR,
onetime Superior General of the Congregation of St. Basil and founder of the federated University of Toronto, who first introduced me to philosophy and to Aquinas

Foreword

WHEN my *Augustine's Quest of Wisdom* was published, in 1945, Mr. William Bruce suggested that I might then undertake a companion volume on St. Thomas Aquinas. After all, Aquinas had carried on the same quest, almost a thousand years later. I started to gather material for the present doctrinal biography. It soon became evident that the life of Aquinas is much harder to write than that of Augustine. Oddly, we know much more about the fourth-century Father than about the thirteenth-century Doctor. So it has taken me almost twenty years to write the present book. The problem was not that I was gathering too much information, rather, the more I read the so-called sources, the less I had in the way of solid biographical facts. Most of the popular *Lives* of St. Thomas are filled with statements that simply are not true. His father was not a count; his mother was not related to the Hohenstaufen family; he did not come upon a little boy who was trying to put the sea into a hole in the sand; and so on.

The earliest Latin biographies of St. Thomas, written by William of Tocco, Peter Calo, and Bernard Gui between 1318 and 1330, contain precious little information. Aquinas himself wrote nothing autobiographical. Apart from a few lines in chronicles, his contemporaries have said little about him. There are a few documents in which he is briefly mentioned. Actually, the records of the two investigations preceding his canonization contain much data not utilized by Thomas' biographers. All these materials had been edited by the Bollandists in the *Acta Sanctorum* but that edition is very faulty. Father D. Prümmer, O.P., started a new edition of these early *Lives,* and other documents, which began to appear as a supplement to the *Revue Thomiste,* in 1911. At his death, Father M.-H. Laurent, O.P., took over and finished this useful edition of the *Fontes Vitae S. Thomae Aquinatis.* They were offprinted in six fascicles, 1911–1937, but complete sets were hard to obtain. Through the kindness of Father Laurent, I was sent a set of these *Fontes,* in 1949, from the Vatican Library. In 1959, Kenelm Foster, O.P., published an English translation of one of the first *Lives* (Bernard Gui's) plus a selection of other biographical documents, in his *Life of Saint Thomas Aquinas: Biographical Documents*. It is a reliable collection of materials. I have also received much help from the several scholarly studies by Father Angelus Walz, O.P.

In this book, I have tried to give only the facts that can be documented in the life of St. Thomas. Some few stories and legends had to be mentioned, if only to brand them as pious fabrications. I have taken care that no reader will be in doubt as to their character. Where dialogue occurs in this book, it is translated directly from the sources. All quotations in English have been translated by the present writer, except where otherwise indicated in the footnotes.

The plan of presentation is simple: my odd-numbered chapters are concerned with the biography; the even-numbered ones deal with the development of St. Thomas' thought. People who are chiefly interested in the life, but not the philosophy and theology, may prefer to skip every second chapter. I hope they will then go back and read the others, for it is the even-numbered chapters that really tell why Thomas Aquinas was a great man.

It only remains to thank the editors of The Bruce Publishing Company for their forbearance and encouragement to a dilatory writer.

Contents

AQUINAS' SEARCH FOR WISDOM

CHAPTER ONE

Boyhood in Southern Italy

So MANY things enter into the making of a wise man — personal ability, a good education, opportune conditions for growth and expression. Probably no member of the family of Landolfo and Teodora d'Aquino suspected that their youngest son was marked for lasting fame. Certainly no one could have foretold from his antecedents how Tommaso d'Aquino was to achieve that fame.

THE AQUINOS OF ROCCASECCA

The name, Aquinas, is a Renaissance Latin variant of Aquino, a small town in southern Italy which dates back to Roman times. From the ninth century onward, the feudal family which owned and ruled most of Aquino and its environs took the place name as its own. Shortly before 890 a Lombard soldier named Rodiperto appeared in Italian history as the head of the Aquinos. Adenolfo II of Aquino received the title of Count in the tenth century. The third Adenolfo became abbot of the great Benedictine monastery at nearby Montecassino. Thus was established the life pattern of many generations of d'Aquinos: wars, petty politics, and an occasional foray into the realms of ecclesiastical preference.

The original title of Count was lost in 1137 with the death of Landolfo IV d'Aquino. His son, Pandolfo, continued as master of the domain of Aquino but Pandolfo's youngest son, Rinaldo I, moved in the mid-twelfth century to that portion of the family estate situated at Roccasecca. The principal branch of the family continued to be known as the Aquinos of

Acerra, while the junior branch into which Thomas Aquinas was born were the Aquinos of Roccasecca and Montesangiovanni.[1]

Thomas' father, Landolfo, was the son of Aimone I; he seems to have been born during the 1160's. It is difficult to keep the various cousins, uncles, nephews, and so on, distinct because the same names crop up in various branches of the family during each successive generation. In any case, it is clear that Landolfo lived in a fortified castle at the country place which would be Dryrock in English. He raised a large family, possibly more than fourteen children. Landolfo's first marriage probably antedated the thirteenth century: there is a record of 1217 telling how one of his sons, Giacomo, was refused the office of abbot of the canons of the Church of St. Peter Canneto.[2] Since Giacomo could hardly have been the eldest son and must have been at least twenty years of age at that time, it appears that Landolfo was a mature man in 1217. Other older sons of Landolfo, and half brothers of Thomas, were Filippo and possibly Adenolfo.

At some time in the second decade of the thirteenth century, Landolfo took his second wife, Teodora, a young lady from Naples.[3] She and Landolfo had eight or nine children. The boys were Aimone, Rinaldo, Landolfo, and Tommaso who was to become known as Thomas Aquinas. Aimone became a soldier, took part in an expedition of Emperor Frederick II in the Holy Land, was captured and held for ransom on the Island of Cyprus, and was eventually released through the good offices of Pope Gregory IX. This occurred in 1233.[4] Aimone supported the papal cause against the Emperor from this time on. He did not die until late in the 1260's.[5] Rinaldo also served in the Emperor's forces and then, apparently

[1] For further details on the Aquino family, see: F. Scandone, "La vita, la famiglia e la patria di S. Tommaso," in *San Tommaso d'Aquino: Miscellanea storico-artistica* (Roma, 1924), pp. 1–110.

[2] *Documents* II and III, in *Fontes Vitae S. Thomae Aquinatis* (6 vols., ed. D. Prümmer et M.-H. Laurent, Saint-Maximin: *Revue Thomiste,* 1911–1937, hereafter cited as *Fontes*), fasc. VI, 532–535.

[3] William of Tocco, *Vita S. Thomae Aquinatis,* caput 1 (*Fontes,* II, 66): "mater ejus Domina Theodora, tam morum quam genitorum claritate conspicua. . . ." That Teodora was related to the royal Hohenstaufen family is now denied. Cf. F. Pelster, "La famiglia di S. Tommaso," *Civiltà Cattolica,* 74 (1923), 404. See also: A. Walz, *Saint Thomas d'Aquin,* adaptation française par Paul Novarina (Louvain: Publications Universitaires; Paris: Beatrice-Nauwelaerts, 1962), pp. 14–21. This most recent revision of Walz's factual biography will be cited as *Walz-Novarina* (*1962*).

[4] *Doc.* V (*Fontes,* VI, 536–537) is a letter from Pope Gregory IX to the Patriarch of Antioch, requesting that "Haymo de Aquino" be freed.

[5] *Doc.* X (*Fontes,* VI, 541) identifies Marotta as the sister of Aimone; the date is March 23, 1254, so he is still living at this time.

at some time in the 1240's, changed sides and fought with the troops defending the Papal States. He was killed by the Imperial soldiers and came to be regarded as a martyr who had died in defense of his Church.[6] Little is known of the career of Landolfo but it is probable that this brother died young and in less heroic circumstances, for Thomas was convinced that Landolfo had to spend some time in purgatory.[7]

Thomas Aquinas had at least four sisters. Marotta became a Benedictine nun and was confirmed as abbess of the convent of Santa Maria de Capua, in 1254, by Pope Innocent IV. She is identified as the sister of Aimone of Aquino who is now evidently the head of the family. Marotta died about 1259.[8] Another sister was given her mother's name, Teodora, and eventually married Count Roger of San Severino.[9] She lived until 1294, managed her husband's properties after his death, and appealed at least three times to the royal court of Sicily for the restitution of possessions that were allegedly despoiled or stolen.[10] Her son, Thomas, became Count of San Severino and lived to take a prominent part in the celebration of the canonization of his uncle in 1323.[11] Maria, a third sister, married another member of the famous San Severino family, Guglielmo. Their daughter, Catherine, was also active at the time of the canonizing of Thomas Aquinas, and she was probably the source of some of the family legends which William of Tocco included in his early biography of St. Thomas.[12] We know that an unnamed fourth sister was killed by lightning while still a child at Roccasecca.[13] It is possible that there was another full sister, Adelasia, the wife of Count Roger of Aquila. She was evidently a close relative of Thomas Aquinas, for he served as executor of Roger's estate in 1272.[14]

---

[6] Tocco, *Vita*, 44 (*Fontes*, II, 118): "de Domino vero Rainaldo pro fidelitate Ecclesiae morienti sub tyrannide persecutionis Frederici Imperatoris sibi mors computata fuit ad martyrum." See the testimony of Bartholomaeus of Capua to the same effect, *Processus Canonizationis* (*Neapoli*), LXXVIII (*Fontes*, IV, 375).

[7] Tocco, *Vita*, 44 (*Fontes*, II, 118) refers to "fratre suo Landulfo." *Doc.* XXXV (*Fontes*, VI, 592–593) mentions an "Adenulfus de Aquino" along with Aimone.

[8] *Doc.* X (*Fontes*, VI, 541–544) is Pope Innocent IV's approval of the election of Marotta d'Aquino.

[9] Tocco, *Vita*, 37 (*Fontes*, II, 111).

[10] *Doc.* XLVIII (*Fontes*, VI, 649–651).

[11] A certain Friar Bentius, O.P., reported on the festivities to the Master General and noted that the banquets were sumptuous (*mensa etiam copiosa fuit*), one being provided by Thomas of San Severino. (See: *Fontes*, V, 513–518.)

[12] Tocco, *Proc. Can. Neapoli*, LXII (*Fontes*, IV, 350).

[13] Tocco, *Vita*, 2 (*Fontes*, II, 67).

[14] Scandone, "La vita," pp. 67–69, thinks Adelasia was a sister.

Because of the duplication of given names in the various branches of the family and the possibility that there were several children belonging to Landolfo's first marriage, it may be seen why estimates as to the size of Thomas' immediate family vary widely. In any event, Thomas was the youngest boy. His birth occurred at some time between 1220 and 1227. There are no extant records of this event, or of his baptism, and any attempt at a more exact date is an exercise in conjecture. Recent biographers give 1225 as his birth year, simply because William of Tocco wrote, in the *Life* which he assembled shortly before the canonization (A.D. 1323), that Thomas had died in his forty-ninth year.[15] We know that his death took place in 1274. However, Tocco wrote almost a century after his birth, and the inaccuracy of chronological details in medieval lives of the saints is notorious. It has recently been argued that Aquinas must have been at least thirty-five years of age when he received the Paris degree of master in theology in the year 1256. This reasoning would place his birth in 1221, or thereabouts.[16] At the other extreme is the claim of several biographers that Thomas could have been born as late as 1226 or 1227.[17] For the sake of simplicity, we shall use 1225 as the conventionally accepted year of birth.

There is no longer any basis for dispute as to the place of Thomas' birth: it was the family castle at Roccasecca.[18] Various Italian towns have claimed him as a native son but without solid documentary proof. Roccasecca lies on the way between Rome and Naples, roughly at the halfway point. Cassino, so much in the news during World War II, is ten miles to the southeast. In the thirteenth century, as now, two roads connect Rome

[15] "Obiit autem praedictus Doctor anno Domini millesimo ducentesimo septuagesimo quarto . . . anno vero vitae suae XLIX." Tocco, *Vita,* 65 (*Fontes,* II, 138). Bartholomew of Lucca, *Historia Ecclesiastica,* XXIII, 10: "obiit . . . quadragesimum nonum annum suae vitae perficiens, quinquagesimo inchoaret aeternae gloriae jubilaeum."

[16] Cf. G. Abate, "Intorno alla cronologia di S. Tommaso d'Aquino (c. 1220–1274)," *Miscellanea Francescana,* L (1950), 231–247; Henricus de Hervordia, *Liber de rebus memorabilibus sive Chronicon,* ed. A Potthast, Göttingen, 1859, p. 186, says: "1221 Sanctus Thomas de Aquino nascitur." Nicholas of Piperno, a Cistercian from Fossa Nova where Thomas died, said that Thomas appeared to be fifty or sixty years old at his death ("videbatur sibi quod fuerit quinquegenarius vel sexagenarius"), *Proc. Can. Neapoli,* XIX (*Fontes,* IV, 290).

[17] F. Pelster, *Kritische Studien zum Leben und Schriften Alberts des Grossen* (Freiburg i. B., 1920), p. 76; J. J. Berthier, *S. Thomas 'Doctor Communis' Ecclesiae* (Rome, 1914), p. XLI.

[18] Cf. *Walz-Novarina (1962),* p. 16.

and Naples: one (the Via Appia) runs close to the seacoast; the other (the Via Latina) parallels the coast but is about twenty to thirty miles inland. Cassino and Roccasecca are on this inland route.

In relation to thirteenth-century political divisions, Roccasecca was situated in the northern portion of the Kingdom of Sicily, over which the Emperor Frederick II ruled from 1220 to 1250. Not far to the north lay the southern boundaries of the Papal States which were under the direction of Pope Honorius III (1216–1227) and Pope Gregory IX (1227–1241). As a Catholic family subject to the Hohenstaufen Emperor, the position of the Aquinos of Roccasecca was most difficult, for these middle decades of the thirteenth century were one long period of warfare between the imperial and papal armies. Landolfo and his older sons were soldiers and civil officials in the service of the Emperor. In 1220 Landolfo had been named by Frederick II to the position of justiciar of the lands about Roccasecca, Cassino, and Aquino.[19] This territory was known as the "Land of Labor" (*Terra Laboris*) and Landolfo functioned, along with his relative, Thomas I of the Aquinos of Acerra, as governor and judge of this district in the Empire. Apparently Landolfo remained a faithful, though possibly troubled, vassal of Frederick until Landolfo's death in 1243.[20] Thomas' father may have been more than eighty years old when he died.[21]

For the first few years of his life, Thomas Aquinas lived under the care of his mother and nurse at Roccasecca. Local tradition regards a building with Gothic windows, which still stands today, as Aquinas' home. Few authentic details are known concerning Thomas' first years. Recent biographers quite properly take many of the stories told in the fourteenth-century lives as pious fabrications.[22] There is the famous legend[23] that a hermit

---

[19] *Doc.* I (*Fontes,* VI, 532): "Tunc (decembri 1220) apud Sanctum Germanum Landulfus de Aquino, filius domini Aymonis, per imperatorem iustitiarius factus Terre Laboris."

[20] *Doc.* IX (*Fontes,* VI, 541): "IX kal. ianuarii obiit . . . Landulphus de Aquino miles. . . ." The year is not given; *Walz-Novarina* (*1962*), p. 13, date his death December 24, 1243. Certain prisoners of war were committed to Landolfo's care in 1239, so he was living at that time. See *Doc.* VII (*Fontes,* VI, 539).

[21] Cf. *Walz-Novarina* (*1962*), p. 13: "il avait sans doute plus de quatre-vingts ans."

[22] E. Janssens, "Les premiers historiens de la vie de saint Thomas d'Aquin," *Revue Néoscolastique de Philosophie,* XXVI (1924), 474–476.

[23] Catherine of San Severino, niece of Thomas Aquinas, is Tocco's source for this story; see: *Proc. Can. Neapoli,* LXII (*Fontes,* IV, 350). Janssens, *loc. cit.,* suggests that the Aquino women elaborated the legend. Cf. Tocco, *Vita,* 1 (*Fontes,* II, 66–67).

bearing the suspicious name, Brother Bonus, came to Teodora during her confinement and greeted her with these familiar words:

> Rejoice, O Lady, for thou art with child and thou shalt bear a son whom thou shalt name Thomas; and with thy husband thou shalt plan to make him a monk in the monastery of Montecassino, where the body of blessed Benedict lies. Thou shalt be in hopes of attaining the great revenues of this monastery, through his advancement to the eminence of the prelacy. But God will ordain otherwise, for he will be a brother in the Order of Preachers, so renowned in science and of such sanctity in his life that, in his time, it will be impossible to find his peer in the world.

Teodora's alleged reply is equally familiar: "I am not worthy to bear such a son; may God carry out the pleasure of His will!"

This parody of the Angelic Salutation has every appearance of being a prophecy after the fact. Among other things, it might be noted that in the early 1220's the Dominican Order was just getting established and was by no means renowned for the scholarship of its members.

Another story, however, about Thomas' infancy contains the sort of details that might be remembered by the women of the Aquino family in the fourteenth century, when it was first recorded.[24] While Thomas was still small enough to be carried by his nurse, his mother took him to Naples for a visit — possibly because Roccasecca was in the area where fighting was going on.[25] One day in Naples, Teodora and the nurse took Thomas to the public baths. When his nurse put the baby in a place where he could sit in the bathing establishment, little Thomas found a piece of paper and held it tightly in his hand. The nurse noticed that Thomas cried when she tried to remove the paper, so she bathed him and took him home, still clutching the paper. Later, Teodora opened his tiny fist and discovered the Hail Mary written on the paper. From that time on, according to the story, the nurse would give him the paper to pacify him, whenever the baby cried. Irrespective of whether this incident prefigures Thomas' eventual devotion to the Virgin Mary, the little story does suggest that he was a normal baby.

On another occasion, when Thomas was still young enough to sleep with his nurse, a terrifying storm hit the castle at Roccasecca. Lightning struck one of the towers where the children slept. A little sister of Thomas' was killed but he was not harmed. Like any concerned mother, Teodora

[24] Tocco, *Vita,* 3 (*Fontes,* II, 68).
[25] Scandone, "La vita," p. 80.

rushed to his bed and found him and the nurse quite safe.[26] The rural character of the establishment is indicated by the fact that it is also carefully recorded that some horses were killed in the stables.

We may suppose that, with the exception of the visit to Naples, Thomas spent most of his time as a little boy in the care of his mother and nurse within the confines of the walled estate at Roccasecca. Doubtless he saw his brothers occasionally practicing the arts of war but it is possible that they and his father were away much of the time on civil or military duties. All that his early biographers say is that his parents brought him up with all due care.

It was probably in his fifth year that Thomas was sent to study at the nearby Benedictine monastery of Montecassino.[27] It is not clear whether he was entered as an oblate (with the intention on the part of his father that Thomas would continue in the normal course of events to become a Benedictine monk), or whether he was sent as a lay student simply to acquire the rudiments of learning with the Benedictines. More probably his parents actually enrolled him as a beginner in the religious life of the monastery. Certainly the later attitude of his family and the reports that his parents hoped that Thomas might eventually become the abbot of Montecassino lend credence to the conclusion that he was formally entered as an oblate at this time.[28]

If Thomas became an oblate at about the age of five, then this means that his father made a simple promise for his son to live the life of a Benedictine and to be educated according to the Rule of St. Benedict. This promise to God, made at the entry of a child into religious life, is quite different from the solemn vow of a more mature monk. It did not mean that Thomas had to remain forever in the monastery, or in religious life. If he persevered, then on reaching the age of full discretion he was free to decide of his own volition whether to continue or to leave. It was not too unusual for boys to begin the religious life in this way. As a mature theologian, Thomas Aquinas often discussed the advisability of admitting

---

[26] Tocco, *Vita,* 2 (*Fontes,* II, 67); Peter Calo, *Vita S. Thomae Aquinatis,* 2 (*Fontes,* I, 18) tells the same story. On most points the early *Lives,* by Tocco, Peter Calo, and Bernard Gui, do not differ on the basic data.

[27] Tocco, *Vita,* 4 (*Fontes,* II, 69): "et quinquennem ad monasterium praedictum montis Cassini per nutricem cum bono societate transmittunt."

[28] T. Leccisotti, "Il Dottore Angelico a Montecassino," *Rivista di Filosofia Neo-scolastica,* XXXII (1940) 522, strongly argues that Thomas was a Benedictine oblate.

young boys to the monastic life.[29] The Dominicans ordinarily required their candidates to be more mature and to have some education before they entered. Aquinas carefully explains the difference between a simple and a solemn vow, insists that young children cannot take solemn vows, and so cannot become professed religious, but he clearly maintains that they can be entered in a monastery by their parents for the sake of being introduced to the religious life. At no point in these discussions does Thomas refer to his own experience; as always, his writing is quite impersonal and gives no help to the biographer.

Of course it is impossible to determine the exact year in which Thomas Aquinas began his studies with the Benedictines at Montecassino. As we have seen, it could have been at any time from 1226 to 1232. If his entry occurred in 1231, as many biographers seem to think, then Thomas was received during the abbacy of one of his distant male relatives, Landolfo Sinnibaldo. This man was the head of the ancient monastery from 1227 to 1236.[30] He appears to have been a nephew of the other Thomas of Aquino (of Acerra).[31]

The fact that Abbot Landolfo played some part in historical events of this period may be of assistance in determining the chronology of Aquinas' early studies. Landolfo Sinnibaldo had gone to Rome in 1228 for his ordination as a priest. (Perhaps it is unnecessary to remind the reader that he could have been a professed monk without being a priest.) At that time, Pope Gregory IX named Landolfo Sinnibaldo as papal ambassador to the court of Emperor Frederick II. If the Abbot's mission was to arrange a peace, he was not immediately successful. There was still sporadic fighting between the papal and imperial armies; Frederick's forces occupied several places around Montecassino and the monastery was fortified as a stronghold for the Emperor's troops. The peace of San Germano brought hostilities to a temporary close in the year 1230.[32] Since it is unlikely that Thomas' father would send his son to Montecassino in a period when it was the scene of bitter fighting, it is quite probable that young Thomas

---

[29] S. Thomae, *Contra pestiferam doctrinam retrahentium homines a religionis ingressu,* c. 3 et c. 12 ad finem; *Quaestiones Quodlibetales,* q. V, art. 11; *Summa Theologiae,* II–II, q. 189, art. 2 et 5.

[30] I. Inguanez, *Cronologia degli Abati Casinesi del secolo XIII* (Montecassino, 1929), p. 421.

[31] *Walz-Novarina* (*1962*), p. 24.

[32] Cf. C. J. H. Hayes and M. W. Baldwin, *History of Europe* (New York: Macmillan, 1949), I, 284.

went to the monastery after a truce had been secured. A document dated May 3, 1231, records the donation by Landolfo d'Aquino of two mills for the support of the monks at Montecassino. The same record mentions that Landolfo had previously given twenty ounces of gold for the building and repair fund at the monastery.[33] No mention is made of young Thomas but these gifts may have been connected with his entry. In the absence of more concrete evidence, 1231 may be taken as the date of this event.

Tocco reports that Thomas made the short journey from Roccasecca to Montecassino in the charge of his nurse.[34] They were accompanied by a group of travelers, or guards, but no mention is made of either father or mother being present at the reception. His father could have made the arrangements well in advance.[35] We can only imagine the little boy's feelings as he left familiar surroundings and companions to begin a new life on the famous hill overlooking Cassino.

THE YEARS AT MONTECASSINO

If Thomas Aquinas came to the Benedictines as a five-year-old, as William of Tocco says, then he must have learned the rudiments of reading and writing from them. He became a great reader and a very poor writer. It is a lamentable fact that St. Thomas' handwriting was so bad in his mature years that it was almost impossible to read it. His back-sloping and ill-formed script came to be noted for its illegibility. We shall see later that several of his writings are partially preserved in his own hand; but these autographs in the *littera inintelligibilis* can only be read by palaeographers who have made a special study of them.

The usual custom in the Benedictine system of education was to put the young students under the direction of one of the older monks as tutor. They did not, as a rule, teach classes. We do not know the name of Aquinas' first master.[36] There is a suggestion in one manuscript that a certain Nicholas of Perugia was his preceptor but there is no other evidence and this monk is otherwise unknown. In any case, Thomas probably did

[33] *Doc.* IV (*Fontes,* VI, 535–536), dated May 3, 1231.

[34] Tocco, *Vita,* 4; see note 27, *supra.*

[35] Cf. *Walz-Novarina* (*1962*), p. 25, with the reference to: M. P. Deroux, *Les origines de l'oblature bénédictine* (Ligugé, 1927).

[36] Tocco, *Vita,* 4 (*Fontes,* II, 69): "Cum autem praedictus puerulus coepisset in dicto monasterio sub disciplina Magistri diligentius educari. . . ." Bartholomew of Lucca, *Hist. Eccl.,* XXII, 20: "Habens secum semper magistrum specialem more nobilium regionis."

much of his studying alone, following tutorial methods. This conclusion is in keeping with the tenor of Benedictine educational practice in the Middle Ages.[37] It also accords with the remarks of William of Tocco who reports: "The little boy frequently avoided the company of the other noble youths who were being educated there."[38]

Certain historical events, of which Thomas may have been a witness, occurred during this decade. On July 1, 1231, an earthquake of great intensity centered in the region about Cassino, causing much material damage and great suffering to the people. Subsequent minor tremors continued throughout the month of July and the terrified countryfolk made a pilgrimage to the famous monastery on the mountain to pray for God's forgiveness and protection. If Thomas was at Montecassino at this time, as seems likely, he must have shared in the general alarm. In any case, he was resident in the affected region.[39] There is a passage in his *Commentary on the Psalms*[40] where he speaks of the terror occasioned by earthquakes. He explains that the will of God is the primary cause of such natural catastrophes and then he embarks on a long discussion of the natural causes of earthquakes and windstorms. Convinced that winds and earthquakes are interconnected, he was inclined to think that the forceful impact of one wind on another caused the earth to ripple into waves. Then he reports Seneca's conjecture that Sicily was separated from Calabria by an earthquake. It was evidently a natural phenomenon with which he was much impressed.

In 1234, the Emperor Frederick visited the nearby town of San Germano. This would have been an occasion of great importance to the people of the district. Frederick had to be greeted by the leading personages, civil and ecclesiastical, of the province. Doubtless some members of the Aquino family of Roccasecca, and quite possibly Thomas' father were present in San Germano. Representatives would be sent from Montecassino. It is not impossible that young Thomas saw the famous Emperor at this time.[41]

---

[37] *Codex Florentinus* (Conventi soppressi, 1, vii, 27) has a marginal note to the text of Tocco: "habitum est a fratre Nicholao de Perusio antiquiori." Cf. P. Delhaye, "L'Organisation scolaire au XIIe siècle," *Traditio,* V (1947), 211–268.

[38] Tocco, *Vita,* 4 (*Fontes,* II, 69).

[39] On this and some of the later incidents mentioned here, consult: T. Leccisotti, *art. cit.,* pp. 519–547.

[40] S. Thomae, *In Psalmos Davidi Expositio,* Ps. 17, sect. 6 (ed. Parma, XIV, 196–197).

[41] *Walz-Novarina* (*1962*), p. 30; Leccisotti, *art. cit.,* p. 540.

An ecclesiastical ceremony of great importance to the Benedictines took place in the same year. The monastery of Montecassino was the scene of the blessing of the newly elected Abbot Stephen of the Benedictine Abbey of Glanfeuil in France. Glanfeuil was a monastery subject to Montecassino and was later to become famous in history as the abbey of Saint-Maur. During the month of April, 1234, Stephen of Glanfeuil, clothed in the pontifical vestments customarily worn by the abbot of Montecassino, received the benediction of Abbot Landolfo. This was, of course, a solemn religious event at which all the residents of Montecassino, including Thomas Aquinas, would assist.[42]

A dispute between the officials of the monastery of Montecassino and Filippo d'Aquino occurred in 1236. Both parties made claim to a mill which was connected with the Church of St. Nazarus at Comino, a dependency of the monastery. Eventually Pope Gregory IX took cognizance of the heated affair and appointed Riccardo, canon of Fondi, to hear testimony and settle the dispute in ecclesiastical court.[43] The outcome is not recorded but the matter must have been of some interest, and possible embarrassment to Thomas. Filippo d'Aquino was either his half brother or a cousin. The Aquinos were zealous guardians of their possessions and no strangers to the law courts.

Toward the end of the decade, matters became more and more difficult for the monks at Montecassino. They were innocently but inevitably entangled in the continuing struggle between Pope and Emperor. Frederick was excommunicated in 1239 but his forces were a threat to the monastery even before this date. Most of the monks were exiled by imperial edict and Montecassino was left without a head, from the death of Abbot Landolfo (1236) until the accession of Stephen de Corbario (1238). In 1239 the monastery was occupied as a fortress by the Sicilian troops.[44]

At some time during these years (one might guess that it was late in 1238 or early 1239), the monks at Montecassino saw that it was no longer a safe and suitable place for a young student such as Thomas. Landolfo of Aquino, still in the good graces of the Emperor,[45] was advised to with-

[42] On this event see the portion of a letter written April 25, 1234, by Abbot Landolfo and printed as Document 15, p. 255, in: H. Bloch, "The Schism of Anacletus II and the Glanfeuil Forgeries of Peter the Deacon of Monte Cassino," *Traditio,* VIII (1952), 159–264. The article contains much information on the history of the two monasteries.

[43] *Doc.* VI (*Fontes,* VI, 538) is Pope Gregory's letter of July 12, 1236.

[44] Cf. Bloch, *art. cit.,* p. 219.

[45] *Doc.* VII (*Fontes,* VI, 539).

draw Thomas from Montecassino. The account of this termination of Thomas' life with the Benedictines, as recounted by William of Tocco and the other early biographers, is curiously innocent in regard to these political difficulties. Tocco blandly explains that the Abbot (this would be Stephen II apparently) looked ahead and advised Landolfo, in view of the promise shown by the boy in his studies, to send Thomas to the University of Naples.[46]

Whatever the reason may have been, Thomas left Montecassino, probably in the spring of 1239. He appears to have spent the summer with his family at Roccasecca.[47] Since he continued to enjoy the friendliest relations with the monks at Montecassino, throughout the remainder of his life, there is no question that Thomas left his first school with the approval of the Benedictines. They had given him a solid foundation for the brilliant career which he was to achieve in later years.[48] Montecassino was not restored to its monastic calm for more than twenty-five years. It was just as well that Thomas Aquinas' destiny lay elsewhere.

[46] Tocco, *Vita,* 5 (*Fontes,* II, 70).

[47] C. Fabro, "Tommaso d'Aquino," *Enciclopedia Cattolica* (Firenze, 1954), XII, 253.

[48] Cf. A. Stehle, "St. Thomas at Monte Cassino," *Catholic Educ. Assoc. Bulletin,* XXI (1924), 658–665.

CHAPTER TWO

The Roots of Wisdom

THERE is little question that his years with the Benedictines at Montecassino left a strong and lasting impression on the mind and character of Thomas Aquinas. He always maintained friendly relations with the Benedictines. One of St. Thomas' last writings is a letter in 1274 to Bernard Ayglier, abbot of Montecassino. Its opening lines read:

> To the reverend Father in Christ, Lord Bernard, by the grace of God the venerable Abbot of Cassino, [from] Brother Thomas of Aquino, his devoted son, always and everywhere in ready obedience.[1]

If this letter is authentic (and it is generally regarded as such[2]) it indicates a surprisingly strong attitude of filial piety toward a Benedictine.

What Thomas learned at Montecassino may be reduced to three things: religious knowledge, basic academic skills, and good study habits. On these detailed points, we are given practically no information by the early biographers; they simply say that he was a brilliant but quiet student who kept much to himself.[3] They do record that Thomas often asked his master, "What is God?" — and that he committed the master's teaching to memory. At the canonization inquiry, Bartholomew of Capua testified that Thomas "grew in life, in moral behavior and in knowledge" under

[1] For the Latin text, see S. Thomae Aq., *Opera Omnia,* ed. Vivès, XXXII, 834; or *Opuscula Omnia,* ed. Mandonnet, III, 249.

[2] Cf. Eschmann, "Catalogue of St. Thomas's Works," in Gilson, *Christian Philosophy of St. Thomas* (New York: Random House, 1956), p. 418, n. 62. (Hereafter cited as "Catalogue.")

[3] Tocco, *Vita,* 4 (*Fontes,* II, 69–70); Calo, *Vita,* 3 (*Fontes,* I, 19–20).

the Benedictines.[4] Actually, our information concerning Thomas' training at Montecassino must be drawn from indirect sources.

The Benedictines had been at Montecassino a long time. St. Benedict had set up a monastery there, in the sixth century, and though it was not his first monastic establishment Montecassino soon became the foremost.[5] In the ensuing six centuries it developed into the center of Benedictine culture and learning. When Thomas entered the monastery, its traditions were already ancient. Through the damage and occupations of many wars, through periods of famine, ravaging disease, and the near eclipse of civilized living, Montecassino had endured and even flourished. Its motto was well merited: "When cut down, it grows again" (*Succisa virescit*).

St. Benedict had devised a Rule of religious life which emphasized prayer and work, both taken in a broad sense. Liturgical exercises, if they were to be performed with meaning and living faith, required careful study and meditation on the Bible and the Patristic commentaries. The chanting of the Psalms led to the development of distinctive musical forms and even to the study of the mathematical bases of music itself. Grammar, rhetoric, poetry, and the other liberal arts had to be cultivated as aids to the interpretation and exposition of Holy Scripture. All of this learning was cultivated in the spirit of early Christian writers, Augustine, Boethius, Benedict, and Gregory the Great. In the beginning, the concept of "work" was interpreted as agricultural and manual labor, as a cure for idleness and spiritual sloth. But there was other work to be done than that of the fields. Libraries were needed, manuscripts had to be copied and bound and preserved. To make a fair copy, without unusual embellishment, of one ordinary-sized treatise, a medieval scribe had to work hard at his writing desk for upward of six months. Other monks had to provide the hand-fashioned materials, well-prepared skins, quill pens, lasting inks, suitable bindings. The *scriptorium* became the focal point of long hours of hard work; its activities required tangential essays into the pictorial arts.

By the late twelfth and early thirteenth centuries, the program of academic studies in Benedictine monasteries was no longer ordered, if it ever had been, under the seven liberal arts. At times in fact, there were definite movements among the Benedictines to minimize secular learning. St. Peter

---

[4] *Proc. Can. Neapoli,* LXXVI (*Fontes,* IV 371): "crescens in vita, moribus et scientia."

[5] Cf. J. Chapman, *St. Benedict and the Sixth Century* (London: Sheed & Ward, 1929).

Damian (in the eleventh century) warmly approved of the fact that Montecassino then had no school for boys.[6] Yet there were always some individual Benedictine scholars who were able to give private instruction.

It seems likely that Thomas Aquinas first learned some simple prayers and used parts of the Bible, or adaptations of Scripture, as texts in reading and writing. The Psalms were part of the everyday Office and the Psalter may have been his first textbook. In chanting the Office, the boys learned not only to read and to memorize but were also introduced to music. In this there was room for some work in arithmetic. While Latin was the language of the Church and of scholarship, which meant that Thomas learned Latin from the beginning of his schooling, some emphasis was given to vernacular instruction.[7] In the thirteenth century, Montecassino customarily held one period of instruction each day in the language of south Italy. Thus Thomas acquired at an early age a correct knowledge of the Sicilian dialect and this was the language that he used in conversations with his compatriots. We shall see later that his longtime secretary and companion was Reginald of Piperno, a south Italian who spoke the same vernacular. He was also able to deliver popular sermons in this dialect, as he did at Naples in the years immediately preceding his death.

The education received at Montecassino was basically a religious formation. In addition to Holy Scripture, the authors read were the Latin Fathers of the Church plus some of the standard Benedictine writers. Depending on the condition of the library in the monastery (which could have been well stocked) and the interests of his preceptor (about whom we know nothing definite), the young Thomas could have read portions of Ss. Ambrose, Augustine, Jerome, Benedict, Gregory the Great, and Isidore of Seville. Of later writers, he doubtless came to know something of St. Anselm of Canterbury and Hugh of St. Victor.[8] Certainly these and other standard religious writers appear as familiar authors in the mature writings of St. Thomas. On certain questions he seems to have a predilection for the views of Benedictine writers. St. Benedict is cited on the problem of obedience to a religious superior,[9] on the problem of man's vision of the

---

[6] *Opusculum 36, De divina omnipotentia,* PL 145, 621: "Hoc mihi non mediocriter placuit quod ibi scholas puerorum qui saepe rigorem sanctitatis enervant non inveni." Cf. P. Delhaye, "L'Organisation scolaire au XIIe siècle," *Traditio,* V (1947), 225.

[7] T. Leccisotti, "Il Dottore Angelico a Montecassino," *Rivista di Filosofia Neoscolastica,* XXXII (1940), 530–533.

[8] Delhaye, *art. cit.,* pp. 232–233.

[9] *S.T.,* I-II, 13, 5, ad 3.

Essence of God,[10] on the one-year period of religious novitiate,[11] and throughout Aquinas' defense of the religious life.[12] More than a hundred references to Gregory the Great, in the *Summa of Theology* and *Summa contra Gentiles,* show St. Thomas' familiarity with this Benedictine moralist. It is not suggested that Aquinas learned all that he knew of Benedictine literature while a child at Montecassino; however, he evidently acquired a special affection for these masters of the religious life. This was not due to his later study of the rule of his own (Dominican) Order, for the rule of the Order of Preachers was not based on the Benedictine but on the Augustinian form of monasticism.

We have seen that the early Latin biographies of Thomas Aquinas provide no exact information concerning his studies at Montecassino. They speak glowingly but vaguely of his brilliant progress as a student and his curiosity about God. William of Tocco also mentions a tendency toward solitary meditation and taciturnity.[13]

In the thirteenth century the text used for elementary studies in Latin grammar was the *Ars Minor* of Donatus.[14] A larger textbook by Donatus, the *Ars Grammatica* or *Major,* was also studied. The more advanced work was Priscian's *Eighteen Books of Grammatical Instructions.*[15] It is unlikely that Thomas studied anything more than Donatus, or some similar summary of Latin grammar, at Montecassino. Possibly he read selections from the Latin classics but the general trend of Benedictine instruction in this period was religious rather than classical or humanistic.[16]

Apart from a solid knowledge of Christian doctrine and the elementary skills of reading and writing, the greatest asset that Thomas gained from the Benedictines was the beginning of good study habits. His later scholarship was founded on a well-trained memory, the ability to read a serious

[10] *S.T.*, II-II, 180, 5, ad 3 (this is actually a quotation from St. Gregory, *Dialogi,* II, 35, concerning St. Benedict).

[11] *S.T.*, II-II, 189, 2, ad 1.

[12] See Chapters 3, 11, 14, and 16 of *Contra pestiferam doctrinam retrahentium pueros a religionis ingressu,* ed. Parma, XV, 103–125.

[13] *Vita,* 4 (*Fontes,* II, 69): "Erat autem praedictus puer non verbis garrulus, sed meditari intra se jam incipiens taciturnus."

[14] For the work of this Roman grammarian of the fourth century A.D., see:*Probi, Donati, Servii de arte grammatica libri,* ex recensione H. Keilii (Lipsiae, 1864).

[15] Priscian taught grammar in Constantinople; his lectures date from about A.D. 500; see: *Grammatici Latini,* ex recensione H. Keilii, Vols. II–III (Lipsiae, 1855–1857).

[16] J. Leclercq, "L'Humanisme bénédictin du VIIIe au XIIe siècle," *Analecta Monastica,* I (Studia Anselmiana, 20) (Rome, 1948), 1–20.

text with understanding, and a fine mastery of the standard works of reference. From the start, Thomas Aquinas had the dedication to learning which marks the true scholar. Much of the credit for these valuable habits may be due to his Benedictine masters.[17]

One early author[18] suggests that Thomas studied some philosophy and natural science at Montecassino. It is barely possible that he read a little logic there but even that seems quite unlikely.[19] We know of one learned Benedictine who might have tried to introduce the boy to philosophy and who was at Montecassino in these years. This was Master Erasmus who was called from the monastery to teach theology in the University of Naples in the year 1240.[20] There is no direct evidence that Erasmus ever taught Aquinas and it is quite possible that Bartholomew of Lucca (who knew Thomas only in his last years at Naples) is confusing the university studies at Naples with the earlier studies at Montecassino.[21]

When Thomas Aquinas had become a famous Dominican scholar, a certain "Brother John" asked him for advice on how to study. The answer was an utterly simple little letter to John (apparently a young novice in the Order of Preachers) which seems to reflect the lessons that Aquinas learned in his own youth. Though extremely elementary in character, the letter is generally accepted as authentic.[22] It probably summarizes some of St. Thomas' own experiences and efforts as a beginner in the world of learning. This is what Aquinas wrote:

> Since you have asked me, my very dear John in Christ, how you should apply yourself in order to gain something from the treasure-house of knowledge, let this be the advice handed down to you by me on this subject.
>
> Make up your mind to start on small streams rather than to plunge into the sea; for one should progress from easier matters to those that are more difficult. This is, then, my advice and instruction for you. I counsel you

---

[17] A. Stehle, O.S.B., "St. Thomas at Monte Cassino," *Catholic Educational Association Bulletin,* XXI (1924), 658–665.

[18] Bartholomew of Lucca, *Historia Ecclesiastica,* XXII, 20; *Walz-Novarina* (*1962*), pp. 28–29, seems to accept this testimony, but we have no other evidence that philosophy was taught at Montecassino in the early thirteenth century.

[19] Cf. A. Walz, "Thomas d'Aquin," *Dictionnaire de Théologie Catholique* (Paris, 1946), XV (1), col. 619.

[20] I. Taurisano, *San Tommaso d'Aquino* (Turin: Unione Tipografico — Editrice Torinese, 1946), p. 41.

[21] J. V. De Groot, *Het Leven van den H. Thomas van Aquino* (Utrecht: Van Rossum, 1907), p. 19, suggests this explanation of Bartholomew's statement.

[22] For the authenticity of *De modo studendi,* see Eschmann, "Catalogue," p. 421, n. 71.

to be slow to speak and slow to take the speaker's stand. Embrace purity of mind; do not neglect prayer; cherish your cell most of the time, if you wish to be admitted to the vintage-room [of knowledge]. Be friendly to all men; do not be curious about the private activities of other people; do not try to be overfamiliar with anyone, for too much familiarity breeds contempt and provides an opportunity for neglecting one's studies.

Do not get interested in any way in worldly talk or deeds. Avoid idle talk on all matters; do not fail to imitate the example of holy and good men; do not be concerned about what speaker you are listening to; instead, when something good is said, commit it to memory. Be sure that you understand whatever you read. Make certain that you know the difficulties and store up whatever you can in the treasure-house of the mind; keep as busy as a person who seeks to fill a vessel.

Do not seek higher positions. Follow in the footsteps of Blessed Dominic who brought forth and increased the buds, the flowers and the fruits that were useful and wonderful in the vineyard of the Lord of Hosts, as long as he lived.

If you follow these words of advice, you will be able to attain your every desire.[23]

To this simple philosophy of life, St. Thomas Aquinas was himself committed by personal temperament and by his early masters at Montecassino. His later learning served but to reinforce these views. He sought no preferments in Church or State; he was friendly with all his associates but formed no strong personal attachments; he prayed whenever faced with difficulties; and he cultivated the life of the intellect.

[23] Latin text in *Opuscula Theologica*, ed. R. A. Verardo *et al.* (Torino-Roma: Marietti, 1954), Vol. I, 451.

CHAPTER THREE

At the Imperial University of Naples

THOMAS AQUINAS probably left the monastery at Montecassino in the spring of 1239 and went to spend the summer with his family at Roccasecca.[1] Both of his parents were still alive at this time. In the fall, he was sent to Naples to study liberal arts at the Imperial University. It is thought that he studied there from 1239 to 1244. These dates are approximate, for we have practically no documentary evidence concerning this formative period in his life.[2]

The notorious Emperor Frederick II had founded the University of Naples in 1224. Concerning its foundation, he is reported to have said: "We think that it is profitable for us to give our subjects the means whereby to instruct themselves; knowledge will render them more able to govern themselves and to govern the State."[3] This may suggest that Frederick had democratic tendencies; in point of fact, he was a very complicated character. His grandfather, Frederick Barbarossa, had been the second Hohenstaufen emperor. From the middle of the twelfth century, Barbarossa extended his power from Germany over the Alps into Italy. As Holy Roman Emperor, the first Frederick met with opposition from political rivals in northern Italy and, in particular, from the papal forces. The supporters of the Emperor were called Ghibellines and their opponents, Guelfs. Thus began one of the most famous feuds in history — one that is familiar to readers of Dante and Shakespeare. The Aquino family were,

[1] C. Fabro, "Tommaso d'Aquino," *Enciclopedia Cattolica* XII (1954), col. 253.

[2] *Walz-Novarina* (*1962*), pp. 33–43, offers the most accurate account of this period.

[3] Quoted by M. M. Gorce, *L'Essor de la pensée au moyen âge* (Paris: Letouzey, 1933), p. 118, from K. Hampe, *Kaiser Friedrich II* (Heidelberg, 1925).

in effect, vassals of the Hohenstaufen Emperors, and thus Ghibellines. Some of St. Thomas' brothers fought against the papal armies in the first half of the thirteenth century.

Frederick II (who did not die until 1250) was still living when Aquinas studied in Naples. This Emperor was much more a Sicilian than a German. A man of considerable intellectual pretensions and dubious religious convictions, Frederick II sponsored the work of many scholars and scientists whom he attracted to his new university. He became the patron not only of Christian but also of Mohammedan and Jewish thinkers. The University of Naples came to rival Toledo as a center of cosmopolitan learning. It was a secular institution, a state university. Doubtless it was an exciting place for an eager young student such as Thomas Aquinas. His personal loyalties would be torn between family ties with the Empire and the devotion of a Catholic to the papal traditions.

We do not know where Thomas lived as a student in Naples. He could have stayed with relatives, for his mother had connections there. It is also possible that he lived at one of the two Benedictine houses in the city, either San Demetrio or San Severino.[4] He was possibly about fourteen years old when he came to Naples. This was quite the usual age to begin the arts course in medieval universities. After mentioning that both of Thomas' parents agreed to send the boy to Naples, William of Tocco gave the names of two of his teachers: Master Martin, for grammar and logic, and Master Peter of Hibernia, for natural philosophy.[5] Some authorities think that Aquinas commemorated the names of these liberal arts teachers in a passage in his *Commentary on the Sentences,*[6] where he is explaining that God has a distinct thought for each individual being and he gives as an example the difference between the divine idea (*ratio*) of Peter and the idea of Martin.

In any case, the identities of these teachers are still subject to dispute. There was a Master Peter de Isernia who taught at the University of Naples in the 1220's, and some have thought that he was the teacher of

---

[4] Cf. De Groot, *Het Leven,* p. 20.

[5] *Vita,* c. 5 (*Fontes,* II, 70): "Unde puer de utriusque parentis consilio Neapolim mittitur, et sub Magistri Martini in grammaticalibus et logicalibus, et Magistri Petri de Ibernia studiis in naturalibus edocetur."

[6] *In I Sent.,* d. 36, q. 2, a. 3: "Ad tertium dicendum quod particularia habent proprias ideas in Deo: unde alia est ratio Petri et Martini in Deo, sicut alia ratio hominis et equi."

Aquinas.[7] It is recorded that this Peter was offered a salary of twelve ounces of gold annually at Naples.[8] However, Petrus de Isernia taught law, not arts, and it is not clear that he was in Naples as late as the 1240's. A more likely candidate for the honor of being Thomas' first university teacher was another Master Peter who was a master of arts and was still actively teaching in the 1260's. This Peter conducted a philosophical disputation before King Manfred between 1258 and 1266.[9] The question that he disputed was: "Whether the parts of the body are made for the sake of their activities, or the activities are produced for the sake of these parts." In the treatment of this question, final causality is much stressed and the teachings of Aristotle and Averroës are clearly distinguished. Obviously this Peter de Hibernia was a learned man with a special interest in the philosophy of nature. He appears to be identical with the author of several commentaries on Aristotle, and one on Porphyry, still extant in Vatican manuscripts.[10] He could have been the teacher of Aquinas.

Concerning the Master Martin who taught grammar and logic to Thomas, there are problems of a different character. Thanks to the pioneering research of Martin Grabmann and the continuing studies of Heinrich Roos, we now know a good deal about a certain Master Martin de Dacia (of Denmark) who became a famous teacher of speculative grammar and logic in the thirteenth century. In his dissertation of 1952, Roos fully agreed with Grabmann that this Martin the Dane was Thomas' teacher.[11] However, Roos later expressed doubts concerning this identifi-

[7] M. Grabmann, "Magister Petrus von Hibernia der Jugendlehrer des hl. Thomas von Aquin," *Mittelalterliches Geistesleben* (München, 1926), pp. 254–255.

[8] *Fontes,* II, 70; H. Denifle, *Die Entstehung der Universitäten des Mittelalters* (Berlin, 1885), I, 456, n. 972.

[9] Clemens Baeumker, "Petrus von Hibernia der Jugendlehrer des Thomas von Aquin," *Sitzungsberichte der Bayer. Akademie d. Wissenschaften,* Philos.-philol. Klasse, 8 (München, 1920). This 1920 study is summarized in Grabmann's article, under the same title, and cited above.

[10] *Cod. Vat. Lat.* 825, fol. 92^r — 102^r contains expositions of *De longitudine et brevitate vitae* and *De morte et vita,* with the explicit on fol. 102^r: "Magister Petrus de ybernia fecit hoc opus." *Cod. Vat. Lat.* 5988 (not 5989 as Grabmann listed it, *art. cit.,* p. 264) has a commentary on Porphyry's *Isagoge,* beginning at fol. 63^r, and one on Aristotle's *Perihermeneias,* starting at fol. 82^r, both ascribed to Peter de Hibernia. They appear to postdate 1250; Averroës is much cited. (Copies are in the Vatican Microfilm Collection at St. Louis University.)

[11] *Die Modi Significandi des Martinus de Dacia,* BGPM XXXVII, 2 (Münster, 1952), p. 59: "Und vielleicht hat M. Grabmann doch recht, wenn er die Vermutung ausspricht dass Martinus de Dacia mit dem Jugendlehrer des hl. Thomas von Aquin identisch sei."

cation.[12] One difficulty is that the famous Danish grammarian seems to have lived until 1304! This would have made him a very old man if he taught Aquinas in 1240. However, Martin de Dacia could have been in his twenties when he taught at Naples and he could have long outlived Thomas. We simply do not know whether he is the Master Martin named by William of Tocco.

The names of other teachers in Naples have been suggested. Due to the dispersal of the Benedictine monks at Montecassino in 1239, Master Erasmus of Cassino came to teach at Naples in 1240.[13] Possibly this monk was friendly with Thomas and he may have functioned for a time as his spiritual adviser. It is unlikely that Erasmus actually taught Thomas, since the Benedictine was a master in theology and there is no evidence that Aquinas studied theology at the University of Naples. Italian traditions also mention Terrisio di Atina and Arnaldo Catalano as possible teachers in this period.[14]

What precise course of studies was followed by Thomas Aquinas in Naples cannot now be ascertained. The old ideal of the seven liberal arts — divided into the *trivium* (grammar, rhetoric, and dialectic) and the *quadrivium* (arithmetic, geometry, astronomy, and music) — was not followed in thirteenth-century schools. Usually it was difficult to find masters proficient in the mathematical and scientific subjects of the *quadrivium.* St. Thomas' later writings show that he acquired a knowledge of the standard works in grammar and logic and that he was by no means ignorant of the quadrivial subjects. At Naples he may have read some of the older Latin translations of Aristotle's treatises on natural philosophy. Indeed, it is quite possible that he took the degree of master in arts there.[15] He was there long enough and this degree would be the normal outcome of a successful course. All the early biographies speak of his outstanding qualities as a student at Naples.[16]

Pierre Mandonnet (whose pioneering studies on the early life of Aquinas are still valuable) has suggested that Thomas wrote some poetry while he

---

[12] Henricus Roos, ed., *Martini de Dacia Opera* (Copenhagen: G. E. C. Gad, 1961), p. XXXVIII. See the review by E. A. Synan, *Speculum,* XXXVII (1962), 460–463.

[13] I. Taurisano, *San Tommaso,* p. 41.

[14] *Ibid.,* p. 43.

[15] A. Walz, "Thomas d'Aquin," *DTC,* XV (1), col. 619.

[16] Thus Tocco, *Vita,* c. 5 (*Fontes,* II, 70); "In quorum scholis tam luculenti coepit esse ingenii, et intelligentiae perspicacis, ut altius profundius et clarius aliis audita repeteret, quam a suis Doctoribus audivisset."

was an arts student. This is not impossible. Mandonnet discusses a vernacular sonnet attributed to St. Thomas. He printed it from an obscure manuscript source, with the comment that it may well be a genuine work of Aquinas.[17] Since the poem has some interest and illustrates the kind of Italian dialect which Thomas may have spoken, it is worth recording here with a rough translation into English.

Tanto ha virtu ziascun, quanto ha intelletto;
(Each man has as much virtue, as he has understanding;)
E a valor quanto in virtu si stende;
(And he has worth to the extent that his virtue is broad;)
E tanto ha 'llhor di ben, quanto l'intende,
(And he possesses goodness, to the extent that he wills it,)
E quanto ha d'honor gentil diletto.
(And to the extent that he has a worthy love of honor.)
E il diletto gentil, quanto ha l'effetto,
(And worthy love, in proportion to its consequences,)
Adorna il bel piacer, che nel chor scende;
(Adorns that fine joy which surges in the heart;)
Il quale adorna tanto, quanto splende
(For such joy adorns its, to the extent that it shines forth)
Per somiglianza del proprio subietto.
(Through likeness with its proper object.)
Dunque chi vol veder, quanto d'honore
(So, he who wishes to see how much honor)
Altrui e degno e di laude perfecta
(And perfect praise another person merits)
Miri in qual disio amante ha il core.
(May consider to what desire the lover turns his heart.)
Pero ch'esser felice ogni uomo affecta,
(For, though every man craves to be happy,)
Massimamente quel che per l'onore
(This is true above all of him who, for honor)
Verace adopra, tal corona aspetta.
(Works faithfully, his gaze on such a crown.)

While the thought of such a poem to *True Honor* may be trite, there are resemblances in it to certain points in the mature works of Thomas Aquinas. Mandonnet has pointed out a passage in the *Summa contra Gentiles* which has some similarity of language.[18] It is not difficult to note

[17] P. Mandonnet, "Thomas d'Aquin, novice prêcheur," *Revue Thomiste,* VIII (1925), 222–249; the text of the sonnet is on p. 239. He took it from *Biblioteca Estense, Cod.* 9.A.27, fol. 37. Grabmann, *Die Werke des hl. Thomas v. Aquin,* BGPM XXII, 1–2 (Münster, 1949), p. 413, is noncommittal about the attribution and points out that the MS is dated A.D. 1347.

[18] Lib. III, 28; translated in *The Truth of the Catholic Faith* (New York: Doubleday Image Books, 1956), Vol. III, p. 114.

other "Thomistic" notions in the poem: the lines about the *"bel piacer . . . che splende"* are reminiscent of St. Thomas' famous description of the beautiful as that which gives pleasure when seen (*quod visum placet*), and as having the quality of shining forth (*claritas*).[19] Moreover, the third last line expresses a Thomistic (but also an Aristotelian) commonplace (every man desires to be happy). It must be admitted that any medieval writer, faintly acquainted with the *Nicomachean Ethics* and with a gift for the Italian *chi ben beve, ben dormira* style of poetry, could have written this little poem.

At some point in his years at the University of Naples, Thomas Aquinas became friendly with some members of the Order of St. Dominic and this encounter sparked one of the most important personal decisions in his life. He determined to become a Dominican friar. During these years, Jordan of Saxony (Master General of the Order of Preachers) visited and preached at the university. In point of fact, Jordan seems to have been in the habit of giving sermons at university centers: at Paris, Bologna, Padua (where Albert the Great entered the Order), and at the schools of Oxford.[20] A vigorous and impressive man, Jordan probably inspired Thomas Aquinas with the desire to take up a new religious vocation. The Order of Preachers had been founded early in the century by St. Dominic and received papal approval in 1216. Combined with a life of poverty and obedience was the Dominican ideal of scholarship and evangelical effort. Such a life appealed to the young Aquinas.[21] Another Neapolitan Dominican was John of San Giuliano (a place not far from Thomas' home); William of Tocco says that this fellow Apulian influenced Aquinas' entry into the Dominican Order.[22]

Landolfo of Aquino, Thomas' father, had died, apparently in December of 1243.[23] It must have been around this time that the young Neapolitan

---

[19] *S.T.*, I, 5, 4, ad 1; I–II, 27, 1, ad 3.

[20] H. D. Scheeben, *Beiträge zur Geschichte Jordans von Sachsen* (Vechta-Leipzig, 1938), p. 96.

[21] Cf. M.-D. Chenu, *Introduction à l'étude de saint Thomas d'Aquin* (Paris: Vrin, 1950), pp. 34–43. (Henceforth cited as *Introduction.*) This title has recently appeared in English as *Toward Understanding St. Thomas* (Chicago: Regnery, 1964).

[22] *Vita,* c. 6 (*Fontes,* II, 71): "Frater autem Joannes de S. Juliano praedicti Ordinis professus . . . praedictum juvenem a Deo sibi destinatum monuit, et ad ingressum praedicti Ordinis mente dispositium inclinavit."

[23] A fragment from the *Necrology* of the Abbey of Montecassino reads: "IX kal. ianuarii obiit . . . Landulphus de Aquino miles" (see *Fontes,* VI, 541); the editor,

student was deciding on his vocation. There is no evidence that he consulted any members of his family, however; indeed, we shall see later that his mother and brothers were shocked when they learned that Thomas had decided to become a mendicant friar. St. Thomas later wrote that the advice of one's family is not to be sought when considering a religious vocation. In one of his short works,[24] there is a rather bitter comment to this effect: "On this decision [to enter the religious life], blood relatives are not friendly but unfriendly. . . . So, in such a case, the advice of relatives is especially to be avoided."

That this observation echoes his own experience can hardly be doubted. Thomas' immediate family did not share his admiration for the life of mendicancy which he now proposed to embrace.

M.-H. Laurent dates this entry, "after 1245." *Walz-Novarina (1962)*, p. 50, and Leccisotti, *Il Dottore Angelico*, p. 545, give 1243 as the probable year of Landolfo's death.

[24] *Contra pestiferam doctrinam*, in *Opuscula Omnia*, ed. Mandonnet, IV, 294: "Propinqui autem carnis in hoc proposito amici non sunt sed potius inimici. . . ."

CHAPTER FOUR

Liberal Arts and the New Science

In his five years at the University of Naples, Thomas Aquinas acquired a working knowledge of traditional logic and became acquainted with certain parts of the Aristotelian philosophy of nature. He never became a specialist in logic or the natural sciences, partly because his later teaching career was not in the arts faculty but also because his personal gifts and interests directed him to other studies. Compared with Albert the Great, for instance, Aquinas was neither as great a logician nor as devoted to empirical science and the observation of natural phenomena.[1] Although logic became a useful tool for St. Thomas, he never succumbed to the medieval disease of logicism.

As far as logic is concerned, many treatises were available for study at the University of Naples by 1240. Aristotle's Greek writings (*the Organon*) had included six treatises: the *Categories, On Interpretation, Topics, Sophistic Refutations,* the *Prior* and *Posterior Analytics*. These works treated terms, propositions, dialectical reasoning, fallacies, syllogistic reasoning, scientific demonstration. In the third century of the Christian era, Porphyry had written a Greek *Introduction* (*Isagoge*) to Aristotle's *Categories*. Of course, Thomas could not read these Greek treatises, for he was not trained in Greek.

At the beginning of the sixth century, Boethius translated most of Aristotle's *Organon* into Latin. He also made a version of the *Isagoge* and

[1] In his *Medieval Logic* (Chicago: University of Chicago Press, 1952), p. xiii, P. Boehner says that Aquinas is not an important figure in thirteenth-century logic; on the other hand (p. 1) he remarks that, "we may regard St. Albert's tracts on logic as a fair approximation of the total heritage bequeathed to the schoolmen of the mid-13th century."

wrote various commentaries on these logical works. Before mid-twelfth century, Latin students of Aristotle had copies of Boethius' versions of the *Categories,* with Porphyry's *Introduction,* plus two commentaries by Boethius on this text. They also possessed Boethius' translation of the work *On Interpretation,* with two Boethian commentaries. These Latin works, plus three simple treatises on categorical and hypothetical syllogisms and a treatise on the *Topics* (including a fragmentary paraphrase of Cicero's *Topics*) formed the collection known as the "Old Logic." By the middle of the twelfth century (almost a hundred years before Aquinas' studies), four more of what were thought to be Boethius' translations were rediscovered: the Aristotelian *Topics, Sophistic Refutations,* and the two *Analytics.* This second group, plus the *Book of Six Principles* (attributed to Gilbert of Porrée), became known as the "New Logic." Peter Abelard had written several logical treatises in the twelfth century but we do not know whether his work was used at Naples. There were also certain translations of Arabic treatises on logic: notably al-Farabi (tenth century) *Liber introductorius in artem logicae demonstrationis,* and the section on logic from Avicenna's (eleventh century) *Kitab-al-shifâ.*[2]

Thomas' teachers at Naples had the New as well as the Old Logic.[3] Moreover, they must have been able to use some of the Latin versions of the Arabic works. By the 1240's, some teachers had prepared their own paraphrases, or textbooks, for the various divisions of this traditional Aristotelian logic.[4]

It is perfectly clear that Thomas Aquinas did learn some Aristotelian philosophy at Naples. The usual statement in histories of philosophy and biographies, that Albert the Great introduced Aquinas to Aristotle, must be taken with some reservations. This is especially true in regard to works on the philosophy of nature. Quite a number of translators were active in Sicilian centers (chiefly Naples but also the nearby medical school of Salerno) in the late twelfth and early thirteenth centuries. A Latin version of the original Greek of Ptolemy's *Almagest* was made in Sicily, about

---

[2] H. Bédoret, "Les premières traductions tolédanes de philosophie. Oeuvres d'Alfarabi," *Revue Néoscolastique de Philosophie,* 41 (1938), 80–97; and "Oeuvres d'Avicenne," *ibid.,* 374–400.

[3] Thus C. H. Haskins, "Translators of the Twelfth Century and the First Latin Version of Ptolemy's Almagest," *Harvard Studies in Classical Philosophy,* XXI (1910), 98: "In philosophy they [Sicilian scholars] appear to have acquired the *New Logic* of Aristotle somewhat earlier than their northern contemporaries."

[4] See Boehner, *op. cit.,* pp. 1–5.

A.D. 1160.[5] Greek scholars such as Aristippus and Eugene of Palermo were active at the Sicilian court. A Master William of Luna was translating at Naples in this period.[6] However, it is sufficient to examine the work of Michael Scottus to see how rich the library of the University of Naples was in books on science and natural philosophy. Michael was a translator from Arabic into Latin and he made his first versions at Toledo, Spain, of Aristotle's *On the Heavens,* with Averroës' commentary, of the lengthy treatises *On Animals,* and possibly of the treatises *On Generation, On Meteorology,* and the *Parva Naturalia.* About the year 1227, Michael Scottus was induced to come to the court of Frederick II and he worked in Naples until 1235, or later. There he translated ten books of Aristotle's *Metaphysics* (the *metaphysica nova*) plus Averroës' commentary, and Avicenna's treatise *On Animals.* He also wrote in Naples several of his own treatises on general science: the *Liber Introductorius* and the *Liber Particularis Physionomia,* which became known as *On the Secrets of Nature.*[7] Michael Scottus may have been more the executive than the scholar. This is what Roger Bacon implies: "Michael Scottus took credit for many translations; but it is well known that a certain Jew named Andrew did most of the work on these."[8] In any event, Michael knew how to produce translations.

Five or ten years later, when another Irishman named Peter came to teach courses on the philosophy of nature at the Neapolitan University, he doubtless used at least some of these books on biological, astronomical, and physical science. It has been noted in the preceding chapter that we have manuscript copies of certain commentaries by Peter de Hibernia on the scientific writings of Aristotle. These expositions employ a very distinctive method, that of the *lectio* plus *quaestiones.* This style of commentary is very different from the Avicennian method of paraphrase which was used by St. Albert. Thomas Aquinas' commentaries on Aristotle employ an adaptation of the Averroistic method used by Peter (a reading and analysis of portions of the text, plus a discussion of key difficulties in Aristotle). In the judgment of Clemens Baeumker and Martin Grabmann, Peter introduced Thomas Aquinas to the natural philosophy of

[5] Haskins, *art. cit.,* p. 78.

[6] F. Van Steenberghen, *Aristotle in the West* (Louvain: Nauwelaerts, 1955), p. 92.

[7] G. Sarton, *Introduction to the History of Science,* Vol. II, Part 2 (Washington: Carnegie Institute, 1931), pp. 579–580; Van Steenberghen, *op. cit.,* pp. 87–92.

[8] *Compendium Studii Philosophiae,* c. 8; in Fr. Rogeri Bacon, *Opera quaedam hactenus inedita,* ed. J. S. Brewer (London, 1859), p. 472.

Aristotle and taught him how to explain the text, long before Aquinas ever met Albert.[9] Peter's influence extended beyond any question of style, however. St. Thomas seems to have been impressed, from the beginning of his career as a thinker, by the realism and what one might call the "naturalism" which are the hallmarks of the Aristotelian. There is no question that he read Avicenna and the Pseudo-Dionysius and St. Augustine with interest, and that he learned much from Neoplatonic metaphysics. As Grabmann points out,[10] there is a strong Avicennian current in Thomas' exposition of the first book of the *Sentences* (which he was to write ten years later).[11] Yet Aquinas was never a medieval Platonist in the strong sense of this term.[12] On the other hand, Albert and most of his pupils always colored their Aristotelianism with Platonism. While it is conjectural to attribute Aquinas' basic philosophical point of view to his masters at Naples, one might at least note that he had many opportunities to examine the main problems of philosophy before studying in the Dominican course.

The question now arises: Have we any written evidence of the character of St. Thomas' studies at the University of Naples? It seems that we do. William of Tocco reports that, during the period when (as we shall see in the next chapter) Thomas was kept at home by his family, the young scholar devoted his time to reading and study. During this confinement, according to Tocco, Thomas "made a compilation of Aristotle's treatise *On Fallacies.*"[13] In itself, this report might not long detain us, for William's biography contains many inaccuracies, rumors, and errors of fact. Yet there is further evidence which suggests that Tocco was right on this point.

Among the *opuscula* of St. Thomas there is a work entitled, *On Fallacies, for Certain Noble Students in Arts.*[14] Though its authenticity and chron-

---

[9] Baeumker's study in the *Proceedings* of the Bavarian Academy, 1920, is not easily available but his conclusions are summarized and reinforced by M. Grabmann, "Magister Petrus von Hibernia," *Mittelalterliches Geistesleben* (München, 1926), I, 259–265.

[10] *Art. cit.*, p. 263.

[11] On the divine *esse,* see *In I Sent.*, 8, 1, 1; on the simplicity of the human soul, see 8, 5, 2; and on *veritas* as the essence of God, see 19, 5, 1.

[12] This point has been very thoroughly studied in: R. J. Henle, *St. Thomas and Platonism* (The Hague: Nijhoff, 1956).

[13] Tocco, *Vita,* c. 9 (*Fontes,* II, 74): "In tali autem carcere iuvene diligentius coarctato . . . tractatum fallaciarum Aristotelis, ut dicitur, compilavit."

[14] *De fallaciis ad quosdam nobiles artistas,* in *Opuscula Omnia,* ed. Mandonnet, IV, 508–538; it is also in the Parma and Vivès *Opera Omnia,* in J. Perrier (ed.),

ology have been much discussed in the past, present-day authorities all tend to accept it as genuine. Grabmann observes: "we have a very old and unquestionable record in the manuscripts of the *De fallaciis* of St. Thomas."[15] Eschmann lists it as an authentic work and notes that Mandonnet, after rejecting the *Fallacies* because it was not included in the so-called "Official Catalogue," found that it is mentioned in other medieval lists of Thomas' writings and eventually regarded its authenticity as very probable.[16] The treatise is accepted as genuine by Walz but he dates it as probably of the period 1272–1273.[17] The main reason for this late date (during the second professorate in theology at the University of Paris) is found in a famous *Letter from the Paris Faculty of Arts.*[18] This document has misled many people. In it the arts teachers at Paris request the Dominican authorities to send them several philosophical manuscripts (of non-Thomistic treatises) together with some works pertaining to philosophy (*quaedam scripta ad philosophiam spectantia*) which, they say, Aquinas had promised them before his death. And the letter adds: "If he composed any works of like character pertaining to logic — just as we humbly asked him when he departed from us — may your kindness deign to share them with our Faculty."[19] This vague reference to "logical writings" is the only basis for the conjecture that Thomas wrote *On Fallacies* during his second teaching period at Paris. This is very weak evidence, indeed.

The treatise, *On Fallacies,* is an ordinary and undistinguished summary of the kind of thing that was regularly taught in the thirteenth century concerning various mistakes in reasoning. It distinguishes the four kinds of arguments known to Aristotle (demonstrative, dialectical, tentative, and sophistical) and then proceeds to discuss various stock instances of sophistical or fallacious reasonings.[20] Another very short treatise, *On Modal Propositions,* is of a similarly elementary character and may be

---

Opuscula (Paris, 1949), and in the Marietti printing of *Opuscula Philosophica,* ed. R. M. Spiazzi (Turin-Rome, 1954).

[15] M. Grabmann, *Die Werke* (1949), p. 351.

[16] Eschmann, "Catalogue," p. 410, n. 49.

[17] *Walz-Novarina (1962)*, pp. 54 and 224.

[18] The *Letter* is printed in *Fontes,* VI, 583–586; it will be more fully discussed *infra,* pp. 218–219.

[19] *Ibid.,* p. 585: "Si qua similiter ad logicam pertinentia composuit — sicut quando recessit a nobis humiliter petivimus ab eodem — ea vestra benignitas nostro communicare collegio dignetur."

[20] See *De fallaciis,* c. 2; ed. Mandonnet, IV, 509.

associated with the work on fallacies.[21] *De modalibus* has been newly edited and studied by I. M. Bochenski, an expert on the history of logic; he regards it as a superficial student exercise, unworthy of the genius of the Angelic Doctor.[22] Yet Bochenski does not deny that it was produced by Thomas Aquinas. Both treatises are mentioned in the early literature and can hardly be excluded from the Thomistic corpus. It would seem most reasonable, then, to place these two logical treatises in, or shortly after, his years as a liberal arts student. The dedication of one of them to some "Noble Students in Arts" could refer to Neapolitan scholars, and could indicate that Thomas wrote the summary of the Aristotelian teaching on fallacious reasoning shortly after leaving the University of Naples. This would date the *De fallaciis* in the years 1243–1244 and would accord with the report of William of Tocco.

We now have printed texts of several logical treatises by William of Sherwood, a typical teacher of logic in the first half of the thirteenth century.[23] There are many similarities between William's works and these two logical treatises by St. Thomas. In exemplifying amphiboly, the *De fallaciis* uses the same irreverent example that is found in William of Sherwood.[24] Such illustrations are, of course, stock examples in most medieval treatises on logic. But the very lack of originality in *De fallaciis* indicates that we are not dealing with a work of Thomas' maturity. There is, however, one example in the treatise which is interesting, in view of what we have seen about Thomas' teachers at Naples. In Chapter 7, illustrating the fallacy of misplaced accent, he speaks of the acute accent which indicates a tonal rise of voice and adds: in the word, *Martinus,*

---

[21] *De propositionibus modalibus,* ed. Mandonnet, IV, 505–507; critically edited by I. M. Bochenski, from four MSS, in "S. Thomae Aquinatis, De modalibus, opusculum et doctrina," *Angelicum,* XVII (1940), 180–221.

[22] Even Bochenski, who is very critical of the content, admits that the attribution to St. Thomas is beyond doubt (*art. cit.,* p. 196); cf. Eschmann, "Catalogue," p. 410, n. 50.

[23] Ueberweg-Geyer, *Die Patristische und Scholastische Philosophie* (Berlin: Mittler, 1928), p. 455, puts William's death in 1249; Grabmann thinks that he died about 1267, *Die Introductiones in logicam des Wilhelm von Shyreswood, + nach 1267* (Sitzungsberichte der Bayerische Akademie, 10) (München, 1937).

[24] *De fallaciis,* c. 5 (Mandonnet, IV, 515): "Quicumque sunt Episcopi, sunt Sacerdotes. Isti asini sunt Episcopi. Ergo isti asini sunt Sacerdotes." (In medieval Latin, one kind of small donkeys were called *episcopi.*) For the same example in William of Sherwood, see Grabmann, *Die Introductiones,* ut supra, p. 87.

this occurs in the middle syllable.[25] It is odd that Aquinas picked this proper name out of all the possible Latin words that would have served the purpose. Is he here, also, commemorating his Neapolitan teacher of logic, Master Martinus?

If the treatises on fallacies and modal propositions were compiled in 1244, then they illustrate the kind of studies in logic that St. Thomas did at Naples. They do not suggest that he was fascinated with logic. Later, in Italy during the 1260's when Thomas was preparing commentaries on most of the works of Aristotle, he paid little attention to the *Organon*. Unlike Albert the Great who covered all of the logical treatises of Aristotle in his Latin paraphrases, Aquinas commented on but two works: the *Posterior Analytics* and a portion of the treatise *On Interpretation*. Both expositions are dated after 1268; they are a far cry from the immature efforts of the *Fallacies* and *Modal Propositions*.[26]

As to St. Thomas' studies in the philosophy of nature under Master Peter, we have no early writings that would indicate their character. It is unlikely that he read the larger Aristotelian treatises: the *Physics, Metaphysics,* or the *Nicomachean Ethics* at Naples. If his teacher was the Petrus de Hibernia who has left commentaries on some minor biological and psychological treatises in the Aristotelian tradition, then we might conclude that Aquinas became acquainted in Naples with the *Parva Naturalia*. It is also probable that he read some of Avicenna there. In both of St. Thomas' early philosophical *opuscula,* the *Principles of Nature* and the treatise *On Being and Essence,* Avicennism is prominent. However, this feature may be due to his studies under Albert rather than to his work at Naples.

It is worth reemphasizing, finally, that St. Thomas later adopted the style of Averroës in his mature expositions of Aristotle, and that Peter of Hibernia favored this type of literal commentary on the text. Quite possibly, one of the most important lessons learned at Naples was how to read the text of Aristotle.

---

[25] *De fallaciis,* c. 7 (Mandonnet, IV, 519): "in media syllaba cum dicitur Martinus, media syllaba acuitur, sive elevatur."

[26] See Eschmann, "Catalogue," p. 401, nn. 28–29.

CHAPTER FIVE

The Dominican Student

IN 1243 or 1244 Thomas Aquinas entered the Order of Preachers as a novice.[1] There is no original document to fix this date. John the Teuton, who was Master General when Thomas entered the Order, had been elected to that office in 1241. Tocco reports that the entry occurred during the pontificate of Pope Innocent IV (1243–1254).[2] Another indirect indication of the date may be drawn from the fact that the Constitutions of the Dominican Order required that a candidate be at least eighteen years of age in order to be accepted.[3] The biographies by Tocco, Bernard Gui, and Peter Calo give no more precise chronological information.

The monastery at Naples was then part of the Roman province and the provincial was probably Humbert de Romans. Tommaso Agni da Lentini was the prior at Naples.[4] It is quite likely that Brother John of San Giuliano assisted at the ceremony. Mandonnet considered it morally certain that the Master General, John the Teuton, was also present.[5]

---

[1] Mandonnet, "Thomas d'Aquin, novice prêcheur," *Revue Thomiste,* VII (1924), 255–257, reviews the available evidence and fixes the reception of the habit in April, 1244.

[2] Tocco, *Vita,* c. 8 (*Fontes,* II, 73).

[3] "Nullus recipiatur infra octodecim annos." See H. D. Scheeben, "Die Konstitution des Predigerordens unter Jordan von Sachsen," *Quellen und Forschungen zur Geschichte des Dominikanerordens,* 38 (1941), 57, n. XIV, 2; cf. *Analecta Ordinis FF. Praedicatorum,* III (1896), 628.

[4] Bernard Guidonis, *Vita,* c. 5 (*Fontes,* III, 171): "Cui habitum ordinis contulit et induit vir per omnia laudabilis et devotus, fr. Thomas Agni de Lentino, tunc prior neapolitanus." Peter Calo, *Vita,* c. 4 (*Fontes,* I, 20) seems to think that John of San Giuliano was then prior at Naples. Tocco, *Vita,* c. 6 (*Fontes,* II, 71), and Bartholomew of Capua, *Proc. Can. Neapoli,* 76 (*Fontes,* IV, 371), say that John of San Giuliano received Thomas but not that he was prior.

[5] "Novice prêcheur" (1924), 375.

Since the ritual for the reception of the Dominican habit has remained much the same, it is possible to reconstruct the scene.[6] Young Thomas Aquinas was brought into the church, or possibly the large hall of the monastery, by the master of novices. Prostrating himself on the floor, the postulant spread his arms wide to form a cross.

"What do you seek?" asked the prior.

"The mercy of God, and yours," was Thomas' answer.

Then the prior bade Thomas to stand while he explained to the youth the austere Rule of the Order, the three vows of poverty, chastity, and obedience, and the constitutional requirements of Dominican life. At the end of these instructions, the prior formally demanded: "Do you wish to observe all of this?"

"Yes, I do wish it," answered Thomas.

Then the prior concluded: "May the Lord bring to completion this work that He has begun."

The friars in attendance added, "Amen."

At this point the master of novices brought Thomas up to the prior, at whose feet he genuflected. The Brother in charge of vestments extended the white tunic and the black hood to the prior who, with the assistance of the master of novices, placed them on the postulant. Meanwhile, the monks present chanted the hymn, *Veni, Creator Spiritus,* and other prayers.

Then the novice master had Thomas stand before the prior who now embraced the postulant with the kiss of peace, as did all the attendant friars. The *Te Deum* was sung.

Finally, the prior turned Thomas over to the novice master, with these instructions:

"If, in the course of this period of novitiate, it turns out that our way of life pleases you, and if your behavior pleases us, then you may make your solemn profession. If not, we shall be free on both sides. Strive then to carry this burden willingly for the love of God, and to obey the master of novices in all things, as you would me."

As events turned out, Thomas was not to live the ordinary life of a Dominican novice. In thirteenth-century practice in the Order, this period of novitiate would not have required him to live apart from the regular community. He would have had to share, under the direction of the novice master, the actual life of the monks. Whether his novitiate was to have

---

[6] *Processionarium Ordinis Praedicatorum* (Roma, 1930), 149; for further details see *Walz-Novarina* (*1962*), 46–47.

actually lasted for a full year, we do not know; this point depends on the exact date of taking the habit, which is impossible to ascertain. If it took place after June 17, 1244, the novitiate required a full year, in accord with the constitution issued on that date by Pope Innocent IV.[7]

Less than ten years earlier (A.D. 1235) the Neapolitan Dominicans had been attacked physically by armed representatives of the family of a young man who had entered the Order without parental permission.[8] It is likely that they now feared similar reprisals from the Aquino family. They decided to send young Thomas Aquinas away to Paris.[9]

Meanwhile Teodora heard the news of her son's reception into the mendicants. She was not pleased. Rushing down from Roccasecca to Naples, she found that Thomas had already left in the company of a group of Dominicans en route to Rome. Nearly all saints have doughty mothers and Teodora was no exception. She sent a messenger to alert her older sons (apparently Aimone and Rinaldo) who were on military service with the army of Frederick II in the vicinity of Acquapendente in Tuscany.[10] The group of Dominicans had stopped but briefly at the monastery of Santa Sabina in Rome. If the Master General was not with Thomas' group in Naples, then John the Teuton may have joined the travelers in Rome, for an early source insists that Thomas was traveling with the head of the Order.[11]

When Thomas and his companions had passed Viterbo and arrived in the neighborhood of Acquapendente (all these land journeys by thirteenth-century Dominicans were made on foot[12]), they were forcibly stopped by

---

[7] This general requirement of the one-year novitiate and the order of Innocent IV are discussed by St. Thomas (*S.T.*, II–II, 189, 2, ad 1) but he says nothing about his own novitiate.

[8] Cf. Mandonnet, "Novice prêcheur" (1924), 388–389; citing *Bullarium Ordinis Praedicatorum* (Roma), I, 74.

[9] Tocco, *Vita*, c. 7 (*Fontes*, II, 72).

[10] Much of this account is from Tocco, *Vita*, cc. 6–11 (Fontes, II, 71–77), who testified to the same details in the *Proc. Can. Neapoli*, 58 (*Fontes*, IV, 350–351), and there reported that his information came from Thomas' niece, Catherine de Morra, who had the story from Teodora.

[11] Thomas Cantimpratensis, *Bonum universale de apibus*, I, 20 (ed. Colvenerius, Duaci 1627, p. 81): "Quidam nobilis adolescens de Romanorum partibus, Thomas de Aquino nomine. . . . Instigavit [diabolus] parentes ejus, et maxime duos fratres illius potentissimos ac feroces . . . furtim a suis fratribus, quos praediximus, raptus est . . . Romam ergo adiens magister Ordinis Praed., piae et beatae memoriae Johannes. . . ."

[12] Mandonnet, "Novice prêcheur" (1924), 538–539: "il était défendu aux Prêcheurs

the Aquino brothers who tried to make Thomas remove the Dominican habit. Failing in this, they apprehended him and took him back to the Aquino castle at Montesangiovanni. Since it is known that Frederick's troops were on military exercises in this area during the spring of 1244 (Frederick himself was at Terni, near Acquapendente, on May 7 of this year), it is probable that this "capturing" of Thomas Aquinas took place in early May, 1244.[13]

The young novice was detained by his family for at least several months. Estimates of the duration of this period of captivity vary widely in the early biographers, ranging up to two years. It is likely that Thomas was first brought to Montesangiovanni and later moved to the main family residence at Roccasecca. Teodora and the older brothers hoped that Thomas would give up his resolution to become a mendicant friar. The general impression that one gets from the various accounts is that the family still expected that Thomas might return to the Benedictines, when affairs had become more settled at Montecassino. Their attitude is understandable; they had no inkling of the career that lay ahead of Thomas in the Order of Preachers. For generations, the main activities of the family had been political and military. Despite the fact that one of Thomas' brothers, Rinaldo, may have studied liberal arts at Naples, the family had little appreciation of scholarship. Moreover, several Aquinos had done well enough as Benedictines and the traditions of this long-established Order were more acceptable to the still feudal aspirations of Teodora and her sons.

In the early descriptions of what happened to Thomas Aquinas during this period of detention by his family, historical facts are inextricably merged with imaginative legends and efforts at pious edification. William of Tocco's account is typical. His seems to be the earliest biography (and he testified under oath to many of the same details, at the canonization proceedings), but he gathered his information some seventy-five years after the detention took place.

In any event, the story is that Thomas steadfastly rejected all the efforts

---

de voyager autrement qu'à pied." The *Bonum universale,* II, 58, says that when John the Teuton became a bishop he continued to travel on foot: "Ipse vero pedes cum fratribus incedebat."

[13] Mandonnet, "Novice prêcheur" (1924), 248–255, studies the evidence and concludes: "l'arrestation de Thomas d'Aquin à Acquapendente tombe pendant la première moitié de mai 1244." Fabro, "Tommaso d'Aquino," *Enc. Catt.,* XII, 254, puts the reception of the habit in 1243–1244.

of his family to persuade him to leave the Dominican Order. This much is historically true. He may have been kept in his room but he was permitted to have books and to continue to wear his habit. There is general agreement that he used these months to good advantage, studying the Bible, possibly instructing his younger sisters, even, as we have seen, doing some writing. It was at this time, according to Tocco, that he wrote the treatise *On Fallacies* and began to read the *Four Books of the Sentences.*[14] Eventually Thomas was permitted to receive some visits from representatives of the Dominican Order.

Where the early biographers differ is in their description of the means used by the family to persuade Thomas to leave the Dominicans. One work written during his lifetime (in 1259–1260) says simply: "They induced him, using whatever means they could, to break his resolution."[15] William of Tocco is more explicit and perhaps imaginative in his account.

> While he [Thomas] was alone in the room in which he customarily slept under custody, they sent in a very attractive girl decked out like a prostitute. She tempted him to sin, using all the devices at her disposal, glances, caresses and gestures. The fighter [Thomas] had taken God's wisdom as his spouse and beloved, and he was not overcome by her appearance. Yet when he began to feel fleshly desire rise within him, which he always had kept under rational control (this exception was allowed by consent of divine providence, so that he might rise to a more glorious triumph from this test), he snatched a burning stick from the fireplace and indignantly chased the girl out of his room.
>
> Internally raging, he strode to a corner of the room, made the sign of the cross on the wall with the point of the burning stick and, prostrating himself tearfully on the floor, prayerfully begged God for the girdle of perpetual virginity to keep himself immaculate in temptation. While praying and in tears, he suddenly fell asleep. Behold, two angels were sent to him from heaven; they told him that he had been heard by God and that he had gained a triumph in a very difficult struggle. Binding him tightly about the loins, they said: "See how, acting on God's behalf, we bind you with the belt of chastity, as you have asked, and it cannot be broken in any temptation. This gift which cannot be gained from the merits of human virtue is granted to you out of divine liberality."[16]

[14] Tocco, *Vita,* c. 9 (*Fontes,* II, 74): "In tali autem carcere . . . quod ibi Bibliam perlegit, et textum Sententiarum didicit; et tractatum fallaciarum Aristotelis, ut dicitur, compilavit, atque sorores suas sacras litteras pro presagio sui magistratus instruxit."

[15] *Vitae Fratrum,* IV, c. 27; in *Monumenta Ordinis Praedicatorum Historica* (Louvain-Rome), I (1896), 201.

[16] Tocco, *Vita,* c. 10 (*Fontes,* II, 75); the same account was given under oath at the canonization proceedings in Naples (*Fontes,* IV, 349) by Tocco, who said that Thomas' *socius,* Reginald of Piperno, was the source of this information.

Few modern biographers accept this whole account literally; some reject it almost entirely.[17] Angelus Walz, a scholarly Dominican historian, notes that the story was first told by William of Tocco who had "a certain tendency toward legends and was ready to enlarge upon and color the most simple facts."[18] Like Mandonnet, Walz thinks that the Aquino brothers were capable of using such means to deter their brother, of course. Teodora could hardly have been a party to such a crude effort to change her son's mind but, of course, some such incident may have occurred at Montesangiovanni in the absence of Thomas' mother. On the other hand, it is possible that Aquinas' younger sister may have innocently tried to talk him out of his vocation and this harmless incident may have become the basis for the legend that he was tempted by a harlot.

As to the story of the angelic girdling, Walz points out that most modern scholars tend to agree with Mandonnet that the belt of chastity was not a material reality but that its significance is moral.[19] We may note that this story is one reason why Thomas Aquinas eventually came to be called the Angelic Doctor. It is not the only reason: a more important one was his later preoccupation with angelology.

With the passage of time, the family came to see that Thomas could not be moved by their arguments against the Dominicans. Possibly the friars complained to Pope Innocent IV, as Tocco says.[20] In any case, this reported appeal shows that William of Tocco thought that the imprisonment took place during Innocent's pontificate (1243–1254). John of San Giuliano visited Thomas and may have persuaded the family that all was not lost even if their son remained a Dominican. So Thomas was eventually released from custody and rejoined the friars in Naples. Political events may also have helped to motivate the family decision. Pope Innocent was soon to leave for France, where (at the Council of Lyons, July 17, 1245) he was to depose Frederick II as Holy Roman Emperor. Now turning against Frederick, the family of Aquino were accused of plotting

---

[17] Joseph Endres, *Thomas von Aquin* (Mainz, 1910), p. 20, rejected the story as unhistorical. Mandonnet, "Novice prêcheur" (1925), 233–236, mentions the attempted seduction but treats the angelic girdling as a dream and not a physical event.

[18] *Walz-Novarina (1962)*, pp. 52–53.

[19] *Ibid.*, p. 53.

[20] Tocco, *Vita*, c. 8 (*Fontes*, II, 73): "Fratres . . . ad Summum Christi Vicarium Innocentium Papam quartum . . . cum gemitu accesserunt."

his downfall and they had to flee northward into the Papal States.[21] By order of Frederick, and so before the Emperor's death in 1250, Thomas' brother, Rinaldo, was put to death.[22]

William of Tocco could not resist the urge to embroider his account of the liberation of St. Thomas. He described how Thomas escaped by being lowered on a rope from a window of the castle into the arms of his exultant Dominican colleagues.[23] As Mandonnet astringently remarks, this story smacks of St. Paul's escape from Damascus by being lowered in a basket over the walls.[24]

Thomas Aquinas thus spent most of his novitiate at home. It was a period that obviously tried his vocation and the Dominicans were glad to take him back without further evidence of the strength of his intentions. At Naples they decided that Thomas should go forthwith to Rome where the Master General, John the Teuton, received him. Possibly he was there dispensed from any further requirements of the novitiate.[25] Then, apparently in 1245, Thomas resumed his northward journey to Paris, possibly going part of the way by ship.[26] Eventually he reached the Dominican house on the Rue Saint Jacques, where some of his most eventful years were to be spent.

There is some vagueness and disagreement in the early sources concerning his whereabouts for the next three years. Tocco says that the Master General took Thomas to Paris, and then on to Cologne where a general house of studies (*studium generale*) was directed by Brother Albert, master in theology.[27] Some of the other accounts speak of his going almost immediately to Cologne for his first Dominican studies.[28] From these early biographical references, we cannot determine where

[21] Mandonnet, "Novice prêcheur" (1925), 411–414, concludes that the Aquino's had to liberate their prisoner because they were leaving Roccasecca.

[22] Bartholomew of Capua so testified, *Proc. Can. Neapoli,* (*Fontes,* IV, 375): "et quod Deus revelaret sibi quid esset de anima domini Raynaldi, fratris sui, quem imperator Fredericus occiderat et ut credebat iniuste."

[23] Tocco, *Vita,* c. 11 (*Fontes,* II, 77).

[24] Acts 9:25; cf. Mandonnet, *art. cit.,* p. 416.

[25] Tocco, *Vita,* c. 12 (*Fontes,* II, 77); *Walz-Novarina* (*1962*), p. 57, discusses the possibility of a papal dispensation.

[26] Tocco, *Vita,* c. 38 (*Fontes,* II, 112).

[27] *Ibid.,* "Magister Ordinis . . . duxit ipsum Parisius deinde Coloniam."

[28] Thus Thomas Cant., *Bonum universale,* I, 20; and Bartholomew of Lucca, *Hist. Eccles.,* XXIII, 20–21. *Walz-Novarina* (*1962*), 59–65, reviews all the evidence.

Thomas first studied as a Dominican. One group of twentieth-century scholars (Denifle, De Groot, Pelster, and Toso) maintains that Thomas studied before 1248 at Cologne. Another equally impressive group (Mandonnet, Grabmann, Castagnoli, Glorieux, Van Steenberghen) insists that he remained in Paris for his studies, from about 1245 to 1248.[29]

In point of fact, the first solid date that we have in the life story of Thomas Aquinas is the year 1248. In this year, probably in the summer or early fall, he accompanied Albert the Great from Paris to Cologne, where a Dominican house of general studies was now established for the first time. To substantiate this, we have the formal record of the general chapter meeting of the Order of Preachers (June, 1248) which states:

> Let the four Provinces, namely Provence, Lombardy, Germany and England, provide that there be forever a general and solemn house of studies, in some suitable convent, and that each provincial prior have the power to send to this place two brothers capable of doing the studies.[30]

No one now doubts that the *studium generale* for the German province was thus founded at Cologne in 1248, or that both Thomas and Albert lived and worked there from 1248 to 1252. It is the period preceding 1248 that occasions controversy. Obviously it would help to know the chronology of Albert's life and work but our information on this period is defective.[31] However, it seems to be established that Albert was bachelor of the *Sentences* at the University of Paris during at least part of the 1240–1248 period and that he continued to teach there until 1248. The first document in which Albert is called *Magister* is dated May 15, 1248.[32] Since Cologne did not have a general house of studies before 1248, and since it is unlikely that Thomas would be sent to the training center of another

[29] It is hardly necessary to repeat the individual references here; they have been gathered in *Walz-Novarina* (*1962*), p. 64, with the exception of F. Van Steenberghen, *Aristotle in the West* (Louvain: Nauwelaerts, 1955), p. 167.

[30] *Acta Capitulorum Generalium,* ed. B. M. Reichert, in *Monumenta Ord. Praed. Hist.,* III, 41.

[31] P. de Loe, "De vita et scriptis Alberti Magni," *Analecta Bollandiana,* XIX (1900), 257–284; XX (1901), 273–316; XXI (1902), 361–371. F. Pelster, *Kritische Studien zum Leben und zu den Schriften Alberts des Grossen* (Freiburg i. B., 1920); plus several studies in the St. Albert issue of the *Revue Thomiste* for 1931 (Vol. XXXVI). See also: F. Van Steenberghen, *Le Mouvement doctrinal du IXe au XIVe siècle* (Paris: Bloud et Gay, 1951), pp. 236–238. (Hereafter cited as *Le Mouvement.*)

[32] *Chartularium Universitatis Parisiensis,* ed. H. Denifle and E. Chatelain (Paris, 1889), Vol. I, n. 178. (Hereafter cited as *C.U.P.*)

province when it was not a *studium generale,* especially when Albert was not there, our best conclusion seems to be that Thomas took his first (the so-called "passive") course in theology under Albert, in Paris, during the years 1245 to 1248. It is not impossible that Thomas spent a short time in Cologne, in 1245, possibly on a visit with Albert, and that this transitional visit has confused the biographers.[33] As we shall see later,[34] Thomas did advanced studies in theology at the University of Paris from 1252 to 1256; taking his degree as a master in theology in 1256. Now the statutes of the University of Paris required eight years of study at this university before a candidate could become a *magister* in theology.[35] Hence, in default of any evidence that the university changed its rules for the sake of Thomas, we must conclude that he had studied there before 1252 — and this could only have been from 1245 to 1248.[36]

When Thomas accompanied Albert to Cologne,[37] in 1248, he may have arrived in time to witness the laying of the first stone of the famous cathedral, on August 15, 1248.[38] Certainly, they found that the Dominican monastery in Cologne was being enlarged to accommodate the influx of students from all over northern Europe. A house on the Stolkgasse, next to the original monastery, had been acquired to make room for this expansion.[39] Thomas Aquinas' ordination as a priest probably took place in the cathedral of Cologne, during these years (1248–1252). We have no record of it but the *Bulla canonizationis* (July 18, 1323) states that Thomas "was promoted to the priesthood at an early age (*etate adhuc juvenis*) and that he later went to Paris and taught theology."[40] This is the basis for dating his ordination during the Cologne years.[41]

There are various intimations in the early literature that Thomas was offered the position of abbot of the Benedictine monastery at Montecassino

---

[33] This is roughly what Pelster finally decided in *Kritische Studien,* pp. 79–81; see also Walz, "Thomas d'Aquin," *DTC,* XV, 1, col. 620.

[34] *Infra,* Chap. Seven.

[35] *C.U.P.,* I, 79, n. 20; cf. C. Thurot, *De l'organisation de l'enseignement des Maîtres en théologie de Paris au XIIIe siècle* (Paris, 1933), I, 210.

[36] M. D. Chenu, *Introduction,* p. 38.

[37] Tocco, *Vita,* c. 12 (*Fontes,* II, 77).

[38] Walz, "Thomas d'Aquin," *DTC,* XV, 1, col. 621.

[39] G. Löhr, *Beiträge zur Geschichte des Kölner Dominikanerklosters in Mittelalter* (Leipzig, 1920), II, 13.

[40] *Fontes,* V, 520.

[41] *Walz-Novarina* (*1962*), pp. 71–72.

while he was still a student at Cologne.[42] It is also rumored that he was invited to accept the episcopacy at various times in his life. Whether these stories have any historical foundation is a point that is difficult to decide. Certainly one can say this: if the Pope had ever insisted that Aquinas take a higher ecclesiastical office, then he would not have refused. In a formal discussion of this matter, Thomas gives his judgment that it is improper to refuse a position of authority, when commanded to take it by a superior.[43] Hence the report by Thomas of Cantimpré that the Pope offered to let Aquinas keep his Dominican habit while he served as head of the monastery of Montecassino, and that Thomas Aquinas fled secretly from the papal court to Cologne in order to avoid the charge, is probably unfounded gossip.[44]

In the next chapter, we shall examine the ways in which Thomas' early Dominican studies and his relations with the famous Albert the Great may have influenced his intellectual development and his search for wisdom.

---

[42] Bartholomew of Lucca, *Hist. Eccl.*, XXIII, 21, and Thomas Cant., *Bonum universale,* I, 20 ("A papa praecipitur ut regimen Abbatiae Montis Cassini susciperet.") are the oldest sources of these rumors. Cf. E. Janssens, "Les premiers historiens de la vie de s. Thomas d'Aquin," *Revue Néoscolastique de Philosophie,* XXVI (1924), 203, who says that Thomas of Cantimpré is repeating secondhand gossip.

[43] *S.T.*, II–II, 185, 2, c.: "ad inordinationem voluntatis pertinet quod aliquis omnino, contra superioris iniunctionem, praedictum gubernationis officium finaliter recuset."

[44] Cf. Janssens, *ibid.*

CHAPTER SIX

Expanding Intellectual Horizons

IN THE early Latin biographies, the story of Thomas Aquinas' first studies in the Dominican Order is told rather sketchily. They indicate that he spent about seven years (1245–1252) under the direction of Albert the Great at Paris and Cologne. William of Tocco's account reads:

> When Brother John the Teuton, Master of the Order, had accepted him [Aquinas] as a son cherished in Christ, he brought him to Paris and then to Cologne, where a general house of studies was flourishing under Brother Albert the Great, Master in theology, of the same Order. He was regarded as outstanding in every science.
>
> When the said young man arrived there and heard him [Albert] teaching profound and marvelous things in every science, he rejoiced that he had so quickly found what he had sought: some source from which he could avidly draw in order to satisfy his thirst, a man to show him the direction of the knowledge for which he had come.
>
> He [Thomas] began to be wonderfully taciturn and silent, zealous in study and devout in prayer, inwardly collecting in memory what he was later to promulgate in teaching. Now, when this quiet student concealed under the veil of astonishing simplicity whatever he was learning from the Master and whatever God in His mercy was infusing into him, the Brothers started to call him the Dumb Ox, for they were unaware of the way that he would eventually roar in his teaching.
>
> Indeed, it was helpful to himself and others that he was rather mute, as far as outward speech goes, so that he could become more loquacious in the intimacy of his own thoughts, with a view to acquiring silently and quickly the habit of knowledge without any hindrance of external talk. And when he had made this progress in his quiet way, unknown to his colleagues, and Master Albert had begun to lecture on St. Dionysius' book, *On the Divine Names*, the said young man listened very attentively to these lectures. On one occasion, another student (who was unaware of the power of intelligence that lay hidden within him) offered to review the lecture for him. He [Thomas] accepted with humble thanks. Then, when this student

started to make the review and was failing to do it well, the said Brother Thomas (as if he were already licensed by God to teach) repeated the lecture clearly and added in his review many things that the Master had not said. As a result, the astonished student begged Brother Thomas to review the lectures for him henceforth. . . .

He [Thomas] agreed to do this but asked him not to tell the others, so that he could still remain concealed in his simplicity. Now, although the student made this promise, he was gravely concerned as to the advisability of keeping silent. So, he told the Master of Students about this newly discovered treasure of unexpected wisdom in the said young man. When the Master arranged to be present, though unseen, at the place where the review was conducted, he understood that it was even more complete than the student's report had suggested. For Master Albert, it was a matter of concern how he might convey to his disciple [Thomas] what a consolation he was for his teacher.

It so happened that, at this time, the Master was conducting a disputation on a difficult question and Brother Thomas had written out his summary of it on a scrap of parchment. By chance some student found this note in front of his room and he gleefully showed it to the Master. When the Master read it, he was amazed at the secret work of his studious disciple. He became aware that in him continued silence accompanied by such simplicity and purity of behavior was not without the privilege of great and hidden grace.

So, he charged the Master of Students to assign him [Thomas] a rather difficult question which he was to answer the next day. Though he [Thomas] was inclined by humility to decline, he did agree as a matter of obedience. Going to his customary place of prayer and commending himself humbly to God, as a beginning for this his first academic exercise, he prepared as well as he could with divine help to answer the question in the next day's class.

When he had restated the Master's arguments, he set forth a distinction whereby he gave a very satisfactory answer to the question and the objections. The Master said to him, "Brother Thomas, you seem to be taking the role of a Master, giving a definitive answer (*determinantis*) and not that of a student disputant (*respondentis*)."

Then with all respect he replied, "Master, I don't see how I could have answered the question differently."

At this point, the Master said, "Now you may answer this question by means of your distinction"—and he presented him four objections so difficult that he thought them entirely conclusive. When Brother Thomas answered them very fully, Master Albert was moved to speak in prophetic mood: "We call this man the Dumb Ox but he will eventually bellow so loudly in his teaching that he will resound throughout the whole world!"[1]

All is sweetness and light in Tocco's story, but he hardly appreciated the temperamental and speculative differences which already distinguished

---

[1] Tocco, *Vita,* c. 12 (*Fontes,* II, 77–79). See much the same account in P. Calo, *Vita,* c. 8 (*Fontes,* I, 25–27).

Albert from his promising student. Born near the beginning of the thirteenth century, at Lauingen (Germany), Albert had entered the Dominican Order in 1223. He was studying liberal arts at Padua when the indefatigable Jordan of Saxony persuaded Albert to take up the life of a Friar Preacher. After teaching in various German monasteries for about ten years, Albert was sent to the University of Paris in the early 1240's. There he was a bachelor of theology and eventually became a master. In what year this degree was received is still a debatable point, but 1245 would not be a bad guess. There is a Paris University document of 1242, signed *Albertus Teutonicus,* which attests to his presence in Paris in that year and to the fact that he was not yet a master. Another Paris document, of 1248, does refer to him as *magister.*[2] As we have seen, Albert apparently stayed in Paris until 1248 and then went with Thomas Aquinas to Cologne to establish the new *studium generale.*[3]

Albert was then an established scholar, doubtless the most learned man the Dominicans had, when Thomas first studied under him. But his learning was of a peculiar sort. As far as philosophy was concerned, Albert was very largely self-taught. He must have been an omnivorous reader. Roger Bacon is the source of a much quoted and caustic report about Albert which probably contains a good deal of truth.

> Another who is still living [Albert] entered the Order as a boy, for he had never lectured in philosophy, nor had he studied it in the schools, nor was he a student in a solemn house of studies before he became a theologian, nor could he have been educated in his Order, since he was the first master of philosophy among them. Yet he taught others, hence what he knew he got from his own efforts. Truly, I praise him more than all the crowd of scholars, because he is a great student with infinite vision and plenty of money. So, he has been able to collect many useful things from the infinite sea of the authors.[4]

Roger was a gossip but he usually knew what he was talking about. He was only a little younger than Albert and had known the Dominican when he, Roger, was teaching liberal arts at Paris in the 1240's. The above report was written by Roger after 1266. It might be just as well to explain first his reference to Albert's wealth. In 1260, Albert was consecrated

---

[2] *Supra,* Chap. Five, note 32; for further information on Albert's career see: B. Geyer, *Albertus Magnus* (Die Grossen Deutschen, I) (Berlin, 1956).

[3] This is the chronology adopted by Gilson, *History of Christian Philosophy,* p. 201.

[4] Roger Bacon, *Opus Minus,* ed. J. S. Brewer (in *Opera quaedam hactenus inedita*) (London, 1859), p. 325.

Bishop of Ratisbon (Regensburg) — much to the displeasure of his Master General, Humbert de Romans. After two years Albert resigned from his episcopal see. Actually, he had encountered much trouble in his diocese. Albert then returned to the life of scholarship but he was also entrusted with various important diplomatic and ecclesiastical missions for his Order and for the papacy. So, after 1262, Albert lived in an odd status. He retained the personal dignity of a bishop but he resided in various Dominican houses and was still regarded as a Friar Preacher. The situation cannot have been without its anomalies. Albert was well aware of his pontifical dignity and jealous of all the perquisites of his office. His last will (which an ordinary Dominican, subject to the vow of poverty, would not think of making) shows that Albert owned an excellent library and had quite a fortune. As he explained in this curious document:

> All know and it can in no wise be doubted that, by reason of the exemption from the rule of the Order granted me by the Pope, I possess temporal goods as my own property and may dispose of them as I think best. . . .[5]

Although this takes us well beyond the period of his first encounter with Aquinas, it tells us a good deal about the rather imperious character of Albert the Great. Even as a master of theology, he was not a man who would suffer the apparent presumption of a brilliant student without rebuke.

The other main point that Roger makes about Albert is also true, in great part. Albert the Great had studied the ordinary course in theology with the Dominicans, before going to Paris, but he had not taken a degree in the liberal arts. Yet Albert reached maturity at a time when many exciting works of foreign scientists and philosophers were being translated for the libraries of Latin scholars. He knew the traditional Christian authors, such as Augustine, Boethius, and Anselm. He read the new translations of the Arabic commentators on Aristotle: Al Kindi, Al Farabi, Avicenna, and eventually Averroës. Jewish authors, Isaac of Israel, Maimonides, and Avicebron, were grist to his encyclopedic mill. By the mid-1240's, Albert had Robert Grosseteste's translations of Aristotle's *Nicomachean Ethics* and of the writings of the mysterious Dionysius the Pseudo-Areopagite. Various anonymous writings, such as the *Book of Causes* and the *Theology of the Pseudo-Aristotle,* fascinated him.

[5] Cited by J. Pieper in *Scholasticism* (New York: Pantheon Books, 1960), p. 180, from the *Testamentum domini Alberti,* ed. Schmeller, in *Gelehrte Anzeigen,* München (Bayer. Akad., Vol. 30) 1850, cols. 45–47.

Albert valued all this knowledge and felt that he had to share it with all Christian scholars. His personal interests were very broad — much more extensive than those of his pupil, Aquinas. Albert's writings show that he was not only a theologian and a philosopher but also a devotee of all the known areas of experimental and observational science. He assembled vast amounts of material in zoology, botany, geology, chemistry, and optics.[6] Of course, much of his scientific writing consisted of paraphrases of information gleaned from dozens of earlier writers. As Roger says, he collected "many useful things from the infinite sea of the authors." Yet Albert tried to develop a general theory of natural science and endeavored to use his broad experience to test his scientific reports.

In this area, natural science and its precise data, Thomas Aquinas never showed as much interest as Albert. It was as if Thomas knew that he could not be a polymath and settled for a much less extensive field of study than that of his Dominican teacher. Possibly Aquinas read most of the books that Albert used but he did not attempt the encyclopedic work in the field of descriptive science which is to be found in Albert's treatises *On Animals.*

More important, perhaps, was Albert's approach to the variety of philosophies which he found in the new translations. It was only in the 1250's and 1260's that Albert wrote his paraphrases of practically all the works of Aristotle. But his earlier writings already showed a tendency toward eclecticism: there is Augustinism and Neoplatonism, Boethian logic and Grosseteste's metaphysics of light, Avicenna's speculation on the necessitated descent of the many from the One, combined with a kind of naturalistic empiricism. It was as if Albert were blind to the inconsistencies of this hodgepodge of conflicting theories that he piled into his lengthy works.

He was the first Dominican scholar to attempt to utilize all of the philosophy of Aristotle in the service of Christian theology.[7] Granted that most of his knowledge of Aristotelianism came initially through secondary sources, it is still obvious that Albert was far ahead of his Dominican contemporaries. One evidence of this is found in his lectures on the *Nicomachean Ethics,* given at Cologne between 1248 and 1252. Thomas Aquinas, in fact, served as the recorder (*reportator*) of this course on

---

[6] See A. C. Crombie, *Robert Grosseteste and the Origins of Experimental Science* (Oxford: Clarendon Press, 1953), p. 192.

[7] M. Grabmann, *Mittelalterliches Geistesleben* (München, 1936), II, 70; cf. Van Steenberghen, *Le Mouvement,* pp. 244–245.

Aristotelian ethics.[8] These lectures are not yet edited in Albert's printed works. At least, we know that Albert did introduce Aquinas to one major work of Aristotle.[9]

Another set of lectures given by Albert, those on the treatise *On the Divine Names* by the Pseudo-Dionysius, illustrates his interest in Neoplatonism. These lectures were also partially recorded at Cologne by Thomas Aquinas. A still-extant Naples manuscript[10] contains portions of this Albertinian exposition, partly in the hand of Aquinas and partly written by another scribe.[11] Thomas' writing during the Cologne period is more vertical than the back-sloping hand of the *Summa contra Gentiles* autograph (of about 1260), but it is already the "unreadable script" (*littera inintelligibilis*) which occasioned so much complaint among his later secretaries.

Two things should be clear from the foregoing. First of all, Thomas Aquinas did serve as a sort of assistant to Albert during part of his course at Cologne. He had the status of a student but he was perhaps better prepared than some of the ordinary students to help his teacher by recording his lectures. Second, this does not mean that Aquinas agreed with the tenor of Albert's thought. His silence on many points may have been due not merely to the marvelous humility, of which Tocco often speaks, but also to the fact that Thomas had his own reservations about the views of his master and was wise enough to keep his thoughts mostly to himself.

There can be little doubt that Albert lectured on parts of the Bible, during the Cologne period. The commentaries on the Psalms, Jeremiah, Daniel, the Gospels, and the Apocalypse were apparently produced at this time.[12] On the other hand, Albert's course on Lombard's *Sentences* was not attended by Thomas. It was given at Paris, before Aquinas arrived.

In comparison with his contemporaries in the Order, Albert was breaking new ground. Hugh of St. Cher, for instance, taught Dominican classes

[8] Cf. A. Pelzer, "Le Cours inédit d'Albert le Grand sur la Morale à Nicomaque recueilli et rédigé par saint Thomas d'Aquin," *Revue Néoscolastique de Philosophie,* XXIII (1922), 333–361, 479–520.

[9] The paraphrase of the *Nicomachean Ethics* printed in Albert's *Opera Omnia* is a different work, from the period after 1254; see Van Steenberghen, *op. cit.,* p. 238.

[10] Naples, *Biblioteca Nazionale,* B. I, 54.

[11] See A. Dondaine, *Les Sécrétaires de saint Thomas* (Rome: S. Sabina, 1956), Fasc. 2: Planches, p. 13; also Fasc. 1, p. 20.

[12] Van Steenberghen, *op. cit.,* p. 237; the biblical commentaries by Albert are printed in *Opera Omnia,* ed. Borgnet, Vols. XV–XXIV and XXVIII.

in theology during the 1230's and eventually became a cardinal.[13] His unedited lectures on the *Sentences* are preserved in a Vatican manuscript.[14] Though he was a capable man, the *Prologue* to this work shows that Hugh knew only the logic of Aristotle. He was unfamiliar with the content of the major philosophical writings of Aristotle.[15] Within ten years, the situation is changed. Albert brought in a wealth of learning which Hugh did not have.

The precise character of Albert's personal thinking, when he taught St. Thomas, is still a matter of discussion. Van Steenberghen thinks that his teaching at Cologne was much influenced by Neoplatonism.[16] If this is so, then Aquinas encountered at Cologne a very different sort of philosophy from the rather simple and straightforward philosophy of nature that he had been taught at Naples. Yet Albert was convinced of the importance of philosophy in the Dominican course of studies. As he wrote in his exposition of the *Letters* of the Pseudo-Dionysius:

> There are some people who are ignorant in all ways and they wish to fight the use of philosophy; this is especially true among the Dominicans, where no one stands in opposition to them. They are like brute animals blaspheming against things they do not know.[17]

Albert was exaggerating the situation in his own Order but there were Dominicans at the middle of the thirteenth century who felt that the Bible contained all the wisdom that a Christian needed and who resented any effort to introduce liberal arts studies into their training program. This attitude continues to be evident, even in the 1260's, in the writings of Vincent of Beauvais and Gerard de Frachet.[18] Albert spearheaded the movement within the Order of Preachers to make the study of philosophy and natural science compulsory in the training of those Dominican scholars

---

[13] P. Mandonnet, "Hughes de Saint Cher," *DTC*, VII (1927), 221–239.

[14] *Cod. Vat. Lat.*, 1098; see the study by John Fisher, "Hugh of St. Cher and the Development of Mediaeval Theology," *Speculum*, XXI (1956), 57–69.

[15] Cf. Fisher, *art. cit.*, p. 68.

[16] Van Steenberghen, *op. cit.*, p. 237, refers to 1248 to 1254 as "la période mystique et dionysienne."

[17] *In Epistolas B. Dionysii Areopagitae*, Epist. 7, n. 2, B; in *Opera Omnia*, ed. Borgnet, XIV, 910; this was probably written before 1254 (Van Steenberghen, *op. cit.*, 237–238).

[18] For this aspect of the *Vitae Fratrum* and of the work of Vincent of Beauvais, see Mandonnet, *Siger de Brabant*, Première Partie (Louvain: Institut Supérieur, 1911), pp. 34–35.

who were to proceed to advanced work in theology. On this point, there is no question that his young Italian pupil, Thomas Aquinas, shared Albert's aims and supported their accomplishment in the ensuing years.

As to what "philosophy" is, there was less agreement. One could say, by way of external description, that Albert considered philosophy to be what was found in Aristotle and his commentators, and also in the Greek and Latin Fathers of the Church. Philosophy consisted in the use of human reason to understand the things and events observed in natural experience. However, Albert had, at least as early as the 1240's, a more definite philosophy which Aquinas could not wholly accept.

Albert's metaphysics explained things in terms of the relationship of the many to the One. In regard to the multiple realities of the created universe, God is the One Source from which they have all come. The many things in this world are real but their existence is imperfect and dependent: they more truly exist in their divine causes, within the creative mind of God. These divine exemplary causes, in turn, are not really multiple; they are identical with the being of God, which is One. Thus far, this might be any standard statement of Christian exemplarism. However, Albert pushed it farther. Only God exists simply, perfectly, and necessarily. The world exists in God as a low-grade manifold is present in a high-grade unity.[19] It remains for one of Albert's disciples, Meister Eckhart, to suggest the next step: all things exist in one supreme *Esse,* that of God.

This sort of metaphysics is not Aristotelian; it lies rather in the tradition of Plotinus, Proclus, the *Liber de Causis,* and Avicebron. Gilbert of Porrée had entertained similar views at the beginning of the twelfth century. The notion that all reality is originally one, and that this unity spreads out and deteriorates by becoming more and more pluralized in its successive stages — this is Neoplatonic emanationism. Albert was fascinated with the theme and applied it to many problems. One of these applications is to the life and understanding of man. This is explained in Albert's treatise on the *Intellect and Its Object,* which is available in an English version.[20]

---

[19] These views are already present in the *Summa de Creaturis* and the *Commentary on the Sentences* (written in the 1240's); see the references and brief exposition in: A. Maurer, *Medieval Philosophy* (New York: Random House, 1962), pp. 160–162, 403–404.

[20] Albert the Great, "The Short Natural Treatises on the Intellect and the Intelligible," in R. McKeon, *Selections from Medieval Philosophers* (New York: Scribner's, 1929), I, 326–375.

As Albert sees it, the human soul is related to man's multiple being and activities as God is to the universe. Man most truly exists in the simple unity of his intellectual soul. As a simple substance, the intellect precontains in a higher unity all the manifold perfections of human life, and even of the many living creatures subordinated to man in creation. This is a modified version of the Neoplatonic metaphysics of a "descent of forms." It was continued and developed by Albert's German followers in the Order of Preachers, Hugh Ripelin (of Strassburg), Ulrich Engelbrecht (of Strassburg), Dietrich of Vrieberg. Eventually it culminated in that extraordinary combination of mysticism and metaphysics which Meister Eckhart achieved.[21]

Thomas Aquinas may have been influenced by this kind of thought but he never belonged to this Albertinist school of philosophy. He was too much impressed by the empiricism and naturalism of Aristotle to adopt a metaphysics which ultimately ran the risk of merging the reality and activities of created things with the transcending unity of the divine *Esse*. Meister Eckhart may not have intended to teach pantheism but he came very close to doing so. There is no such tendency in Thomism.

What Aquinas did share with Albert was an open-minded interest in the writings of both Christian and non-Christian thinkers of many schools. Albert's desire to make philosophy known to the Latins became an important part of Thomas' life work. But where Albert proceeded to accomplish this aim by composing huge encyclopedic treatises in which a variety of philosophic positions is incorporated, in a rich but undigested medley, Aquinas undertook to use this literature in rethinking the problems of philosophy. There is an internal unity and consistency in Thomistic wisdom which is simply lacking in Albertinism.

---

[21] On this German Albertinian school, consult B. J. Muller-Thym, *The Establishment of the University of Being in the Doctrine of Meister Eckhart of Hochheim* (New York: Sheed & Ward, 1939); and Gilson, *History of Christian Philosophy*, pp. 431–442.

CHAPTER SEVEN

Bachelor of the Sentences at Paris

John the Teuton directed Master Albert, in 1251 or early in 1252, to select a suitable Dominican student to go to Paris as a bachelor in theology. Albert named Thomas Aquinas. When the Master General did not immediately accept Thomas for this assignment, Cardinal Hugh of St. Cher sent John a letter warmly recommending the young Italian for this special course. With this backing, Thomas was approved by the Master General and ordered to start at the University of Paris in the fall of 1252.[1]

By the middle of the thirteenth century, the University of Paris had become a great institution. It was the center of scholarly activity for the Christian world; courses were offered in arts, medicine, law, and theology, but Paris was especially noted for the quality of the theologians that it trained. During Peter Abelard's brilliant but troubled career as a teacher, in the first half of the twelfth century, there were three distinct schools in Paris: the Cathedral School at Notre Dame, the School of St. Victor, and the School of Ste. Geneviève, the last founded by Abelard. The university grew out of a merger of these schools; its effective foundation may be dated at the start of the thirteenth century.[2] At first Paris was staffed mainly by diocesan priests as teachers. The bishops of Paris and the papal representatives in Paris saw to it that theology became the main field of study at this university. The liberal arts were encouraged because of their value as a preparation for theology, and grammar became a key subject in the teaching of the arts faculty. Courses in law and medicine were

[1] Tocco, *Vita,* c. 14 (*Fontes,* II, 80).

[2] See H. Daniel-Rops, *Cathedral and Crusade,* trans. by J. Warrington (London: Dent; New York: Dutton, 1957), pp. 308–310.

taught at Paris but there were occasional efforts to keep these professional courses away from Paris.

Unlike the equally old University of Bologna, a civic institution in which the students hired their teachers and had a good deal to do with the administration, the University of Paris was controlled by the teaching faculty under the general direction of the bishop. As the thirteenth century moved on, various popes took more and more interest in this growing center of theological studies. Papal delegates figure largely in the university records.[3] Paris was a Church school, with a papal charter. Its graduates were soon recognized as qualified to teach anywhere in the civilized world.

Within a few years of the foundation of the Order of Preachers by St. Dominic, a group of Dominican friars was sent to Paris to establish a monastery. They arrived on September 12, 1217. Soon, able and learned men were attracted to the possibilities of a combined life of scholarship and active preaching, as provided by the Rule of this new mendicant Order.[4] The first Dominican professor at the university was Roland of Cremona; he was licensed to teach theology at Paris in May, 1229. Roland taught for one year and was succeeded in his chair by his pupil, Hugh of St. Cher. Thus one line of Dominican theology professors was established during a period when they were much needed; for the secular priests who taught at the university had gone on strike in 1229 and something had to be done to provide continuity in teaching. Naturally this way of getting into the faculty did not endear the Dominicans to their diocesan colleagues, who tended to regard the friars as strikebreakers.

On September 22, 1230, an elderly English scholar, John of St. Giles, took the habit in the Order of Preachers but retained his position as professor of theology at the university. Up to this time he had been a secular priest. John thus secured a second chair of theology for the Dominicans at Paris.[5] Guerric de Saint-Quentin, O.P., succeeded to John's professorship and served as *magister regens* from 1233 to 1242. Once they were established in the university, the Dominicans took care to keep these two teaching posts. Writing in his *Short Chronicle,* in the 1260's, Gerard of Frachet lists the first Dominican professors of theology at Paris.

---

[3] M. Grabmann, *I divieti ecclesiastici di Aristotele sotto Innocenzo III e Gregorio IX* (Roma: Herder, 1941).

[4] P. Mandonnet, M. H. Vicaire, and R. Ladner, *Saint Dominique, l'idée, l'homme, et l'oeuvre* (Paris: Desclée, 1937), I, 62.

[5] *C.U.P.*, I, nn. 42–44.

From the time of Master Jordan of holy memory [1222–1237] down to 1258 the following Friars Preacher received the licentiate as Masters from the Paris Chancellor and lectured on the sacred texts to the brothers and to students in the University:
Brother Roland of Cremona,
Brother Hugh of Vienne [Saint Cher] (afterwards a Cardinal),
Brother John of Saint Giles, an Englishman,
Brother Guerric of Flanders [Saint-Quentin],
Brother Godfrey of Bléneau, a Burgundian,
Brother Albert the German,
Brother Lawrence of Brittany,
Brother Stephen of Auxerre,
Brother William de Scampis,
Brother John Pointlasne of Paris,
Brother Bonhomme, a Breton,
Brother Elie of Provence [Brunet],
Brother Florent [of Hesdin], a Frenchman,
Brother Thomas of Aquino, an Apulian,
Brother Hugh of Metz,
Brother Peter of Tarentaise,
Brother Bartholomew of Tours,
Brother William of Alton, an Englishman,
Brother Balduin, a Frenchman,
Brother Hannibald, a Roman (later Cardinal priest of the basilica of the Twelve Apostles).[6]

A similar listing, made by Stephen of Salanhac, O.P., in 1277, after naming Brothers Bonhomme and Elie Brunet of Bergerac, adds a significant note:

These last two men were the regents of our schools at Paris, in the time when the Paris *studium* rose up against our brothers, instigated and led in their evil deeds by William of Saint-Amour, as is recorded in the letter of Pope Alexander III which begins, *Quasi lignum vitae.* [A marginal note in the Toulouse MS 490 adds: *Anno Domini MCCLV*.][7]

This allusion to the problems faced by the Paris Dominicans during the regency of Elie Brunet requires further explanation, for this was the time of Thomas Aquinas' studies as a bachelor of theology. Open conflict had developed during the early 1250's between two groups in the theology faculty: on the one side were the teachers who belonged to the two mendicant Orders, the Dominicans and Franciscans; on the other side were the masters of theology who belonged to no religious Order but were secular priests. The latter group was led by William of Saint-Amour, as Stephen

[6] Gerard de Frachet, *Cronica Brevis,* ed. Reichert (MOPH III), pp. 334–335; English in Foster, *op. cit.,* pp. 149–150.

[7] Stephen's list is printed in Douais, *L'Organisation des études,* p. 164.

mentions. Reasons for the friction and growing bitterness of feeling are not hard to find.

It will be recalled that the Dominicans had come into the university faculty at the time of the strike by the seculars in 1229–1230. On Shrove Tuesday, 1229, some university students quarreled with a Paris innkeeper. Jurisdictional disputes arose between the civic and university authorities. As consequence of this "town and gown" episode, twenty-one overseers of the university, on March 21, 1229, decided to suspend the studies in Paris for a period of six years. We have seen how Roland of Cremona, though a member of the theological faculty, did not obey this decree but continued to teach in the Dominican house of studies. The bishop of Paris, William of Auvergne, was a former master of theology at the university. No doubt his position in the crisis was very difficult, for he probably was opposed to the removal of the courses in theology from Paris, but some of his personal sympathies may have been with his secular colleagues. In any case, William was unable to control the situation. In November of 1229, Pope Gregory IX wrote to the Bishop, pointed out his failure to deal with the crisis and lamented the fact that he had been raised to the episcopacy.[8]

Gradually the Paris masters returned to their posts and, on the surface, accepted the Dominicans and Franciscans as teaching colleagues. The truce was not long-lived. The professors at the university formed a sort of guild, with special rights and privileges but also with solemn obligations to the growing structure of university statutes. Professors who belonged to religious Orders were expected to conform to the regulations of the academic guild — but they were also solemnly bound by the rules of their own Orders and by vows of obedience to superiors who were not necessarily members of the university faculty. Understandably, the secular masters came to feel that their religious colleagues were in an anomalous position, that their duties as religious inevitably conflicted with their obligations in the academic guild.[9]

As mid-century approached, the friction came into the open. Because

---

[8] Grabmann, *I divieti,* p. 91; Van Steenberghen, *Aristotle in the West,* p. 81.

[9] See the appropriate years in *C.U.P.*, I, for the basic documents; cf. Mandonnet, "Novice Prêcheur," *Rev. Thomiste,* XXX (1925), 489–533; Chenu, *Introd.*, pp. 14–22. On the whole problem: Max Bierbaum, *Bettelorden und Weltgeistlichkeit an der Universität Paris* (Paderborn: Franziskanische Studien, Beiheft 2, 1920); D. L. Douie, *The Conflict between the Seculars and the Mendicants at the University of Paris in the Thirteenth Century* (London: Blackfriars, 1954) (Aquinas Papers, 23).

they remained on the job during periods of stress, and because they brought in men of outstanding ability as teachers of theology, the Dominicans and Franciscans attracted more and more students to their classes at the university. Meanwhile, the secular professors found their student enrollments dwindling. In February, 1252, William of St. Amour (as spokesman for the seculars) accused the Dominicans of illegally holding more than one chair of theology in the university. As he wrote plaintively: "Everyone follows their courses; everyone flocks to their church."[10] A proscription was issued, in April, 1253, against any person being accepted as a master who had not fully accepted the faculty regulations and decrees at the University of Paris.

News of the conflict at Paris soon reached Pope Innocent IV, now occupied with his own problems in Italy. At the beginning of 1254, some of the secular masters at Paris issued a defamatory booklet against the teaching friars. Four of the diocesan professors were called to Rome where they presented their case against the "invasion" of the university by the mendicant scholars. Meanwhile, the Dominicans had lost their Master General, through the death (November, 1252) of the noted John the Teuton. Two years elapsed before a new General was elected. This left the Dominicans leaderless in a period of stress at Paris. Pope Innocent at first defended the university privileges of the mendicants, but on November 21, 1254, he issued the Bull, *Etsi animarum,* canceling these privileges.[11] Shortly thereafter, on December 7, 1254, Innocent died. His papal successor, Alexander IV, immediately annulled his predessor's Bull! By April, 1255, Pope Alexander (in the new Bull, *Quasi lignum vitae*[12]) had canceled all regulations of the University of Paris that were restrictions on the religious members of the faculty. Rebellious secular masters at Paris replied with an ultimatum to the Pope: "We would renounce all our privileges and our teaching, close the university and leave Paris, rather than accept the Dominicans among us — they are our persecutors."[13]

One version of William of St. Amour's treatise, *On the Dangers of Recent Times,* was issued in 1255. It detailed the case of the secular masters against the mendicant scholars.[14] In the heat of his argument, William did not hesitate to label his opponents as antichrists. Feeling ran

[10] Taurisano, *San Tommaso d'Aquino,* pp. 101–106.

[11] *C.U.P.,* I, nn. 236 and 240.

[12] *Ibid.,* n. 247.

[13] Taurisano, *op. cit.,* p. 103.

[14] Cf. P. Glorieux, *Répertoire des Maîtres,* I, 343–345.

high on both sides. Writing to the Dominican general chapter meeting at Florence (1257), the new Master General, Humbert de Romans, reported on the situation.

> Our Order has been exposed in this period to tribulations in several areas, and especially in France at Paris. By the disposition of divine Providence, this has turned out for our good, that He should have permitted more serious trouble where our forces are greater and better, gathered from various parts of the world, equipped with all the weapons, they can stand more powerfully against their adversaries and fight them with greater force.[15]

News of the friction at the University of Paris spread far and wide. Distorted rumors of the scandal circulated through the medium of popular poems in the vernacular. As Rutebeuf had it in the *Lay of Master William of St. Amour:*

> You've certainly heard of the quarrel
> (Let's only mention it)
> That lasted a good length of time,
> (Seven full years its duration)
> Between the Men of St. Dominic
> And the teachers of Logic.[16]

Of course, it was not the arts faculty (the "logicians") who opposed the Dominicans, although most of the secular professors of theology came up through the faculty of arts and taught philosophy for a few years before studying theology. But popular poets are not given to fine academic distinctions. What is important to the story of Thomas Aquinas is the fact that these disturbances occurred during the course of his graduate studies in theology, in 1252–1257. He is usually pictured as marching serenely through life, protected in his cloister, enjoying one academic success after another. In point of fact, young Thomas must have felt his urbanity ruffled at many points during these years of turmoil. Here he was, a south Italian in his twenties, far from home and family, unfamiliar with the vernaculars of most of his associates, educated in a philosophic tradition different from theirs, living in a house of studies whose leading professors were anathema to the controlling forces in the university where he was expected to take his doctorate in theology! Inevitably, Thomas Aquinas was drawn into the bitterness of the secular-mendicant quarrel.

In spite of these troubled conditions at the university Aquinas continued his studies and taught as a bachelor, under the supervision of the Do-

[15] Mandonnet, *Siger de Brabant,* p. 89.

[16] *Oeuvres complètes de Ruteboeuf,* ed. A. Juvenal (Paris, 1839), I, 73.

minican master, Elie Brunet. As we shall see in the next chapter, his lectures on the *Sentences* of Peter Lombard were delivered between 1252 and 1256, in the Dominican house of studies on the Rue Saint-Jacques.[17] By 1256, Thomas had completed his studies as bachelor of theology and was almost ready to receive his degree as master of theology. As the early biographers describe the situation, the Chancellor of the university (Aimeric de Veire) directed the Dominican Prior in Paris to have Brother Thomas prepare himself for the reception of the magistrate (the equivalent of our present doctorate).[18] Tocco's account is a little fuller than the others.

> When the course of study had been zealously and fruitfully completed and the time had arrived for the bachelors in theology to be presented by the Paris Chancellor, although the regulation concerning the customary amount of time had not been fulfilled, the Chancellor directed the Paris Prior of the Order of Friars Preacher to command on his part the aforesaid Brother Thomas to get ready to receive the magistrate in theology, in spite of and without objection arising from the fact that he might be given special preference over other candidates. Although he humbly excused himself on the basis of his lack of knowledge and of age, Thomas was unable to refuse, because he was subject to his vow of obedience. So, he humbly accepted the burden imposed on him and, retiring to his customary place of prayer, tearfully prostrated himself and prayed to God that he be granted infused knowledge and grace to receive and carry out the magistrate, and that he might be made worthy by many graces.
>
> He then began the Psalm [11:1, Vulgate]: "Save me, O Lord, for truths are decayed from among the children of men." When he had prayed for a long time in tears, he fell asleep. Behold, a heavenly messenger was sent to him, an ancient Brother revered in the same Order, who said, "Brother Thomas, why are you praying to God with such tears?"
>
> He replied, "because the burden of the magistrate has been put upon me and my knowledge is not enough for it. Moreover, I have no notion of what subject to treat in my inaugural lecture."
>
> "Your prayer has been heard," the old man said, "take up the burden of the magistrate, for God is with you. Take this text for your inaugural lecture: *Thou waterest the hills from thy upper rooms; the earth shall be filled with the fruit of thy works* [Ps. 103:13]."
>
> When these words had been uttered, Brother Thomas awakened and gave thanks to God for so quickly hearing his prayer. For this text not only provided a theme for his lecture but a basis for all his studies; since, from these origins which he took from the heights of divine speculation, he watered the whole Church, as a field planted with divine seed is irrigated by the rains of wisdom. Indeed, it is clear to all that, throughout the world

[17] Cf. *Walz-Novarina (1962)*, p. 85, note 54.

[18] B. Gui, *Vita,* c. 12 (English in Foster, *Life,* p. 34); Tocco, *Vita,* c. 16 (*Fontes,* II, 84–85).

among faithful Catholics, nothing else is read in all the schools of philosophy and theology than what is drawn from his writings.[19]

The general view in the Dominican monastery in Paris, during the thirteenth century, was that the ancient monk who appeared to Thomas in his dream was St. Dominic himself.[20] This is not a likely identification, because St. Dominic was not an old monk when he died.

Also during the same year (1256), the tide was turning against the secular masters at Paris. Bull after Bull issued from Rome in support of the mendicant scholars. Humbert de Romans, who had become Master General in 1254, was a forceful personality. He called a general meeting of the Dominican Order in Paris at the climax of the struggle. The Pope summoned a commission of cardinals at Anagni to examine William of St. Amour's defamatory booklet. Important representatives of the Dominican and Franciscan Orders presented their case at the papal court. In the fall of 1256, Thomas Aquinas completed his first defense of the religious Orders in answer to the charges of William of St. Amour. This first controversial work is entitled: *Against the Attackers of the Religious Life*.[21]

The quarrel at Paris was more than a battle of the books, however. When Thomas' colleague, Florent de Hesdin, started his lectures at the Dominican house on the Rue Saint-Jacques in September of 1255, it was necessary to call on the royal archers to protect him from violence.[22] In the Franciscan monastery, Brother Bonaventure had been qualified for several years to receive his magistrate in theology, but the theology professors used every possible delaying tactic to block the awarding of the degree to this noted Franciscan scholar who was seven or eight years older than Thomas. Several papal letters were sent to the University of Paris ordering the professors to agree to the granting of these degrees and

[19] Also see: *Vitae Fratrum* (MOPH I), Pars IV, c. 24, 8; the testimony of Cistercian Brother Peter de Castro Montis Sancti Johannis, *Proc. Can. Neapoli*, XLIX (*Fontes*, IV, 331); and of Brother Peter de Caputio, O.P., *op. cit.*, XCII (*Fontes*, IV, 398–399).

[20] Peter de Caputio, *loc. cit.*, p. 399: "dixit quod opinio erat Parisius inter fratres Praedicatores quod ille fuit sanctus Dominicus." But see Foster, *Life*, p. 148.

[21] *Contra impugnantes Dei cultum et religionem*, in *Opuscula Theol.* (Turin: Marietti), II, 1–109; English in Procter, *An Apology for the Religious Orders* (Westminster, Md.: Newman, 1950). Cf. Glorieux, "Le *Contra Impugnantes* de saint Thomas," *Mélanges Mandonnet* (Paris: Vrin, 1930), I, 51–81.

[22] Glorieux, *art. cit.*, p. 75.

to admit both Thomas and Bonaventure to full faculty privileges.

Thomas was busy on the preparation of his inaugural lecture during the spring of 1256. He was not quite old enough, perhaps, to take the degree, for the university statutes required that a candidate be thirty-five years of age before becoming a master in theology. Although we do not know his precise age in 1256, Aquinas was likely in his early thirties. Moreover, he seems to have been genuinely doubtful of his readiness for this major step in his career. However, he dutifully proceeded with the task. The actual granting of the degree seems to have taken place in the spring of 1256, for Pope Alexander wrote to the Chancellor on March 3, 1256:

> It gives Us pleasure to hear that you have shown readiness and diligence in this matter, which attitudes manifest loyalty or savor of decency, as may evidently be observed; for you have granted the licentiate to teach in the theology faculty to Our beloved son, Brother Thomas of Aquino, O.P., a man of noble origin, distinguished by the uprightness of his behavior, who has through the grace of God obtained the treasure of literary knowledge — and you did this before receiving Our letter which We sent to deal in particular with this matter. Now, since it is quite fitting that this affair, so laudably begun by you, should come to a quick and happy conclusion, observing your loyalty, We have asked and ordered by means of Apostolic commands directed to you in writing that you arrange for the aforesaid Brother to hold his inaugural lecture in the aforementioned Faculty as quickly as possible.[23]

It is not entirely clear what degree Thomas received just prior to the writing of this papal letter of March 3, 1256. In the letter, it is referred to as the licentiate (*licentiam in Theologica Facultate docendi*), but most Dominican historians now insist that he became a *magister* in 1256.[24] On June 17, 1256, Pope Alexander wrote again:

> What further difficulties are there? The aforementioned masters and scholars have no interest in keeping, as We have understood, the peace that is surrounded by pricks of discord; for they are maliciously opposed to those who wish to attend the lectures, disputations and sermons of the Friars, and also to those who desire Our beloved son, Brother Thomas of Aquino, to hold his inaugural lecture.[25]

---

[23] *Doc.* XI (*Fontes,* VI, 544–545).

[24] G. Abate, "Intorno all cronologia di S. Tommaso d'Aquino," *Miscellanea Francescana,* L (1950), 231–247, argues that Thomas received the licentiate before March, 1256, gave his *principium* between April and September, 1256, and became *magister regens* only on August 12, 1257. I think that Abate may be right. Chenu, *Saint Thomas d'Aquin et la théologie* (1959), p. 33, and *Walz-Novarina* (*1962*), p. 92, both claim that he became *magister regens* in 1256.

[25] *Doc.* XII (*Fontes,* VI. 548–549).

Under circumstances which are not clearly documented, Thomas did deliver this inaugural lecture (*principium*), at some time between June and September of 1256. This sermon is in very formal academic style and includes Scripture texts in almost every sentence, which makes it very difficult to translate. The following is the substance of the lecture, minus the biblical quotations.[26]

The King and Lord of the Heavens, in His providence, has established from eternity a law according to which His gifts may reach the lowest creatures by going through intermediate ones. This law applies not only to spiritual creatures but also to bodily ones. That is why, in this text from the Psalms (103:13), the Lord presents this law, as it is observed in the communication of spiritual wisdom, under a corporeal metaphor. So we see the meaning of the rain flowing forth from the heights of the clouds, by which the mountains are flooded with rivers, by which in turn the earth is fecundated with their richness. In like manner, the minds of teachers (signified by the mountains) are watered from the heights of divine wisdom, and by means of their teaching ministry the light of divine wisdom is channeled down to the minds of their listeners. Thus, in our text, we can consider four points: the profundity of spiritual teaching, the dignity of its teachers, the status of its listeners, and the order of its communication.

I. Its *profundity* as sacred doctrine may be shown from three points of view. First, in its origin, this wisdom comes from above, from the Word of God. Second, from the difficulty of its subject-matter, for there are certain profound truths of divine wisdom which all men attain, even though imperfectly, since the knowledge that God exists is made available naturally to all men; and there are other higher truths which are grasped only by the ingenuity of wise men, trained in the use of reasoning; and there are some highest truths which surpass all enlightened reasoning: these are handed down by sacred teachers, learned in the text of Sacred Scripture; for it is on this highest level that Wisdom itself is said to dwell. Third, its profundity is manifested from the sublimity of its end. It has the highest end, namely, eternal life.

II. The *dignity of its teachers* is demanded by reason of the profundity of this teaching. Hence, they are symbolically represented as mountains, for three reasons. First, because of the height of mountains which are elevated above the earth to the region of the heavens. Thus do sacred teachers contemn earthly matters and aspire to heavenly things only. Second, because of their splendor, for the mountains are the first to be illumined by the rays of sunlight. Likewise, the sacred teachers are the first to receive mental splendor. For, like mountains, teachers are the first to be illumined by the

[26] On the date of this *principium,* Eschmann, "Catalogue," p. 428; Grabmann, *Die Werke,* ed. 3, p. 394; and Tocco, *Vita,* c. 16 (*Fontes,* II, 85). The text of the *principium* is printed in Mandonnet, *Opus. Omnia,* IV, 481–490; and in *Opus. Theol.* (Turin: Marietti, 1954), I, 435 ff. My version follows the French translation by Chenu, *Saint Thomas d'Aquin et la théologie,* pp. 83–84, in omitting the scriptural passages.

rays of divine wisdom. Third, because of the protective function of mountains, in the sense that an earthly territory is defended by its mountains. So too, should the Church's teachers stand in defense of the faith against errors. The sons of Israel do not put their trust in spears or arrows; instead, the mountains defend them. Thus all teachers of Sacred Scripture should be elevated by the eminence of their lives, so that they may be suitably equipped to preach effectively. For the heart cannot be pricked or pierced by the fear of God, unless it be fixed on the highest level of life. They should be enlightened, so that they may be worthy to teach through their preaching. They should be strengthened by learning, so that they may refute errors in their disputing. It is to these three functions, preaching, teaching and disputing, that the text of Titus 1:9 refers: *able both to exhort in sound teaching and to confute opponents.*

III. The *status of its listeners* is signified by the comparison with the earth. In like manner, they should be like the earth, providing a foundation through their humility, standing firm in their grasp of what is right, being fruitful so that the words of wisdom, when received, may fructify in them. So, humility is required in them for the acceptance of instruction as listeners; a feeling for rectitude, so that they may be discriminating listeners; but fecundity is required for discovery, so that the good listener may promulgate many words of wisdom from the few that are heard.

IV. Finally, the *order of development* of sacred teaching is touched upon here, from three points of view: in regard to the order of communication, the amount, and the quality of the gift that is received. First of all, the minds of teachers are not able to grasp the whole of the content of divine wisdom. Moreover, the entirety of what teachers do understand cannot be poured forth on their listeners. The teacher should not preach all that he knows to the uninstructed, for he himself is unable to appreciate the greatness of the divine mysteries. In the second place, this order is touched on, from the point of view of the manner of possession. God possesses wisdom by His nature. Teachers, however, possess knowledge in part, even though abundantly. This is why they are said to be watered from above. The listeners share in it sufficiently, and this is what the satiety of the earth means. In the third place, this order is viewed from the aspect of the power to communicate this doctrine. God communicates wisdom by His own power; so He is said to water the mountains by Himself. But the teachers communicate wisdom only as intermediaries. Hence, the fruit of the mountains is not attributed to themselves but to divine operations. God, then, requires His ministers to be immaculate in their lives, understanding in the acceptance of their ministry, obedient to the prompting of His will. Though no person by himself and of himself is adequate to such a ministry, he may hope that sufficiency will come from God — and he should seek it from God.

Let us pray: May Christ grant us . . . Amen.

This learned and beautiful discourse of St. Thomas Aquinas, preached when he was on the threshold of his public career as a teacher of divine wisdom, has never (to my knowledge) been printed before in English. It contains the germs of many of the strands of wisdom which were to grow in his future works. We should note that a young man with his origins in the district of Montecassino and Roccasecca knew what he was talking about when he spoke of the way in which mountains are a protection in time of strife. Is it possible, too, that his remark, "the sons of Israel do not put their trust in spears or arrows," is couched in gentle irony? Surely, most of Thomas' listeners could remember that one year ago the Dominican house had to be protected by soldiers bearing arrows.

Thomas and Bonaventure both taught theology in their respective houses of study in Paris but they were still not accepted as full members of the theological faculty at Paris. On this point, the secular masters were adamant. In October, 1256, Pope Alexander sent a lengthy message to the university, sternly commanding the recalcitrant administrative officers:

> to receive, insofar as it is within their power, into the academic society and into the University of Paris, the Friars Preachers and Minors now stationed at Paris, and also their students; and in particular and by name, the Friars, Thomas of Aquino, of the Order of Preachers, and Bonaventure, of the Order of Minors, as Doctors of Theology.[27]

This document shows two things. The Pope was a patient man but his patience was running out. And, as far as Pope Alexander knew, neither Bonaventure nor Thomas had yet been granted the master's degree.

It was in the next year (1257), on the Sunday preceding the feast of the Assumption (August 12), that the two friars were summoned to the hall of the Franciscan house of studies in Paris, to receive a grudging admission into the faculty of theology. There, in the presence of a delegate sent by Bishop Reginald of Paris, Canon Christian of Verdun admitted Thomas and Bonaventure to full magistral privileges in the university. He did so with obvious ill grace, for he was acting under duress. He and his associates had fought long and hard against this step. Now they had lost. Even the following extracts from the official record ill-conceal the reluctance of Master Christian. The document begins with a statement by the Bishop of Paris who did not attend the event.

> Reginald, by divine compassion the unworthy minister of the Church in Paris, to all who read this document: Greetings in the Lord. We make it known that, in the year of our Lord 1257, on the Sunday before the Assumption of the Blessed Virgin Mary, in a complete oral statement made in the residence of the Friars Minor of Paris, Master Christian of Verdun declared in public all and each of the things below recorded, according to

[27] *C.U.P.*, I, 338–340, n. 293.

this form, in the presence of our delegate who was specially designated and sworn by us for this purpose.[28]

Apparently, Bishop Reginald wished to dissociate himself as much as possible from the proceedings, but he knew that the Pope expected a proper and legal record of what was done. After all, several of the recalcitrant professors of theology (who were represented by Christian) were canons of the Bishop's own Cathedral of Notre Dame. What follows in the document is given as an exact record of Christian's terse and bitter words.

> My purpose is twofold: first to say why I came and then to do it. . . . [Several quotations from Scripture are inserted here.] Some persons have reported to my Lord the Pope that I have been a rebel against him and that I was the instigator of rebellions — which I never was. And yet the Pope believed this, and those who made this report to my Lord the Pope took away my good name as an obedient man.
>
> For this reason, I have taken pains to recover that name. I knew no other way than to go to my Lord the Pope, so that he might excuse me of disobedience. To this end, I did four things. First, I stated that I had never, to my knowledge, been a rebel. Second, I requested that I be shown whether I had been a rebel in any matter, so that I might do penance. To those who said that I had not accepted the Friars, I stated that this was false. On the contrary, after they were removed from the University, I was with them in the school of Master James [de Guérande, Canon] of Tours and I took their side. Thus I excused myself, as some of those who heard me at the [papal] Court have reported, for they were present when I defended myself in a public audience.
>
> Then I took a further step, desiring to show myself obedient in all matters: I promised the Pope that I would obey in all matters. Next, he has ordered that I take an oath. I have stated that for a Christian there is no difference between one's simple word and an oath. Yet I have sworn to do what the Pope has ordered. Then, I was ordered to do certain things in the Court, and I did them. Also, I was ordered to do the same at Bologna but this order was rescinded because I did not know the language. Further, I was ordered to do the same at Paris. This is why I have come: to say what I have been commanded to say.

Christian proceeded to argue that he had been unjustly harmed by his accusers. Then he denied that he had revoked anything that he had previously said, insisting that his present statement should not be understood as an act of revocation but as one of obedience. Finally Christian made the statement which was the reason for the convocation.

[28] For the full Latin text, see *Doc.* XIV (*Fontes,* VI, 554–559); also edited in *C.U.P.*, I, 364–367.

I, Master Christian, insofar as lies within my power, henceforward accept and henceforward obey, and I shall obey in the future unless my Lord the Pope order otherwise, the command of my Lord the Pope which has these opening lines: *As the tree of life, etc.* And I shall not knowingly act against it, nor shall I give help or counsel, in public or in private, to opponents of this papal document. Second, henceforward insofar as is within my power, I do accept into the academic society and into the University of Paris the Friars Preachers and Minors residing in Paris as Masters, together with their students, and especially and expressly Friars Thomas of Aquino, of the Order of Preachers, and Bonaventure, of the Order of Minors, Doctors of Theology. And I expressly accept the aforementioned Doctors as Masters; and in keeping with the aforementioned command, I shall see to it that these men are received in good faith by the University — that is, by the Masters and students dwelling in Paris; and against the foregoing I shall never offer counsel or consent.[29]

Next in the lengthy deposition, Christian stated that he would exact no obligations or oaths contrary to the papal Bull, *Quasi lignum vitae.* He further promised to permit no more trouble, strikes, or removals of the university from the city of Paris. He agreed to the condemnation of the booklet written against the Friars, recognized the power of the Pope to send the mendicants anywhere as preachers and confessors, without the added consent of lower ecclesiastical authorities, and he admitted that mendicancy is a state of religious perfection. At this point, Christian could not resist adding a qualification: in his statement to the cardinals at the Curia,[30] he understood his words concerning the perfection of the mendicants to mean, "provided they live according to the regulations of their Order," and he now insisted that the cardinals and friars at the papal court so understood his declaration. It was a humiliating occasion for Master Christian.

The document ends with an appendix by the Bishop of Paris who is obviously endeavoring to observe all the due formalities. This appendix further manifests the desire of Bishop Reginald to have as little to do with the proceedings as possible.

We, Reginald, by the grace of God Bishop of Paris, in order to remove all ambiguity, have inserted a word into this document, to which this present note is added, and it is this: in the formula, "in witness to the aforesaid we have affixed our seal to the present document," We have understood and do understand the words, "in witness to the aforesaid," to mean that the said Master Christian so testified in the presence of Our delegate. And

[29] *Doc.* XIV (*Fontes,* VI, 557–558).

[30] For Christian's statement at Anagni, see *Doc.* XIII (*Fontes,* VI, 551–554).

it is not known to us what the Cardinals said, or what the Friars say, concerning their past or present understanding of the statements about the disciples of Antichrist, or whether their understanding agrees with that of the aforesaid Master [Christian].

Given in the Year of Our Lord, 1257, in the month of August.[31]

Thus, grudgingly, the University of Paris accepted a new master of theology. It cannot have been a very pleasant inauguration for Thomas and Bonaventure. Nor did this convocation in the hall of the Franciscans mark the end of friction between the mendicants and the secular scholars at the university. However, from this point onward Aquinas was a fully accredited professor in the greatest university in Christendom.

---

[31] *Ibid.*, XIV (*Fontes,* VI, 559).

CHAPTER EIGHT

Merging Traditions of Wisdom

MANY students of the work of St. Thomas take it that, after going to the University of Paris in 1252, he spent two years teaching Scripture (*Baccalaureus Biblicus,* 1252–1254) and then a second biennium lecturing on the *Sentences* of Peter Lombard (*Baccalaureus Sententiarum,* 1254–1256).[1] Strangely enough, it is difficult to document this usually accepted division of his time as an advanced student in theology at Paris. At least one recent writer questions the assumption that Thomas served as Bachelor of the Bible.[2] We do know that he lectured on the *Sentences* in this period and that his *Scriptum in libros IV Sententiarum* was completed by 1256–1257. This treatise represents the tenor of his theological teaching before 1256, but the text, as we have it, may have been written by Thomas, or revised by him, at the end of this period.

What we do not know is whether he actually taught the two-year course on parts of the Bible in 1252–1254. First of all, if he did, then we have no direct evidence of it, either in historical documents or in biblical commentaries produced by Thomas in those years. Tocco is no great help on the matter: his description of Thomas' work as a bachelor is very vague.

> Having been made a Bachelor, when he had begun as a lecturer to communicate what he had deliberately hidden in his silence, God infused such great knowledge in him, and there was such great teaching divinely expressed by his lips, that he seemed to excel all, even the Masters, and by the clarity of his teaching to stimulate the students to the love of knowledge more than other teachers did.[3]

[1] Cf. M. D. Chenu, *Introduction à l'étude de s. Thomas,* p. 226.

[2] Eschmann, "Catalogue," p. 428: "The fact that Aquinas ever was *Baccalaureus biblicus* in Paris is not quite sure." For the same doubt, see *Walz-Novarina (1962),* pp. 80–81.

[3] Tocco, *Vita,* c. 14 (*Fontes,* II, 81).

This is all very well but it does not tell us what St. Thomas taught. To settle this question all that we can do is to consider the conditions under which Thomas worked and the actual writings that he produced between 1252 and 1256.

The intellectual situation in the Paris faculty of theology during the early 1250's was already complicated by several traditions of learning. We can distinguish four trends of thought which Thomas encountered there: on the Christian side, there were Augustinianism and Boethianism; from the non-Christian literature, there were the views of Aristotle and of Avicenna. Of these four, there is little doubt that the thought of St. Augustine of Hippo was dominant and primary. We are not here concerned with the problem of whether Augustinianism may be called a philosophy;[4] whatever it was, the wisdom of Augustine was still very influential at Paris. Not only were St. Augustine's major works (*Confessions, City of God, On the Trinity, On Christian Doctrine*) being read, the *Books of Sentences* by Peter Lombard were used as a textbook for the teaching of all advanced students in theology, and the content of the *Sentences* was very largely excerpted from Augustine's writings.[5] The master in theology who directed Thomas' teaching as a bachelor in theology was Elie Brunet, O.P., the occupant of the Dominican chair for foreign (non-French) students at the College of Saint Jacques. Little is known of the character or work of this Dominican theologian.[6] His name has never been mentioned by Aquinas. Two regent masters in theology were in charge of the Dominican courses at that time: Brother Bonhomme from Brittany and Brother Elie Brunet from Bergerac in Provence. The former was the director of theology courses for the students of the French group (*natio*) and the latter (Elie) was the director for the students from other Dominican provinces.[7] It is probable that Elie Brunet was a quiet, retiring man of conservative Augustinian views. Our reason for this estimate is very indirect.

The main work of St. Thomas stemming from this period is his *Scriptum in IV Libros Sententiarum*.[8] The *Four Books of Sentences* had been com-

[4] Van Steenberghen argues throughout his *Aristotle in the West* (1955) that there was no Augustinian "philosophy" in the thirteenth century.

[5] See F. Cavallera, "S. Augustin et le Livre des Sentences de P. Lombard," *Archives de Philos.*, VII (1930), 438–451.

[6] Cf. Glorieux, *Maîtres de Théologie*, I, n. 12.

[7] See the list of Dominican masters given *supra* in Chapter Seven.

[8] Probably the best edition is that of P. Mandonnet and M. F. Moos (Paris: Lethielleux, 1929) — (incomplete, the fourth volume appeared in 1947); in ed. Parm., Vols. VI–VIII.

piled at the middle of the twelfth century by Peter Lombard. Originally from North Italy, Peter taught theology in the Paris School of Notre Dame from about 1135–1150.[9] He produced a textbook in theology which was a digest of the "views" (*sententiae*) of earlier Christian writers (Hilary, Ambrose, Jerome, Gregory the Great, Cassiodorus, Isidore, Bede, Boethius, John Damascene, Hugh of St. Victor, Abelard) but in which 80 percent of the material was directly quoted from St. Augustine.[10] In other words, the four books of *Sentences* was a compendium of Augustinian theology.

It might be well at this point to notice the medieval attitude toward authorship. It is bluntly expressed by St. Bonaventure in his introduction to Lombard's *Sentences*:[11]

> To understand these words, it should be observed that there are four ways of producing a book. A man may write down another writer's material without any addition or change: he is simply called a scribe (*scriptor*). A second man may write another man's material, adding something that is not his own: he is called a compiler (*compilator*). A third man may write both the views of another and his own — but principally the other's, his own being attached for clarification: and he is called a commentator (*commentator*) not an author. A fourth man may write down both his own and another's material — but principally his own, the other man's material being used only for confirmation: and such a writer is entitled to be called an author [*auctor,* i.e., an increaser of knowledge].

This throws an interesting light on the literary methods of the Middle Ages. Bonaventure, of course, concludes that Peter Lombard was truly an *auctor,* because he expressed his own opinions (*sententias*) and backed them up with quotations from the Fathers.[12] It is true that Peter had certain views which were not traditional in theology. In Christology, he followed the lead of Abelard in claiming that the humanity of Christ is not that of a concrete individual man (*Christus ut homo non est hoc aliquid*),[13] and in treating the notion of charity, Lombard said that it is not something created in the human soul (a gift) but is identical with the Holy Spirit dwelling in the soul.[14] However, Peter Lombard left a work which was a

[9] He was Bishop of Paris from 1159 to his death in 1160; see A. Forest, *Le Mouvement*, p. 158.

[10] Cf. Grabmann, *Die Geschichte der scholastischen Methode* (Freiburg: Herder, 1911), II, 385–386.

[11] S. Bonaventurae, *In I Sententiarum,* Proem., q. 4, resp; ed. Minor (Quaracchi, 1934), I, 12a.

[12] *Ibid.,* "Talis fuit Magister [i.e., Petrus Lombardus] qui sententias suas ponit et Patrum sententiis confirmat. Unde vere debet dici auctor hujus libri."

[13] P. Lombardi, *Sententiae,* III, c. 10.

[14] *Ibid.,* I, c. 1; see Forest, *op. cit.,* p. 159.

veritable anthology of Augustinian opinions, and this was the textbook which Aquinas was required to teach in preparing for his doctorate in theology.

It is obvious that Thomas Aquinas was not entirely in agreement with some of the philosophical aspects of Augustine's thought.[15] In general, the young bachelor diplomatically accommodated his teaching to the character of his textbook and never openly criticized Augustine. However, the careful reading of his *Scriptum in Sententiis* will reveal certain reservations in the mind of the young lecturer. As an example of this sort of thing, let us briefly look at an article in which he starts with the Augustinian view that the "Image" of the Divine Trinity in the human soul is found in mind, memory, and will.[16] He asks whether the rational powers of the soul are always in act in regard to their objects. In the first part of his answer, Thomas explains Augustine's psychology and says that, according to Augustine, the soul is always understanding itself and God, and loving such objects, indeterminately. Then abruptly he says:

> However, in another explanation, according to the Philosopher [Aristotle], the fact that the soul always understands itself is taken to mean that everything that is understood is only comprehended when illuminated by the light of the agent intellect and when received in the possible intellect.

And in answering a second objection, he adds: "The Philosopher speaks of understanding as a perfect intellectual operation of distinguishing or thinking, and does not take understanding in the sense that it has here."[17] It is clear that Thomas knows that Augustinian psychology is different from that of Aristotle.

Later, discussing two views of how the human soul is related to its body,[18] Thomas says that erroneous answers to this problem are based on two improper ways of thinking about the soul: some imagine it as a sort of mover (*motor*) of the body; other people picture the simplicity of the soul in terms of a mathematical point. Then, with surprising abruptness, he remarks: "Now, each of these views is stupid!"[19] He next cites Augus-

[15] E. Gilson, "Réflexions sur le controverse saint Thomas-saint Augustin," *Mélanges Mandonnet* (Paris: Vrin, 1930), I, 371–383.

[16] S. Thomae, *In I Sent.,* d. 3, q. 4, art. 5.

[17] *Ibid.,* ad 2m: "Philosophus loquitur de intelligere secundum quod est operatio intellectus completa distinguentis vel cogitantis, et non secundum quod hic sumitur intelligere."

[18] *Ibid.,* d. 8, q. 5, art. 3.

[19] *Ibid.,* "Et utrumque horum stultum est."

tine and Albert with benevolent approval as saying that the soul is wholly present in every member of its body and concludes with an explanation of how the soul informs the body. This is obviously an effort to adjust the Augustinian explanation to the Aristotelian one. The young Aquinas (he is approaching thirty) feels that he has to present and somehow defend St. Augustine's views, but he also takes care to introduce various explanations from the Aristotelian tradition.

Yet, as a Bachelor of the Sentences, Thomas Aquinas already has his own personal points of view. To see the young teacher at work, let us examine one of his solutions to the touchy problem of the manner in which human souls are individuated. It is well known that he eventually differed from many of his contemporaries on this question. Here is how he handled it when he first began to teach:[20]

> In accord with the foregoing, we must say that there is nothing in the soul whereby it is individuated. Those who denied that it is a complete substance (*hoc aliquid*) understood this and maintained that it does not have a distinct act of being. Now, I say that it is only individuated from the body. Hence arises the fact that the error of people who claim that souls are first created and then afterwards put into bodies is impossible, because souls do not become plural unless they are infused into plural bodies.
>
> Yet, although the individuation of souls depends on the body as far as their origin is concerned, this does not hold true in regard to their end, in the sense that, when bodies cease to exist, the individuation of souls will stop. The reason for this is the fact that every perfection is infused into matter according to the capacity of that perfection, hence the nature of a soul is not infused into different bodies according to the same nobility and purity. Consequently, the soul in each body will have an act of being (*esse*) that is limited (*terminatum*) in accord with the measure of the body. Now this limited being, though it comes to the soul in the body is not from the body, nor does it depend on the body.
>
> Hence, when bodies cease to exist, there still will remain for each soul its own being, limited in keeping with the modifications or dispositions which have accrued to the soul by virtue of the fact that it has been the perfection of such and such a body.
>
> This is Avicenna's solution and it can be made clear by an example from the sense area. Suppose there is something that is one but incapable of keeping the shape whereby it is distinguished when present in various vessels: something like water. When the vessels are taken away, the definite shapes will not remain in each case but it will continue to be but one amount of water. This is the way it is with material forms which do not retain their own act of being. However, suppose there is something that does retain the shape by which it is differentiated in various containers,

[20] *Ibid.*, art. 2, ad 6m.

even when they are removed, then the distinction of these shapes will remain: this is evident in the case of wax. Now, this is true of the soul, for it retains its act of being after the destruction of the body and this act of being remains in it as individuated and distinct.

One can almost hear the young Italian scholar taking his stand on this thorny problem. It is a position for which he will be criticized later. It does not have the backing of earlier Christian tradition but is the explanation offered by a Mohammedan scholar, Avicenna. Yet Thomas thinks that it is a good answer to the question and he courageously acknowledges its foreign source.

St. Thomas' *Scriptum in IV Libros Sententiarum*[21] follows in a general way the division of theological material made by Peter Lombard. The Master of the Sentences had explained in his prologue that he would arrange his treatise according to the Augustinian distinction of *frui* (the human will-act of enjoying or cherishing that which is good-in-itself) and *uti* (the human act of willing goods that are desired as means to the attainment of a good-in-itself). Students of scholastic philosophy will recognize in this the distinction of the *bonum honestum* (desired for its own sake) and the *bonum utile* (desired as a means to be used to attain a *bonum honestum*). So, the first book of the *Sentences* treats of God as the Absolute Good, enjoyed but never used. Book Two considers creatures as goods to be used in seeking God. Book Three continues this creaturely theme, in respect to the development of man, his salvation and perfection by the virtues. Another Augustinian theme (the difference between *realities* and *signs*)[22] appears in Lombard's fourth book, where he treats of the sacraments, sacramental signs, and the resurrection and final glory of those who are saved.

Thomas Aquinas analyzes each section of Lombard's work faithfully but then he proceeds to discuss in his own way various questions arising out of the text. These *Questions* contain the meat of Aquinas' first course in theology. As he moves into the last two books, he seems to feel freer to pass over many of the details of Augustinism and to use explanations based on philosophies which Augustine did not know. Throughout his course on the *Sentences,* Thomas shows that he is now much impressed by the thought of Avicenna.[23] The importance of Avicennism will also be

---

[21] There is no English translation of this commentary.

[22] For the distinction of *res* and *signa,* and *frui* and *uti,* in St. Augustine, see *De doctrina Christiana,* I, c. 2–5.

[23] Cf. Chenu, *Introduction,* p. 236.

noticed in the other writings of his period as a bachelor. Another feature of the commentary on the *Sentences* is the attention paid to contemporaries. There are many passages which are verbally close to the *Commentaria in IV libros Sententiarum* which Bonaventure wrote during the same years. This is true particularly of the long series of difficulties or objections which preface each article in the *Sentence* commentaries of the two saints. It is unlikely that Bonaventure and Thomas had close personal relations but it is obvious that the latter knew what was being taught in the Franciscan classes in theology.

Albert the Great appears in many parts of Thomas' argument, but in the explanations of the fourth book of his commentary he shows that he is ready to abandon the Neoplatonic and Dionysian themes which are characteristic of Albert's thought. From this point onward, Aristotelianism is the most important philosophic element in Thomism.[24]

This is particularly evident in two philosophical treatises written during these years: one entitled *On Being and Essence* and the other *On the Principles of Nature*. We have the early testimony of Bartholomew of Lucca concerning the writing of these treatises.

> He was twenty-five years of age when he first came to Paris, where he lectured on the *Sentences* before the age of thirty and received his degree or licentiate in theology. Before becoming a Master, (1) he produced *Four Books on the Sentences,* viz. the first, second, third and fourth. He also composed some smaller books. One was (2) against William of Saint-Amour, which begins: *Domine, ecce inimici tui sonuerunt.* (3) The second was *On Quiddity and Being* (*De Quidditate et esse*). (4) The Third was *On the Principles of Nature* (*De principiis naturae*).[25]

Passing over the treatise against the views of William of St. Amour for the moment, let us examine the last two works mentioned by Bartholomew.

That these two philosophical *Opuscula* were written before 1256 is not questioned today. Some authorities feel that it is not possible to fix their chronology more definitely.[26] One of the editors of *On Being and Essence* argues that this work was finished before the second book of the *Commentary on the Sentences;* he also suggests that *On the Principles of Nature* is prior to *On Being and Essence*.[27] However, in the best edition of *On*

---

[24] *Ibid.*, pp. 233–237.

[25] *Hist. Eccles.*, XXII, c. 21 (in Muratori, *Scriptores Rerum Italicarum,* XI, 571).

[26] Eschmann, "Catalogue," p. 411.

[27] M. D. Roland-Gosselin, "Introduction," to *Le 'De ente et essentia' de s. Thomas d'Aquin* (Paris: Vrin, 1926), pp. XXVI–XXVIII.

the Principles of Nature, the editor points out that in both works the philosophic teaching of Aquinas is strongly influenced by Avicenna.[28] In Averroës' *Commentary on the Physics,* it is stated that,

> Avicenna was much mistaken when he said that the first philosopher [i.e., the metaphysician] demonstrates the first principle of being and then proceeds on the basis of this, in his book on Divine Knowledge [Metaphysics] by an argument which he thought necessary and essential in this science — and he erred with an obvious mistake.[29]

What Averroës says is true; Avicenna did think that a philosopher should move from the broad considerations of metaphysics to deduce the character of more limited types of being, such as the properties and activities of physical nature.[30] As a young teacher, Aquinas was much more impressed by Avicenna than by Averroës (whom he probably did not know well during the 1250's) so it is probable that the more general treatise *On Being and Essence* preceded the work *On the Principles of Nature.* It is noteworthy that most lists of St. Thomas' works put them down in that order.[31]

An indication of the approximate contemporaneity of these two philosophical treatises, and also of their priority to most of the work *On the Sentences,* is found in the citations of Aristotle's *Metaphysics.* In *De Principiis Naturae* and *De Ente et Essentia,* Thomas quotes the twelfth-century version of the *Metaphysics* made from the Arabic by Michael Scottus. However, the exposition of the *Sentences* makes use of the translation from the Greek.[32]

Some early documents give the title as *De ente et essentia, ad fratres socios,* which suggests that it was written by Aquinas to define and explain for his Dominican associates at Paris some of the key terms in the new Aristotelian philosophy which he had studied and was using in his teaching but which was comparatively unfamiliar to the other scholars in the monastery.[33] The treatise is divided, in some editions,[34] into six chapters.

---

[28] J. J. Pauson, "Introduction," to *De Principiis Naturae* (Fribourg: Société Philosophique; Louvain: Nauwelaerts, 1950), p. 72.

[29] Averroës, *In I Phys.,* tr. 82, is cited by Pauson, *op. cit.*

[30] Avicenna, *Metaphysica* (St. Bonaventure, N. Y.: Franciscan Institute, 1948), p. 9 E.

[31] Bartholomew of Lucca, *Hist. Eccles.,* XXIII, c. 12, lists *De prin. nat.* before *De ente* but his listing is not chronological.

[32] See Pauson, *op. cit.,* pp. 67–70, and note 3, on p. 70.

[33] Chenu, *op. cit.,* pp. 280–281.

[34] This is true of the Roland-Gosselin text; *supra,* note 27.

In the first chapter, Thomas defines *ens* (being) and *essentia* (essence); in the second he explains the composition of bodies in terms of matter and form, the individuation of bodies by signate matter, and something of the meaning of essence in the case of these composite substances. Chapter Three discusses the relationship of essence to genus, species, and difference. Then in Chapter Four he turns to the character of essence in immaterial substances: human souls, angels, and God (here there is a long criticism of Avicebron who thought that finite spirits were composed of matter and form). Chapter Five summarizes the foregoing and situates these metaphysical notions in relation to other philosophical views, such as those of the anonymous *Liber de Causis*. Finally in the sixth chapter, Thomas turns to the problem of essence in the case of accidents.

Clearly, the little work *On Being and Essence* is a preliminary essay in metaphysics by a young teacher who has not read Aristotle with the completeness that characterized the expositions which Aquinas was to write some fifteen years later. Essence is the central concept and the meaning given this term is very dependent on Avicenna. Yet, even at this early point, Thomas Aquinas has established many of the basic themes of his own metaphysics. The *opusculum* has remained a favorite among followers of the thought of St. Thomas.[35] More than a dozen commentaries have been written on it, of which the most famous is that produced by Cardinal Cajetan in the Renaissance.[36]

Some manuscript titles of *On the Principles of Nature* include the words "to Brother Sylvester." Nothing is known of this friar Sylvester — though it is probable that he was a Dominican. The treatise is usually[37] divided into six chapters. It opens with a discussion of various meanings of *esse* (to be): after pointing out that it is one thing *to be* actually and quite a different matter to be *able to be,* Thomas distinguishes the *esse* of a substance (say, a man) from the *esse* of an accident (to be white). So, where the treatise *On Being and Essence* studies various aspects of "essence," the *Principles of Nature* deals with *esse*. Developing this existential theme, Aquinas turns to the meaning of generation (a moving toward *esse*) and corruption (a moving toward *non esse*) and introduces various

[35] English: *On Being and Essence,* trans. A. Maurer (Toronto: Pont. Inst. Med. Studies, 1949); with an excellent introduction.

[36] M. Grabmann, "De commentariis in opusculum S. Thomae Aquinatis De ente et essentia," *Acta Pontificiae Academiae Romanae,* 1938, 7–20.

[37] I say "usually" — that is, in modern editions; the earliest MSS lack chapter divisions. Cf. Pauson, *op. cit.,* p. 75.

precisions in regard to potency and act, matter, form and privation. These (matter, form, privation) are explained as "principles" of natural (i.e., physical) things. Chapter Three introduces the theme of causality and treats in particular the agent and final causes as extrinsic to what is generated. The fourth and fifth chapters present a further analysis of the Aristotelian four causes: material, formal, efficient, final. Noting that it is possible to use the term "principle" in various senses, Thomas devotes the final chapter to a short explanation of different ways of speaking about a subject. He here discusses univocal, equivocal, and analogical predication. This teaching is briefly applied to the various ways of understanding "principles." Hence the *Principles of Nature* terminates with a little essay on the use of analogy — probably St. Thomas' first attempt to deal with this difficult but metaphysically important theme.[38]

A third work, *On the Nature of Matter,* has been attributed to St. Thomas and associated with these early philosophical studies.[39] While this work is interesting, its authenticity has not been proved. The most recent editor concludes his survey of the problem with this judgment: "In its negative aspect, it seems impossible to maintain that St. Thomas was the author of the *De Natura Materiae.*"[40] We need not stop on it here.

Of a quite different character is Aquinas' treatise *Against the Attackers of the Religious Life.*[41] This is Thomas Aquinas' contribution to the controversy between the secular masters and the Dominican and Franciscan scholars which has been discussed above in our Chapter Seven. St. Thomas wrote the *Contra Impugnantes* in Paris during the autumn of 1256. Much of the work is concerned with refuting the charges of William of St. Amour against the Mendicant friars who were teaching at the University of Paris. Although William's position was condemned at Rome, on October 5, 1256, this pertinent fact is nowhere mentioned in the *Contra Impugnantes.* It seems, then, that Thomas finished writing this book before he learned of the condemnation.[42] Though lengthy and full of information, the *Contra Impugnantes* is not well organized, nor is it as well written as Aquinas'

[38] There is a complete translation in *Pocket Aquinas,* pp. 61–77.

[39] *De natura materiae,* ed. J. M. Wyss (Fribourg: Société Philosophique, 1953).

[40] Wyss, *op. cit.,* p. 64.

[41] *Contra impugnantes Dei cultum et religionem,* in *Opus. Omnia,* ed. Mandonnet, IV, 1–195. English: J. Procter, *An Apology for the Religious Orders* (Westminster, Md.: Newman, 1950).

[42] P. Glorieux, "Le 'Contra Impugnantes' de saint Thomas," *Mélanges Mandonnet,* I, 74. This study cites pertinent passages from William of St. Amour.

later controversial efforts.[43] It is divided into twenty-six chapters, some using the question style and others simply listing itemized charges and replies. If some biographers give the impression that Thomas Aquinas was from earliest youth a genius of the first order, they have not carefully read this treatise. Eventually he became a sober, disciplined controversialist — but he had to learn this skill as he grew older.

Glorieux has shown that the first twelve chapters are directed against various criticisms of the friars that are found in the documents of the University of Paris, from 1253 to 1256. These criticisms include many points which we have seen in the preceding chapters: the friars teaching at the university have divided loyalties and obligations; their way of life is not suitable for professors at a university; the rules of their Orders are not in keeping with Christian traditions; the teaching friars do not live in accord with these rules — and so on. Thomas answers these attacks, charge by charge, but his writing shows signs of obvious haste in composition.

Chapters Thirteen to Twenty-Six are directly concerned with William of St. Amour's treatise, *On the Dangers of Recent Times.* However, it is clear that Thomas Aquinas had at hand a different version of William's inflammatory booklet from the one which appears in his printed *Works.*[44] William wrote several revisions of his work. Pope Alexander IV, in 1256, condemned the third version (and that is what was published in the seventeenth century) but Thomas was answering a fourth or fifth edition of the *De Periculis.*[45] Apparently, he had only a few weeks in which to digest this attack and prepare his answer. Seven criticisms are listed by Thomas Aquinas: (1) the religious try to gain favorable attention to their work; (2) they do not meekly suffer the attacks of their detractors but fight back; (3) they are litigious and even use force to defend themselves; (4) they try to get their persecutors punished; (5) they try to "please men" (Gal 1:10); (6) they glory in the things that God does through them; (7) they frequent the courts of kings and rulers.[46] We need not record in detail the responses which Thomas makes to these charges. As a modern historian remarks: "One feels on each page of the *De Periculis* . . . equivocation, wicked insinuation, sophistry."[47] The last chapters of Thomas' reply review

[43] This is the judgment of Glorieux, *ibid.*, p. 74.

[44] Magistri Guillelmi de Sancto-Amore, *Opera Omnia* (Constance, 1632).

[45] Glorieux, *art. cit.*, p. 71, dates this version approximately in August, 1256.

[46] These are detailed in *Contra Impugnantes,* c. 13 (Mandonnet, IV, 147) and are answered in Chapters 13–19.

[47] P. Glorieux, *art. cit.*, p. 79.

the basic issues and explain something of the general principles of the religious life. These seven chapters are much better written than the early ones.

Some scholars now think[48] that Thomas engaged in academic disputations in 1255–1256 and that two sections now printed in his *Quodlibetal Questions* are actually *Disputed Questions* from these years. It is known that bachelors were the actual disputants in the case of the disputed questions of the thirteenth century, but the records of these academic exercises were usually published under the name of the master who presided over and directed them. In this case, the master would seem to have been Elie Brunet. Anyhow, in our editions of St. Thomas' *Quodlibetal Questions,* there is found a discussion "On Manual Labor for Religious."[49] One of the charges directed against the mendicant professors in the 1250's was that they should be doing manual labor as stipulated by their religious Rules and in conformity with the traditions of Apostolic times.[50] Indeed, it seems that the subject matter of the two articles under consideration deals with such an attack. St. Thomas first faces the question: *Whether manual labor is a matter of precept.*[51] His answer is long and thorough (which corroborates the view that this is a *Disputed,* not a *Quodlibetal, Question*). Briefly, he says this. There are three purposes for the requirement of manual labor: to combat idleness, to control sensuality, and to provide for the necessities of life. He then shows that each of these ends may be achieved by means other than manual work. Then he considers the precept requiring manual labor as a rule of natural law and concludes that it is the kind of precept which binds men as a species but not all individuals of the human species. That is to say, the obligation to do physical work is like the obligation to propagate the species, it may be fully fulfilled by *some members* of the species and does not apply to all men as individuals. He further shows that "manual" labor should not be interpreted as restricted to work with the hands but should include the use of other bodily organs. Then he argues forcibly that it is not reasonable

---

[48] See P. Castagnoli, "Regesta Thomistica," *Divus Thomas* (Piacenza), XXX–XXXII (1927–1929); cf. Eschmann, "Catalogue," n. 4, p. 389.

[49] See S. Thomae, *Questiones Quodlibetales,* VII, art. 17–18.

[50] For the charges, see the *Letter* from the university officials to Pope Alexander IV (1255) in *C.U.P.,* I, n. 256; a reference is made to St. Paul (2 Thess 3:8): "neither did we eat any man's bread at his cost, but we worked night and day in labor and toil, so that we might not burden any of you."

[51] *Quaest. Quodl.,* VII, 17–18 (Marietti, 1931), pp. 152–156.

to claim that a mechanic should be provided with food (even though he grows none) and that a master of the liberal arts or a lawyer should not be entitled to a living by virtue of his work. This answer is masterful, very important for its illumination of the theory of natural law, and if it was actually written by Aquinas in 1255–1256, it shows that he was already a very brilliant disputant.[52]

In the next article, the question is: *Whether those who devote themselves to spiritual works are excused from manual labor.* This problem is also thoroughly discussed. Thomas distinguishes spiritual work (like preaching), which is directed to the common good, from that (like personal spiritual exercises) which is directed to the individual good of the agent. He argues that, under certain proper conditions, both types of spiritual work may excuse one from the general precept of bodily labor. Thomas does not deny that manual labor is required of some people, nor that under special circumstances any person may be obliged to do such work, but he vigorously argues that there are other proper means of gaining a livelihood and that the principle of the division of labor makes it obvious that not all people must work as farmers or artisans.[53] For the Thomistic philosophy and theology of work, these disputations are very significant. They might be read with profit today, in connection with controversy concerning the activities of "worker priests" and the need for specialization in complex social organizations.

Still another "extra-serial" set of disputed questions may have been produced by Aquinas in 1256. These have also been printed with the *Quodlibetal Questions*.[54] Here Thomas discusses the various meanings, or "senses," which may be found in the Bible. The four meanings (literal, spiritual, moral, and mystical) described by St. Augustine, Venerable Bede, and others in the Patristic tradition are here explained. It is noteworthy that the answers to the three articles devoted to this problem are much shorter than those concerned with manual labor. Possibly these articles on Scripture are associated with the commencement of Thomas' teaching as a master of theology in the autumn of 1256. We should remember that he was a master for a whole year before he was formally

[52] *Ibid.*, art. 17, c., plus the answers to six of the primary objections and five arguments *Sed contra*. Chenu, *op. cit.*, p. 242, suggests the date 1257; *Walz-Novarina (1962)*, p. 223, dates it 1255–1256.

[53] *Quaest. Quodl.*, VII, art. 18, c., plus the answers to eight objections.

[54] *Ibid.*, art. 14–16: *De sensibus Sacrae Scripturae*. See *Walz-Novarina (1962)*, p. 223.

accepted as a member of the theology faculty at the university. During this year (from the spring of 1256 to August 12, 1257) Thomas Aquinas apparently taught theology in the Dominican house at Paris.

In these years, from 1252 to 1256, Thomas learned a great deal by teaching, as many scholars do. He was forced to consider what views seemed to him best on many of the basic problems of philosophy and theology. Moreover, the requirements of teaching demanded that he become less taciturn. As a student he thought much and talked little. Now he had to explain his thought to others. This he did in a manner which was remarkable for its novelty. There is a famous and much-quoted passage in William of Tocco's biography which stresses this newness of St. Thomas' teaching.[55] "In his lectures," Tocco says, "he presented new problems, discovered a new and clear way of solving them, and he used new arguments in making these solutions." He continued to be an innovator in all his later teaching.

---

[55] Tocco, *Vita,* c. 14 (*Fontes,* II, 81).

CHAPTER NINE

The First Paris Professorate

THE years in which Thomas Aquinas first taught as a master of theology at Paris (1256/7–1259) appear on the surface to have been comparatively tranquil and uneventful. Partially, this judgment may be due to the poverty of our sources of information. What can be discovered about St. Thomas' life at this time must largely be drawn from indirect references and general historical information. He lived at the Dominican house on the Rue Saint-Jacques and probably taught his classes in a large room there. As master in their school for non-French students, he served as one of two Dominican professors of theology. His colleague who taught the French students was Master Florent of Hesdin. Thomas' ordinary classes were held in the mornings between the canonical hours of Prime and Tierce. Some of his time, in these classes, was devoted to the explanation of selected parts of the Old and New Testaments.

Thomas also directed what we might call the "practice teaching" of several Dominican bachelors in theology. One of these bachelors must have been the English Dominican, William of Alton (or Dalton), for this scholar succeeded Aquinas as *magister regens* in the chair for foreign students during the year 1259–1260. Another Dominican student bachelor was Hannibald Hannibaldi; he studied under Thomas at this time and then served as regent master at Paris from 1260 to 1262. Doubtless Thomas took a special interest in the work of Brother Hannibald, because he was from the Roman Province, would know somewhat the same vernacular, and was the nephew of Richard Hannibaldi, the cardinal with whom Thomas enjoyed a close friendship during the 1260's. In his lectures on the *Sentences,* Hannibald Hannibaldi used so much material from Aquinas'

Commentary that, in the collected works of St. Thomas, Hannibald's exposition has been printed under the name of Aquinas![1] This mistake has contributed to the legend that Thomas produced in the 1260's a revision of his own *Commentary on Peter Lombard*. There is no evidence that he did such a revision. Hannibald's lectures show that he was a loyal follower of his teacher's course. After teaching for two years at Paris, Hannibald returned to Rome and was made a cardinal. Aquinas later dedicated a portion of his *Catena Aurea* to this illustrious pupil.[2]

Through the research of Martin Grabmann, we now know of a man who is never mentioned by Thomas but was his close friend throughout most of his adult life. This was Adenolf of Anagni.[3] When Thomas came to Paris in 1252, he found this fellow Italian there. Adenolf was a diocesan priest who had become a master in arts at Paris by 1250. It is even possible, according to Grabmann, that Thomas and Adenolf had been fellow students in arts at the University of Naples.[4] We know that the Neapolitan university had deteriorated before 1250; many of its scholars and teachers moved elsewhere. It is possible that both Martin of Dacia and Peter of Hibernia came to Paris for this reason before mid-century. Certainly Adenolf did, and in 1255 he became a canon of the famous Cathedral of Notre Dame. Years later (1269–1272), he attended the theology lectures given in Paris by Thomas. Even though he was associated with the diocesan clergy, Adenolf supported Aquinas during the Paris controversies that occurred around 1270. The friendship appears to have been very close; Adenolf provided the money for making Reginald of Piperno's copy (*reportatio*) of Thomas' *Exposition of the Gospel of St. John* in the years 1270 to 1272. As yet, no writings by Adenolf of Anagni have been discovered. If any are eventually identified, they might provide precious information on the life and thought of Thomas Aquinas.

As *socius* in the first Paris professorate, a fellow Dominican, Raymond Severi, is thought to have assisted Thomas.[5] Less well known than Reginald of Piperno (who probably took over as *socius* to Aquinas in 1259),

---

[1] *Scriptum in IV Sententiarum ad Hannibaldum*, in *Opera Omnia*, ed. Parm., XXII, 1–436.

[2] Cf. Eschmann, "Catalogue," p. 397; see *Epistola Dedicatoria, Catena super Marci Evangelium*, ed. Parm., XI, 335.

[3] M. Grabmann, "Adenulf von Anagni, Probst von Saint-Omer (d. 1290). Ein Freund und Schüler des hl. Thomas von Aquin," *Traditio*, V (1947), 269–283.

[4] *Art. cit.*, p. 271.

[5] *Walz-Novarina* (*1962*), pp. 105–106.

Raymond doubtless contributed much to St. Thomas' early writing and teaching. The position of *socius* was much more important than would be suggested by the English term "secretary." Both Raymond and Reginald were men of considerable stature and scholarly attainment. Ordained priests in the Order of Preachers, they were much more than scribes or hack writers. Raymond and Thomas probably occupied adjacent rooms in the monastery, for there are stories in the early biographies that speak of Thomas calling on his assistant at night to record various portions of his writings. During these years at Paris, Raymond regularly heard Thomas' confessions and served his daily Mass — and Aquinas did the same services for Raymond. Unfortunately, no written record of this close collaboration has been left by Raymond Severi. There is a secondhand report in the Naples' canonization proceedings which is our source for the meager information given above. Raymond also testified that Thomas lived a life of great purity and chastity.[6] It has recently been argued that Raymond could only have had the status of a student, during the years 1256 to 1259, and that his transcription of Thomas' *Commentary on St. Matthew* was simply a student *reportatio* of his teacher's notes.[7] However, Peter of Caputio's testimony at Naples suggests that Raymond was something more than a mere student.[8] There is a long tradition that he was in the status of *socius*.[9]

Besides his regular lectures in theology, Thomas Aquinas was much occupied with the more public exercises that were called "Questions" or disputations. Of these, there were two types: *Disputed Questions* and *Quodlibetal Questions*. Both involved oral exercises but they differed in several ways. The disputed questions were the product of class meetings at which the bachelor of theology was the disputant. The master supervised the proceedings, sitting in a higher chair than the student disputant. It was the function of the master to "determine" the question, that is, to give a definitive answer to the problem under discussion. These "determinations" were written by the master, after the initial discussion, and were delivered orally on the following class day. Doubtless, they were further edited for publication. It is not known how frequently St. Thomas conducted such disputations but he was very active in holding these academic exercises.

---

[6] *Proc. Can. Neap.*, XCII (*Fontes*, IV, 398).

[7] Dondaine, *Secrétaires*, p. 199.

[8] *Proc. Can. Neap.*, *loc. cit.*

[9] J. Destrez, *Etudes critiques sur les oeuvres de s. Thomas d'Aquin* (Paris: Vrin, 1933), p. 201: "Or on sait que c'est Raymond Severi qui fut socius de saint Thomas pendant le séjour de celui-ci à Paris 1252–1259."

In the case of Aquinas' *Disputed Questions,* there is a general unity of theme for the work of each year.

Thus, during the years 1256 to 1258, Aquinas held a series of such disputations devoted to the problems of knowledge and reality. In the last year of this professorate (1258–1259), he directed disputed questions on problems associated with the meaning of "good." The records of these years of disputation are now edited in the collected works under the title: *Disputed Questions on Truth.* Their content will be further discussed in the following chapter.

On the other hand, the *Quodlibetal Questions* resulted from special assemblies held each year in the weeks preceding Christmas and Easter. Quodlibet means "what one wills" — this suggests the character of these disputations. Almost any question could be asked of the disputant. In this case, the master was the disputant and those in attendance included not only his own students but also other masters and visitors. Thomas Aquinas conducted *Quodlibets* during these first years as a professor and their records are now edited. We shall also return to the *Quodlibetal Questions* in our next chapter.

Although the name of St. Bonaventure is linked with that of Aquinas in several documents from the 1250's, it is unlikely that they were close associates. Bonaventure was a fellow Italian (from Bagnorea) and he received his degree in theology at the same time as Thomas. However, Thomas was a good deal younger, they lived in different monasteries and studied under different masters, since Bonaventure was a Franciscan. By 1257, Bonaventure had been made head of the Order of Friars Minor and the remainder of his life was devoted to administration rather than to teaching. There would have been little opportunity for a friendship to have developed. A very pious and holy man, Bonaventure was less interested in philosophy and speculative problems than Aquinas. The legend that they were schoolfellows and intimate friends is based on imagination rather than on facts.

Thomas Aquinas was now living far away from his family and news of them was infrequent. His father had died before he entered the Order. Apparently his mother lived until about 1255.[10] The older brothers, like their father, had been supporters of the Emperor Frederick II and had served him in various military and political capacities, as we have seen. At about the time that Thomas was studying in Cologne, the Aquinas

[10] Scandone, *La vita, la famiglia,* pp. 51–55.

family broke off relations with Frederick, and some of the men joined forces with the papal armies. As a consequence, they were exiled from Roccasecca and fled to their smaller property at Montesangiovanni, where they lived in more straitened circumstances. Aimone lived there from 1254 onward and died at the end of the 1260's.[11] Rinaldo fought on the side of the papal forces and was killed before 1257. The fate of the other brothers is not clearly recorded, but by the time that Thomas had become a professor it seems that he had no further contacts with them.

At the period of the investigations of Thomas' claims to sanctity (1318–1320), the only relatives from whom testimony was gathered were those who stemmed from the female side of the family. Thomas' sister Teodora married Count Roger of San Severino and Marsico. One of their sons, Thomas of San Severino, figured in the canonization ceremonies. Another sister, Maria, also married into the San Severino family. She and her husband, William, had a daughter named Catherine of San Severino who was still active at the time of the canonization of her uncle. The oldest sister seems to have been Marotta who became a nun and was named abbess of the Benedictine Convent of Santa Maria in Capua.[12] Marotta died while Thomas was in Paris, apparently in 1257 or 1258, for the *Vitae Fratrum* (its first version is from 1259/60) records that she appeared to Thomas in a vision while he was still in Paris.[13] According to this account, Marotta was now dead and in purgatory. She asked Thomas for a number of Masses to be said for her soul's release from punishment. Later, when Thomas was in Rome, in the mid-1260's, Marotta again appeared in a vision and told her brother that she was in heaven and that he would soon join her there.[14] Thomas is reported to have inquired about the whereabouts of his dead brothers. Marotta assured him that Landolfo was in purgatory but Rinaldo had reached paradise. It was further intimated that Rinaldo had joined the ranks of the martyrs, as a result of being put to death by the Emperor for his loyalty to the Church[15] Whatever credence one gives to these visions, their record has some historical

---

[11] *Doc.* XXXV (*Fontes,* VI, 592–593).

[12] See Pope Innocent IV, *Epistola* (*Fontes,* VI, 541).

[13] Gerard de Frachet, *Vitae Fratrum,* c. 16 (MOPH, I, 215); the same story, with embellishments, is in Tocco, *Vita,* c. 44 (*Fontes,* II, 118).

[14] Tocco, *Vita,* c. 44 (*Fontes,* II, 118).

[15] *Ibid.:* "de Domino vero Rainaldo . . . nomen fratris Doctor reperit inter lineas aureas, quae erant Martyrum, quia pro fidelitate Ecclesiae morienti sub tyrannide persecutionis Frederici Imperatoris sibi mors computata fuit ad martyrium. . . ."

significance. Most of Thomas' brothers and sisters had died by the middle of the 1260 decade.

On the twenty-sixth of June, 1259, Pope Alexander addressed a letter to Reginald of Corbeil, Bishop of Paris, asking that further measures be taken to compose the situation at Paris.[16] This letter shows that all was not well, even in the last year of Thomas' first professorate. The Dominicans and Franciscans were still not being properly treated at the University of Paris. Revised copies of the infamous pamphlet by William of St. Amour were still being circulated. (William himself had been exiled by King Louis IX and had gone to Rome to present his side of the dispute. He there defended himself adroitly before four cardinals and was eventually permitted to return to France. He did not die until September 13, 1272.[17])

Pope Alexander's letter gives a good deal of information on the continuation of the attacks on the mendicants. He deplores the fact that there are now certain poems and songs in the vernacular, in which the friars are indecently ridiculed.[18] With special reference to Thomas Aquinas, the letter reveals what must have been an embarrassing episode during a university sermon that Thomas was preaching. The beadle of the Picard group (*natio*) of students interrupted the sermon, on Palm Sunday (April 6, 1259), and read a libelous booklet directed against the mendicants. Pope Alexander excommunicated this beadle, named Guillot, deprived him of his office and income in perpetuity, asked that he be expelled from Paris, placed under *ipso facto* excommunication anyone who kept or publicized such books, or who permitted the beadle to return to Paris. What St. Thomas thought of the incident, we do not know; he never mentioned it even in his later controversial writings.

An important meeting of Dominican scholars took place at Valenciennes, in the month of June, 1259. It may be noted that Valenciennes is about halfway between Paris and Cologne and was a convenient place of assembly for scholars from both key centers. Those present in this commission were Masters Bonhomme, Florent of Hesdin, Albert the Great (within

---

[16] *Doc.* XVI (*Fontes,* VI, 562–565).

[17] See E. Faral, "Les *Responsiones* de Guillaume de Saint-Amour," *Archives d'Histoire doctrinale et littéraire,* XXIV (1949), 337–394.

[18] *Fontes,* VI, 564: "in infamiam et detractionem eorundem fratrum ab eorum emulis in litterali et vulgari sermone necnon rismis et cantilenis indecentibus. . . ." The editor, M.-L. Laurent, suggests that Pope Alexander has reference to the poems of Rutebeuf.

a year to become bishop of Ratisbon), Thomas of Aquino and Peter of Tarentaise (later to become Pope Innocent V in 1276). All were doctors of theology from the University of Paris and they met to revise the regulations governing the course of studies in the Order of Preachers.[19]

This group ordered a general raising of standards for the training of young men in the Order of Preachers. Among other things, the Valenciennes regulations required that the general houses of study (*studia generalia*) be sent good students, of exemplary character, that properly trained lectors (the ordinary teachers of theology) be provided in these houses, and that these teachers should not be burdened with other tasks or duties. Young brothers with the ability to study were to be released from other occupations, so that they would be free to study. All residents of the monastery were required to attend the lectures in theology, even the prior, and friars were not to celebrate Mass or go to town during the lecture periods except for grave necessity. Lectors not actively teaching were also to attend the classes (in the thirteenth century, at least, theology was a lifelong study) and they were especially ordered to attend all disputations. Each lector was to be assisted by a bachelor. The necessary books were to be taken to class — and no others.

One brief item in the Valenciennes report is now regarded as the *magna charta* of philosophical studies in the Dominican Order.[20] Actually the document does not mention philosophy, as such, but the eighth regulation reads:[21]

> Arrangements are to be made in the Provinces that lack them for one or more centers for the study of Arts (*aliquod studium artium vel aliqua*) in which the young men may be instructed.

Since philosophy had become the key part of the program in liberal arts at Paris, and since all members of this Commission were familiar with the situation at Paris, it is no doubt true that the intent of this regula-

---

[19] *Doc.* XV (*Fontes,* VI, 560): "Apud Valencenas anno Domini MCCLIX de mandato magistri et diffinitorum pro promocione studii ordinatum est per fratres Bonumhominem, Florentium, Albertum Theutonicum, Thomam de Aquino, Petrum de Tharantasia, magistros theologie Parisius, qui interfuerunt dicto capitulo, quod lectores non occupentur. . . ." A shorter version of this document, taken from *Bibl. Munic. de Toulouse,* MS 490, is printed in Douais, *L'Organisation des études,* pp. 173–174.

[20] Walz, *Thomas von Aquin* (1953), p. 67: "Hauptsächlich durch Alberts Einfluss und Bemühen rüchte darin das Philosophiestudium im Orden noch stärker in der Vordergrund."

[21] *Fontes,* VI, 560.

tion was to stress the importance of philosophical training. Certainly Albert was a vehement supporter of more work in philosophy and there is no question that Thomas Aquinas was also fully in agreement with this order.

In point of fact, the Master General at this time was also a man who gave solid encouragement to the promotion of philosophical studies by the Dominicans. Humbert de Romans had been provincial of the French Province for ten years before he became head of the Order for the period 1254 to 1263. No great scholar himself, his administration was distinguished by common sense and a full appreciation of the scholarly ideals of men like Albert and Thomas. At some time between 1256 and 1263, Humbert wrote his influential *Commentary on the Rule of St. Augustine.*[22] Since it illustrates the mind of the Master General under whom St. Thomas began his career as a teacher, a representative passage from Humbert's *Commentary* may be helpful here.[23]

> The question now arises concerning philosophical books and study in them, as to the value of this among the Friars.
>
> I answer: Some friars are altogether unsuited to making progress in these matters; others are fitted to make some progress in them, but not much; still others are of the type from which, as a result of great aptitude in these matters, much profit and fruit may be expected in regard to Holy Scripture. No permission should be given the first group to study such books; some study should be conceded to the second group, but discreetly and rarely; but for the third group the reins should be loosened for this kind of study. And just as it may be conceded that, in general, this study is bad in the general run of cases, so can it be bluntly denied that it arises from a bad spirit. On this, there is the text of I Kings, 13:19, "Now there was no ironworker to be found in all the land of Israel; for the Philistines had taken this precaution, lest the Hebrews should make them swords or spears." The *Gloss* says, "The Devil takes care to prevent, through the pagans, through the heretics, through false Christians, the development of learned teachers in the Church, for they might make spiritual arms with which we could fight." Indeed the pagans did prohibit Christians from learning the liberal arts. Therefore, permission must be granted for studies of this kind, because of the many useful results which can come from them.
>
> One result is the defense of the faith. For, just as heretics and pagans may attack the faith, so may some of them do so through their philosophy. That is why the Apostle says, Col. 2:8, "Beware lest any man deceive by philosophy and vain conceit." Now, just as a man cannot defend himself

[22] After 1256, because Humbert appears to cite Thomas Aquinas' *Commentary of Boethius On the Trinity;* see note 24, *infra.*

[23] The present translation is made from a text of Humbert de Romanis, *Expositio regulae Beati Augustini,* taken from *Bibl. Munic. de Toulouse,* MS 417 (I.302), fol. 136d–138a, as transcribed in Douais, *L'Organisation des études,* pp. 175–176.

against fallacies, if he knows nothing about them, so can he not against such philosophers, if he knows nothing about philosophy.

Another result is the destruction of their errors. Among the philosophers there are many errors and many truths, just as there is both poison and its antidote in the serpent. And just as this antidote is more efficacious than all else against poison, so are their truths more effective in opposing their errors than are the truths of faith, for they do not accept the latter. Hence, Augustine shows in the *City of God* that Plato made some statements through which their error on the resurrection of bodies, in which they did not believe, was refuted. He says, "Plato states that souls without bodies cannot exist for ever; and Porphyry states that the completely purged soul, on returning to the Father, will never return to the evils of the world. It may be maintained that both tell the truth: the consequence being that the soul will rejoin the body, but not on an unhappy condition." Now, this is what the faith teaches concerning resurrection.

Another result is the understanding of the Scriptures. There are innumerable things in the text and commentaries, and in the source writings of the Saints, which cannot be understood without some knowledge of philosophy. Thus the Hebrews are enriched with the Egyptian spoils, as is said in Exodus 11–12. All things that are found in the possession of the philosophers may be applied to the explanation of Scripture.

Another result is the confirmation of the faith. There are many things which they have that are of great value in confirming the faith. Hence, in the *Commentary on Boethius' De Trinitate,* it is said that our faith has been drawn from the inner truths of philosophy.[24] "Because what is known of God is manifest in them" [Rom. 1:19].

Another result is sharpness of wit, to cut into the bread of Sacred Scripture. Prov. 27:17, "Iron sharpeneth iron." That is to say, the iron of natural wit is sharpened with the iron of philosophical writing which truly is iron in relation to Sacred Scripture, which is now called silver, now gold.

Another result lies in the power of motivation. For sometimes philosophical points are more moving than theological ones. I saw a certain friar, who was a great man in both philosophy and theology, who said that while he was still living a secular life he was studying astronomy and he discovered in a book by Albiranasar [either Albumasar or Alpetragius] that the ancient philosophers found that there was in the sky a sign of the following kind: the Virgin holding her Son in her lap and beside her an elderly man who had not touched her. This was taken to mean the glorious Virgin and her Son and Joseph. As he thought back over this, he was more moved to good than by some of the sermons that he had heard. Similarly it is said of Dionysius and the Magi that the eclipse of the sun which they knew through philosophy to be miraculous moved them and led them to Christ, as the new star of philosophy.

Another reason is the bringing of honor to the monastery; this was a

---

[24] Cf. Boethius, *De Trinitate,* Proemio: "Idcirco stylum brevitate contraho, et ex intimis sumpta philosophiae disciplinis novorum verborum significationibus velo. . . ." Cf. S. Thomae, *Expositio,* ad loc. cit, et q. II, art. 3. I know no other commentary to which Humbert could have reference.

matter of concern to the Apostle. For many religious are held in contempt by various people, and their Order along with them, because they are thoroughly ignorant men. On the other hand, this kind of knowledge redounds to the honor of their Order. For example: Brother Roland (of Cremona), a great man in philosophy and theology, when he was living happily in Cremona, learned from some of the friars who had come from the army of the Emperor Frederick stationed at Brescia that his philosopher had much confounded them with his philosophy and they did not know how to answer him. Moved by his zeal for the honor of the Order, Roland said immediately: "Saddle a donkey for me." Now he had gout and was unable to go on foot. When the preparations had been made, he went on the donkey with some friars to the army and began to inquire for the whereabouts of this philosopher. A good many important people who knew and respected him heard this and they gathered together. When the philosopher was summoned, Roland said: "So that you, Master Theodore, may know that the Order of Friars Preacher does have philosophers, I'm giving you a choice, before all these people. You may either argue against me on any point of philosophy that you select, or you may choose to answer my questions." When he had chosen to oppose him in argument, the disputation started and Roland defeated him so gloriously that he brought great glory and honor to the Order. And the philosopher held him in great esteem from that time onward. Surely it is with such honor that the Apostle seems to be concerned, when he says, "As long, indeed, as I am the Apostle [of the Gentiles] I will honor my ministry" [Rom. 11:13].

Another result is a less exalted opinion of philosophical knowledge. There are many who, while they do not know what the philosophers have, think that it is a greater subject than it is. After they know it, they do not value it as anything in comparison with theology. That is why Augustine, as if judging their books in comparison with ours, says: "These pages do not have much about piety."

So, for these reasons and many others, the study of philosophy can be permitted, but care should be taken not to grant it to everyone. In these books there are some good things and some bad. It is a good thing when Augustine said that he read in the books of Plato, though not in the same words, that in the beginning was the Word, and the Word was with God.[25] It is a bad thing to read in them about the cyclic movement of things in the Great Year, and many similar things. So, it is not safe for just any man to read them, unless he knows enough to distinguish the good from the bad; for he might perhaps gather bad plants instead of good ones. There is an example in the *Ecclesiastical Hierarchy* of Bishop Dionysius. He was chided by the brethren for reading heretical books but a vision appeared to him, saying: "Read everything whatever that comes into your hands, because you can put it all to the test and see through it all." The upshot of this is that it is not safe for those lacking in discernment to read a mixture of the good and the bad, for they may gather in the evil with the good. Thus, Theophilus, the teacher of Origen, says: "So grasp the good that the thorns do not harm you."

[25] Augustine, *Confessiones,* VII, 9, 13.

Humbert de Romans was much more typical of the Middle Ages than Thomas Aquinas. He was a practical man, not much given to speculation. Some of his reasons for giving limited approval to philosophical studies must have amused men like Thomas and Albert. Yet, without the support of an administrator like Humbert, the enactments of Valenciennes could have become dead wood. Humbert saw to it that these scholarly regulations came into actual practice, to the extent that circumstances in the various Dominican provinces permitted.[26]

Thomas Aquinas' participation in the Valenciennes conference was but the first of many such services that he was to render to the administration of his Order and his Church. It also marked the end of his first professorate in the University of Paris. After this meeting, he started the long journey from northern France to Rome.

[26] Cf. Douais, *op. cit.*, p. 51.

CHAPTER TEN

First Essays in Thomism

THE years 1257 to 1259 were fruitful from the point of view of Aquinas' intellectual development. Now, for the first time, he was fully in charge of his own teaching and writing. It was a period in which he began to mature as a thinker and to establish his grasp on the relations between science, philosophy, and wisdom. He was teaching theology at the most stimulating place in the world, at a time when Christian learning was ready for the emergence of a new type of wisdom. In this present chapter, we shall examine some of the key writings of the first Paris professorate in order to observe his thinking as a young professor in his thirties.

Many points remain unsettled concerning the chronology of St. Thomas' writings. There is no list from his own hand, nor is there one written by a contemporary, which gives us exact dates or chronological sequence for his many literary products. Early listings, such as those of Bartholomew of Lucca[1] and Bartholomew of Capua,[2] put the titles down in the order in which the works were to be found in early manuscript collections. Other catalogues of his writings group the various treatises according to subject matter: major theological works, Scripture commentaries, expositions of Aristotle, disputed questions, miscellaneous short works. Little or no attention was paid to the dates at which Thomas started and finished his various treatises. Some writings are not too difficult to date, with the resources of modern scholarship, but it would be well to admit that, even today, there is much doubt and disagreement concerning the times at which he wrote various items.[3]

[1] *Hist. Eccles.*, XXIII, 12–15 (see English in Foster, *Life*, pp. 136–139).

[2] *Proc. Can. Neap.*, LXXXV (*Fontes*, IV, 386–389).

[3] This inexactness of our present knowledge is fully admitted in the only treatment of the problem that we have in English: I. T. Eschmann, "Catalogue," pp. 381–437.

It is especially difficult to date Aquinas' biblical commentaries. We are not really certain that he taught a course on Scripture during 1257–1259, for instance, but it is most probable that he did. The portion of Scripture which he lectured on during his first years as a professor may have been the Book of Isaiah. As printed among the works of St. Thomas, the *Exposition of Isaiah the Prophet,*[4] is not in the original form given it by its author.[5] Some time after St. Thomas' death, one of his secretaries, possibly Jacobinus Astensis who had worked for Thomas in Naples, transcribed the commentary on Isaiah from the illegible handwriting of Aquinas into an ordinary text. It is this transcription of 1274–1278 which forms the base for our present noncritical editions.

The fact that Thomas wrote at least a part of the exposition in his own hand is one of our best evidences that it is an early work and probably from the first Paris professorate.[6] We shall see shortly the reason for this statement: fundamentally, it was simply the fact that Aquinas found, while he was still a student at Paris, that his handwriting could not be read. Thus he soon had to give up writing his own manuscripts.[7] Thomas wrote his original *Exposition of Isaiah* before he had abandoned his efforts to write in his own hand. This decision was made only gradually, but by 1259 he had rather definitely determined to use other scribes. The transcription by Jacobinus does not mean, as some scholars have suggested,[8] that Thomas only commented on Isaiah in his Naples teaching period. Jacobinus apparently worked on the "edition" after Aquinas' death, when the Neapolitan Dominicans were assembling a collection of his manuscripts.

As to its content, the *Exposition of Isaiah* is not a good example of a Thomistic Scripture commentary, another good reason for giving it an early date. It cannot compare in interest with the *Exposition of the Gospel*

---

[4] *In Isaiam Prophetam expositio,* ed. Parm., XIV, 427–576.

[5] Cf. J. Destrez, *Le commentaire de s. Thomas sur Isaïe, d'après la tradition manuscrite,* in *Etudes critiques* (Paris: Vrin, 1933), pp. 161–224.

[6] One portion of the autograph is in *Vat. Lat.,* 9850, fol. 105^r–114^v. See the transcription of fol. 112ra, lines 5–28, in Dondaine, *Secrétaires de saint Thomas* (Roma: S. Sabina, 1956), p. 261.

[7] This is one of the main points in the still debated study of Antoine Dondaine. On p. 200, Dondaine judges that the *Expositio in Isaiam* was written in the hand of Thomas, during the period 1252–1256; however, his argument would not exclude the possibility of its being partly written by St. Thomas, in 1256–1259, or even later. *Walz-Novarina* (*1962*), p. 221, now dates the exposition in 1256–1259. I think St. Thomas may have returned to this commentary, in the Naples regency; see *infra,* Chapter Eighteen, notes 26, 27.

[8] Chenu, *Introduction,* p. 209.

of St. John (which dates from the second Paris professorate).[9]

Another product of St. Thomas' efforts as a young professor is much more rewarding for the modern reader. It was customary for such a teacher to conduct academic exercises called *Disputed Questions*. Aquinas was most assiduous in this respect and we have the written record of his efforts at the University of Paris from 1257 to 1259 in the work that is entitled the *Disputed Questions on Truth*.[10] Disputed questions of this type were oral exercises in which a disputant (who was a bachelor) considered a problem set beforehand, stated various difficulties (in numbered "objections"), cited various authorities or reasons opposed to the objections (the *Sed contra*), and then answered the problem and difficulties as well as he could. All of this was done by a "graduate student" in theology under the advice and direction of a master of theology who presided over the student's performance before an audience of other students and interested persons. On disputation days, all other classes in the faculty of theology were suspended. After this first oral session, the master (in our present case, Thomas Aquinas) wrote out a "determination" of the question, summarizing the main parts and giving his own final answer (*Respondeo* or *Responsio,* called also the *corpus* or body of the question), plus definite replies to the objections and to parts of the section "to the contrary," if they merited answers. The written version of the master's summary of the disputed question was the work of the professor and formed (in the case of Thomas Aquinas and other teachers in the last half of the thirteenth century) an important part of his literary output. This question style of writing[11] was used by St. Thomas in many other writings, notably throughout his *Summa Theologiae*.

The *Questions on Truth* were conducted and written up by Thomas, at

---

[9] For a survey of the Scripture commentaries, see Chenu, *op. cit.*, pp. 199–225.

[10] *Quaestiones disputatae de Veritate,* ed. R. M. Spiazzi (Turin: Marietti, 1949). The Leonine edition announces that this work will appear in its Volume XVII. English: *Truth,* trans. by R. W. Mulligan, J. V. McGlynn, and R. W. Schmidt, 3 vols. (Chicago: Regnery, 1952–1954).

[11] See my *Introduction* to *Truth,* I, xiii–xxvi, for further details. I now think that the assertion that each article was a separate disputed question is not correct. Each oral session must have included the content of several articles; however, I still do not think that each of the *Quaestiones* in our printed editions corresponds to one oral session. Question 8 of *De Veritate,* for instance, includes seventeen articles and could hardly have been covered in one session. There was some revision of these *Questions,* for publication. Consult: Eschmann, "Catalogue," p. 390; Dondaine, *Secrétaires,* pp. 209–216, who argues that each oral session corresponds to an edited *Quaestio.*

Paris, from 1256/7–1259. Possibly Brother Hannibald Hannibaldi, who was bachelor of theology under him for at least part of this period, was the student disputant for some of the sessions. In content, this work falls into two parts: Questions One to Twenty deal with problems of knowledge and truth, while the remaining questions (Twenty-One to Twenty-Nine) treat of appetition and the good. Since the first section (168 articles) is twice as long as the second (85 articles), it has been suggested that Aquinas planned a two-year series dealing with intellection and then added a one-year series (1258–1259) on appetition and its object.[12]

When we look at the actual text of these *Questions on Truth,* we begin to realize how much learning he had now assimilated. The Bible, ancient classical writers, many Patristic and early medieval authors, contemporary theologians and chroniclers are perhaps to be expected. But Aristotle, Porphyry, Boethius, and a dozen other philosophers now fill his pages. Nor does he neglect the Jewish and Mohammedan writers: Maimonides, Avicebron, Isaac of Israel, Algazel, Avicenna, and Averroës. Aristotelianism has become very important to St. Thomas but it is balanced by frequent citations of St. Augustine, St. John Damascene, and Dionysius the Pseudo-Areopagite.[13]

Questions One and Twenty-One are essays on the transcendental properties of being: unity, truth, goodness, and the meaning of "thing" and "something." Knowledge in God, in angels, and in the human mind is thoroughly discussed in Questions Two to Nineteen. The appetitive functions of will and sensory appetition are taken up in Questions Twenty-Two to Twenty-Six and are related to the themes of grace and justification in the last two questions.

St. Augustine, in Books Nine to Fifteen of his great treatise *On the Trinity,* had offered a profound analysis of the human soul and its conscious functions. The Augustinian soul was an extremely unified entity. As knowing, it was mind (*mens*); as holding all its contents (even itself and God), it was memory (*memoria*); and as capable of initiating any and all of its activities, it was will (*voluntas*). These were not three faculties or powers; each member of this psychological trinity was regarded by Augustine as identical with the whole soul. In such triads, Augustine found a remote "image" of the Divine Trinity.

[12] P. Synave, "La Révélation des vérités divines," in *Mélanges Mandonnet* (Paris: Vrin, 1930), 358. These views of Father Synave have been severely criticized recently.

[13] See these names in the "Index of Sources," in *Truth,* III, 492–498.

This psychological teaching was so entrenched in Christian learning, after nine centuries, that St. Thomas could not bluntly oppose it. Yet he could no longer wholly accept it. In the tenth question *On Truth,* he courageously undertakes to discuss the whole problem. It is rather generally known that Aquinas had already developed a psychology which incorporated many elements of Aristotelianism: the essence of the soul was really distinct from its powers; these powers were many. On the level of understanding, Thomas was already convinced that there were two intellectual potencies (possible and agent intellects) and a distinct appetitive power, the will. On the level of sense, he distinguished five external and four internal cognitive powers, plus two sensory appetites, the concupiscible and irascible. Several other powers were concerned with the vivifying of the body.[14]

Now this kind of analytic psychology is quite different from that of St. Augustine. Hence, what St. Thomas did was this: he pointed out that Augustine used different terms (e.g., *mens* for *intellectus*), that he gave somewhat different meanings to terms (e.g., will is the whole soul as active), and that he cast his explanations in the framework of Platonic philosophy. There is never any suggestion in the *Questions on Truth* that St. Augustine was wrong and, in fact, Thomas did not think that he was wrong. He simply felt that Augustinism was no longer adequate as a wisdom in the thirteenth century. Thomas interpreted Augustine respectfully but he changed the meaning of Augustinism whenever he felt it necessary. As one writer puts it: "No one is duped by this procedure, and St. Thomas knows it full well, when he transposes Augustine's psychological descriptions into an Aristotelian vocabulary, that Augustine cannot be treated to that extent as a peripatetic."[15]

Throughout the *Questions on Truth,* Thomas Aquinas is developing his own explanations of reality, knowing, willing, and of truth and goodness. His many citations of earlier writers are due in great part to the scholarly practices of the thirteenth century. Certain writers in the past were important; certain texts from these writers were called *auctoritates* (authoritative passages) and one was expected to explain how he stood on such

[14] This psychology of plural potencies of the soul was already evident in Book III of the *Commentary on the Sentences.* Much the same analysis is found in Albert the Great.

[15] Chenu, *op. cit.,* p. 122. For a vigorous affirmation of the fundamentally Augustinian character of Thomas' view of human nature, see: A. C. Pegis, *At the Origins of the Thomistic Notion of Man* (New York: Macmillan, 1963).

texts, when he taught or wrote. In these *Questions,* Aquinas does this over and over again but, in particular, he orients his own thinking in relation to traditional Augustinism.[16]

Another type of academic discussion in which Thomas engaged at Paris is called *Quodlibetal Questions.* These somewhat resembled the *Disputed Questions,* but there were these differences. *Quodlibetum* means "whatever you wish," so the topics or problems faced by the quodlibetal disputant were not set in advance but were posed by members of the audience at the oral session. No previous preparation of answers was possible. Second, the disputant was not a bachelor but the master himself, in the case of the *Quodlibeta.* Finally, these free-style discussions were held more rarely, usually during the weeks preceding Christmas and Easter, and so they were more fully attended even by other professors who proposed problems and difficulties intended to confound the quodlibetal disputant. The *Quaestiones Disputatae* were also called "ordinary" while the *Quaestiones Quodlibetales* were sometimes known as "solemn." Our printed versions are from the master's revisions and, indeed, they may have been further edited by later collectors of the manuscripts.

In the case of St. Thomas, we have a man who was eager to play his full part in the academic life of the university, so he seems to have engaged in more quodlibetal questions than his contemporaries. Pierre Mandonnet was of the opinion, in fact, that Aquinas had invented this type of exercise.[17] However, this is not so; both Franciscan and Dominican professors conducted quodlibetal disputations as early as the 1230's.

As printed today, St. Thomas' *Quodlibetal Questions* are twelve in number, but their numbered sequence is not chronological.[18] It is now generally agreed that Questions VII to XI (inclusive) belong to the first Paris professorate.[19]

Since they deal with a wide diversity of miscellaneous problems, it is

---

[16] W. Schneider, "Die Quaestiones disputatae 'De veritate' des Thomas von Aquin in ihrer philosophiegeschichtlichen Beziehung zu Augustinus," BGPM, XXVIII, 3 (Münster, 1930), 1–97.

[17] P. Mandonnet, "Saint Thomas créateur de la dispute quodlibétique," *Revue des sciences philos. et théol.,* XV (1926), 477–506; but see Grabmann, *Die Werke,* p. 310.

[18] There is no critical edition; a standard text of the *Quaestiones Quodlibetales* is that of Turin: Marietti, 1949. No English version has been made.

[19] Studies by Glorieux, Pelster, Isaac, Axters, and others are summarized by R. M. Spiazzi in his *Introd.* to the edition just cited. The other Quodlibets belong in the second Paris professorate. Cf. Eschmann, "Catalogue," pp. 392–393.

not possible to offer a general analysis of the doctrine of Aquinas' quodlibetal discussions. Generally speaking, the questions put to him ranged over the vast fields of theology, Scripture studies, philosophy, and even canon law. He was asked things like this: Could any created intellect see the divine essence directly? Could God make a bodily quality, such as white, exist without quantity? Do the divine Ideas refer primarily to singular natures rather than to specific natures? Can God make an infinity of actually existent things? Does the soul separated from its body after death exercise any sensory functions? Suppose a person makes a simple vow of chastity and then gets married, may he engage in sexual relations with his wife? May one attend Mass celebrated by a priest who is a fornicator without committing a mortal sin?[20] No matter how tricky or embarrassing the problem, St. Thomas analyzes it carefully and gives a sober, well-considered answer.

Perhaps the best way to show St. Thomas at work is to quote one of these questions in full. Since the reader may be wondering what he said in answer to the last one mentioned above, let us take it as our example.

> It has been asked, whether a person could hear the Mass of a fornicating priest without sinning mortally.
>
> It seems that he could not hear it without mortal sin. For the Church commands under pain of excommunication that no one may hear the Mass celebrated by a fornicating priest. But to act against such an order is a mortal sin. Therefore, etc.
>
> To the contrary is the fact that in many places in the world it is permitted.
>
> I answer that we should make our consideration of this problem in this way: something may be evil in itself from the point of view of natural law (*jus naturale*), and something may be evil from the point of view of positive law. Whenever a priest who is in a state of mortal sin celebrates, he sins mortally. Consequently, if it were evident to me that he is in a state of mortal sin and if I induced him to celebrate Mass, I would commit a mortal sin. This is so according to natural law, for it is a case of provoking him to mortal sin. Now positive law adds something more, that not only must I refrain from inducing him to celebrate but also that, if I hear his Mass, I sin mortally. This was established as a punishment for a fornicating priest.
>
> Now we should pay attention to this point: this is not so understood in regard to any and every fornicating priest but in regard to public fornicators. Those are called "public" who, in the judgment and sentence of the Church, are so named. Hence, whoever hears Mass celebrated by such a public fornicator sins mortally.
>
> In answer to the objection [to the contrary], we must say this: if it is

[20] These are, in sequence, *Quaest. Quodl.*, VII, art. 1 and 10; VIII, art. 2; IX, art. 1; X, art. 8 and 11; and XI, art. 8.

> tolerated by prelates, then this is no reason for excusing it, because this toleration would be due to negligence, or to the wretchedness or deficiency of those prelates who did not dare to correct others, since they know that they have many things to correct in themselves, or it may even at times be due to fear. Consequently, these are not reasons for an excuse.[21]

We might notice several things in this answer. First of all, it is a commentary on the times that such a question would be asked at a public academic function. Thomas is not abashed by the moral dimensions of the query; he takes it in his stride, making no effort to deny that there are unworthy priests. What is more calculated to embarrass him is the allegation that some bishops fail to check on such behavior. Let us remember that this is a period of tension between the diocesan clergy and the members of the religious Orders. Moreover, it is generally recognized that a bishop exercises a good deal of discretion in regard to the detailed application of ecclesiastical laws in his diocese. St. Thomas cuts through these difficulties by putting the matter, first, in terms of what is naturally right or wrong. What he means is this: irrespective of the interpretation of any Church official, there is something wrong when a priest celebrates Mass in a state of mortal sin. This is not "unnatural" in all senses — but it is unreasonable in the judgment of an informed person who knows all the facts of the case. The fact that ecclesiastical law has also condemned it, and assigned a certain punishment for the infraction of this judgment, simply adds to the original unreasonableness of the case. Though brief, this is a typical portion of a quodlibetal discussion.

One other major work illustrates Thomas Aquinas' thinking at this time. He undertook to explain one or two of the short theological treatises written by Boethius in the sixth century. Anicius Manlius Severinus Torquatus Boethius was obviously a man of some importance; even his name would show that. A Roman senator and a Catholic, in the service of a Gothic and Arian Emperor during the sixth century, Boethius had been imprisoned and executed. Among his many writings were five theological treatises which made an important contribution to Christian learning.[22] Not the least of Boethius' accomplishments was the establishment of a Latin terminology (definitions of nature, person, substance, eternity, and so on) suited to the discussion of the problems of medieval philosophy and theology. The first of his tractates was *On the Trinity;* the third had

---

[21] *Ibid.,* XI, 8, in toto.

[22] For English readers, a useful edition is *The Theological Tractates,* ed. H. F. Stewart and E. K. Rand (New York: Loeb Classical Library, 1946).

a very long title (*How Substances May Be Good, in That Which They Are, and Yet Not Be Substantial Goods*). It came to be known as *On the Weeks* (*De Hebdomadibus*), because this phrase occurs in its opening lines.

Among the writings of St. Thomas we find expositions of both these treatises. He commented on the *Trinity* during the years 1256 to 1258, and it is thought that he wrote the explanation of *De Hebdomadibus* at the same time.[23] William of Tocco and the other early biographers mention his "dictating" of the exposition *On the Trinity* in the following little story which is intended to convey the concentrated attention which characterized Thomas' procedure as an author.

> One time when the aforementioned Doctor was in his cell, dictating (*et dictaret*) the summa of the treatises *On the Trinity*, having taken a candle in his hand, he said to his scribe: "Whatever you may see happening to me, don't tell me about it." Then, while he was wrapt in his thinking, the candle burned for more than an hour, right down to his fingers. The Doctor did not perceive that the flame of the candle was sticking to his fingers. He simply let the flame burn without any movement of his fingers until it died out.[24]

At this point it is important to investigate the significance of the verb *dictate* as used by the first biographers. Until rather recently, it has been taken in a very general sense to mean "authored." However, in 1956, the then Director of the Leonine Commission (entrusted with the task of editing the works of St. Thomas Aquinas with the official aid and support of the Catholic Church) published a book which hinges on the meaning of this word.[25] Putting the thing bluntly, Dondaine argues that "dictated" must be taken in its literal sense. St. Thomas was composing his work *In Boethii de Trinitate* by oral dictation to a secretary, or secretaries. Of course, what makes this suggestion difficult to grasp is the fact that we still have an extant manuscript in which a portion of this Thomistic commentary is to be found *in the handwriting of Aquinas himself*.[26] How

---

[23] Eschmann, "Catalogue," pp. 405–406.

[24] Tocco, *Vita*, c. 47 (*Fontes*, II, 121); cf. P. Calo, *Vita*, c. 24; and B. Gui, *Legenda*, c. 28 (trans. in Foster, *Life*, p. 47).

[25] Dondaine, *Secrétaires*, *supra*, note 6.

[26] A portion of the *Expositio in B. de Trinitate*, starting near the end of q. III, art. 2, and continuing to the end of the commentary, is found in autograph in MS *Vat. Lat.*, 9850, fol. 90–104^v. This has been known for a century; A. Uccelli used this manuscript in the nineteenth century (S. Thomae Aq., *In Isaiam prophetam*, etc. [Roma, 1880], *Praefatio*). See Grabmann, *Die Werke*, pp. 428–434, for a description of MS 9850.

can we explain the fact that Thomas was at this time still writing some parts of his works in his own hand and yet dictating to other scribes? Dondaine's answer to this question is ingenious and is based on a very thorough study of several early manuscripts in which the hand of St. Thomas is alternated with the script of other writers on one and the same folio of the manuscripts. With reference to the *Questions on Truth,* also written at this time as we have seen, Dondaine tries to picture Thomas Aquinas at work:

> The manuscript of the Disputed Questions *De veritate* enables us to open the door of the cell in which the Master is at work and to look around in it. Brother Thomas is reading aloud a text already composed and hastily jotted down in the *littera inintelligibilis* (his own undecipherable script) on scraps of parchment useless for anything else. A secretary — whose back is turned to us and whose identity escapes us — is writing rapidly at the dictation of the Saint; he imbeds his text on sheets of parchment of uniform dimensions that are not yet bound. At certain points, Brother Thomas hesitates, repeats a phrase already spoken, asks to have a word struck out, or the beginning of a sentence, in order to give a new cast to the expression of his thinking. Here, now, he stops his dictation in the middle of an authoritative text; he goes and takes up a volume from among several others distributed on a piece of furniture; he opens it, looks for a moment and then dictates word for word the text cited from Augustine, from Boethius, or from Aristotle. At another moment, it is the secretary's turn to interrupt the joint work; he must trim a worn quill pen which is depositing too much ink and obscuring his writing, allow the ink to dry before starting a new column, get another sheet of parchment from a corner of the cell and smooth it out flat.
>
> But, actually, are we facing the private cell of St. Thomas? Isn't there another workroom on the side in which there are several people? At times the secretary has to leave for a few minutes and yet Master Thomas is always dictating. Another secretary hurriedly takes the vacated place and grasps the pen. He will hold it until his colleague returns, whether this absence lasts three minutes or is prolonged for an hour or more.[27]

This is a vivid, breathless description by a man who was not there. Yet it must be admitted that Father Dondaine has a peculiar sort of documentary evidence for this lifting of the veil of ignorance and secrecy that has shrouded Thomas Aquinas as a literary figure. No contemporary biographer tells about this scene in the *scriptorium* in the Jacobin convent. The basis for this description of Brother Thomas at work is simply the character of certain thirteenth-century manuscripts now in the possession of the Leonine Commission in Rome.

Briefly the reasoning reduces to this. Several of these manuscripts show

[27] Dondaine, *Secrétaires,* pp. 10–11; the original is, of course, in French.

the hand of now one scribe and then another at work. Corrections are found which would not ordinarily be made by a *scriptor,* unless the actual author were present telling him to make them. There are places in these manuscripts where some lines are written in the actual text in the hurried and illegible hand of Brother Thomas. These are not merely marginal notes. Whole sections in autograph suggest that Thomas sometimes had to take over at the writing desk and continue to do the writing himself. The interpretation of this manuscript evidence takes on something of the uncertainty of a poorly recorded detective story. But the main lines of the plot are fairly clear, as a result of Father Dondaine's patient study.[28]

Even during his first period as a professor at Paris, Thomas Aquinas realized that his handwriting was so bad that it was better for him to dictate to other writers. Doubtless there were other reasons. He was now an important and busy man. If he could do more and better work with secretarial assistance, then the monastery was ready to provide it for him. There are other examples of this. St. Albert used a variety of assistants and so did many thirteenth-century authors. While Dondaine's conclusions remain conjectural in some details, the general description of St. Thomas and his secretaries has not been seriously challenged. Who these secretaries were remains something of a puzzle, as Dondaine admits. It has always been known that a fellow Italian, Reginald of Piperno, a priest and a Dominican, served for many years as *socius* to Thomas. We do not know when this association started; possibly it was as early as the first Paris professorate, as Dondaine now thinks.[29] However, the handwriting of Reginald has not been identified and it is not possible to say with certainty that he actually did some of the writing on these manuscripts.

One type of handwriting (Hand A in Dondaine's nomenclature) is Italian. This could be Reginald; it could also be Peter d'Andria who is mentioned by Bartholomew of Capua[30] as the *scriptor* for the commentary on St. Matthew which some scholars date in the first Paris period. However, Dondaine thinks Peter d'Andria was too young for such service in the 1250's.[31] There is also the possibility that Jacobinus of Asti (who is known to have been able to read the *littera inintelligibilis* during Thomas'

---

[28] The details of Father Dondaine's work cannot be summarized.

[29] *Secrétaires,* p. 200. Most biographers of St. Thomas take it that Reginald became his *socius,* in Italy, about 1261.

[30] *Proc. Can. Neap.,* LXXXV (*Fontes,* IV, 389): "Lecturam super Matheum. Idem frater Petrus [de Andria] quidam scolaris parisiensis que defectiva est."

[31] *Secrétaires,* p. 199.

teaching period in Naples) may have been associated with him in Paris.[32] Raymondus Severus was a young Dominican who may have helped Thomas at Paris, but it is questionable whether he was his *socius,* since he only entered the Order in 1250.[33] Moreover the Dominicans were able to secure the services of other scribes who were diocesan clerics. Evenus Garnit is mentioned as a *scriptor* who took dictation from Thomas — but we are not told in what period.[34] Hence it is not possible to say with precision who these men were who served as helpers to St. Thomas at Paris and later. As far as the editing of the works of St. Thomas is concerned, the view that the author himself supervised the writing of a master manuscript, sometimes dictating, sometimes writing in his own revisions, is of primary importance. If Father Dondaine is correct, then the older method of collating many early manuscripts to establish a critical text could, and should, be supplanted by the text of these unique and personally edited folios. One reason why the issuing of volumes in the Leonine edition has been suspended in recent years is precisely this unusual theory that Dondaine has proposed.

Under conditions such as these, Thomas produced several of his first Paris writings. The so-called "commentary" on Boethius' *De Trinitate* is rather a set of *Questions* suggested by the original text.[35] Of these, the fifth and sixth questions are most important for understanding the whole plan of Thomistic thought. It was chiefly on the basis of the older standard text of this work that Jacques Maritain wrote his very influential *Degrees of Knowledge,* published in French in 1932.[36] More recently the manuscript (*Vat. Lat.,* 9850) containing the autograph section of the *Expositio de Trinitate* has been restudied.[37] Thomas corrected his own manuscript, sometimes changing it several times, but the older editions printed the

---

[32] *Ibid.,* p. 202.

[33] See Tocco, *Vita,* c. 27 (*Fontes,* II, 101); *Proc Can. Neap.,* XCII (*Fontes,* IV, 398). *Walz-Novarina* (*1962*), p. 105, confidently asserts that Raymond was *socius,* 1252–1259.

[34] Tocco, *Vita,* c. 17 (*Fontes,* II, 89).

[35] The best edition: *Expositio super librum Boethii de Trinitate,* ed. B. Decker (Leyden: Brill, 1955). The important Questions V and VI are well translated in: A. Maurer, *Division and Methods of the Sciences* (Toronto: Pont. Inst. of Med. Studies, 1953).

[36] *Distinguer pour Unir: ou, Les degrés du savoir* (Paris: Desclée de Brouwer, 1932); in English, *Distinguish to Unite, or the Degrees of Knowledge,* trans. under the supervision of G. B. Phelan (New York: Scribner's, 1959).

[37] The key article: L. B. Geiger, "Abstraction et séparation d'après saint Thomas," *Revue des sciences philos. et théol.,* XXXI (1947), 3–40.

uncorrected text! Newer editions (by P. Wyser and B. Decker) now take account of the changes made by St. Thomas and we find that there are doctrinally significant revisions to be made in our understanding of Aquinas' notions on science and wisdom.[38]

The first attempt made by Thomas, in writing Questions V to VI, to interrelate different kinds of knowledge was based on the idea that there are three levels of intellectual "abstraction," and consequently three main types of intellectual knowledge. In accord with earlier Aristotelian tradition,[39] Aquinas distinguished the subject matters and intellectual procedures of philosophy of nature (physics), mathematics, and metaphysics (called "theology" in the ancient literature). As he first worked it out, each of these levels of intellectual knowledge required a distinct type of "abstraction." The physical philosopher abstracts from the individual characteristics of material things but retains the universal qualitative, quantitative, and substantial features of bodily beings. The mathematical philosopher uses a higher degree of abstraction, because he abstracts from the qualities (whiteness, etc.) of his objects and attends to their quantitative aspects. The metaphysician is working at the highest level of abstraction, because he is not interested in quality or quantity, as such, but solely in the "being" of his objects.[40] At the same time, St. Thomas was well aware that there are, properly speaking, only *two* types of intellectual abstraction: that of the whole from its part, and that of the form from matter. So Thomas revised and corrected this explanation on his own manuscript. In his final version he made it clear that physics employs the abstraction of the whole, mathematics the abstraction of the form, while metaphysics uses a third kind of intellectual differentiation which involves *judgment* (and not mere abstraction on the level of simple apprehension) and is now called "separation."[41]

If these questions arising from Thomas' meditations on Boethius' work *On the Trinity* are, then, important to the development of his views on the methods appropriate to the various divisions of philosophy and theology, his *Commentary on the De Hebdomadibus*[42] makes a significant con-

[38] Cf. Maurer, "Introduction," *Division and Methods of the Sciences,* pp. vii–xxxvi.

[39] Cf. Ptolemy, *Almagest,* trans. R. C. Taliaferro (Chicago: Encyclopaedia Britannica, Inc., 1948), pp. 5–6.

[40] See *In B. de Trinitate,* q. V, art. 3, c.

[41] Cf. Geiger, *art. cit.;* the corrected text of q. V, art. 3, c., may be read in Decker's edition.

[42] The *Expositio in B. de Hebdomadibus* is not yet critically edited; it is in *Opusc. Theol.* (Turin: Marietti, 1954), II, 391 ff.

tribution to the actual content of Thomistic metaphysical wisdom. In recent years, scholars have paid more and more attention to the theory of "participation" and its role in metaphysics.[43] This explanation is given its first full-scale examination in this commentary on Boethius. Participation was originally a Platonic notion: Plato felt that lower things in the world of "the many" share in some way in the perfection of the One Ideal Form which they more or less remotely resemble. Thus, for Plato, all imperfectly beautiful things participate in the Form of Beauty which is one in itself.[44] So far as we know, Aquinas did not read the original dialogues of Plato but he learned a great deal about Platonism from his reading of later authors, such as Cicero, Augustine, Boethius, and Dionysius the Pseudo-Areopagite.[45] In Boethius' treatise he found the suggestion that all created good things are good by virtue of their participation in one supreme Goodness. The commentary that Thomas wrote on this work is not in the form of questions but is rather a literal exposition of the text. This style of literal comment will be used by Aquinas, during the next decade of his life, in his famous explanations of the major works of Aristotle.[46]

After explaining that being (*ens*) applies properly to *substances* (which subsist) and less properly to *accidents* (which are supported in being, as it were, by substances), Thomas proceeds to show how some items participate in being.

> To participate is, in a sense, to take a part (*quasi partem capere*). Hence when something receives in a particular way what belongs to another, it is said in a general way to participate in it. Thus "man" [a species] is said to participate in "animal" [a genus], because it does not have the intelligible character (*rationem*) of animal in its whole generality. Similarly, "Socrates" [an individual] participates in "man" [a species]; likewise, too, an accident participates in its subject [substance], and matter in form, because the substantial or accidental form (which is general in its own character) is determined to this or that subject. Likewise, an effect is said to participate in its cause, especially when it is not an adequate resultant of the power of its cause (thus, we might say that air participates in the light of the sun, because it does not receive it in that clarity that is present in the sun.[47]

[43] L. B. Geiger, *La participation dans la philosophie de s. Thomas d'Aquin* (Paris: Vrin, 1942); C. Fabro, *La nozione metafisica di partecipazione secondo S. Tommaso d'Aquin* (Milano: Vita e Pensiero, 1950). [44] This is the doctrine of the *Symposium*.

[45] Cf. R. J. Henle, *Saint Thomas and Platonism* (The Hague: Nijhoff, 1956).

[46] We are not sure that the commentary on *De Hebdomadibus* was written in the first Paris period; it may date from a later period; cf. Eschmann, "Catalogue," p. 406.

[47] *In B. de Hebdomadibus,* lect. 2 (ed. Parm., XVII, 342). Cf. G. Klubertanz, *St. Thomas Aquinas on Analogy* (Chicago: Loyola U. Press, 1960), pp. 56–57.

It is evident that St. Thomas is now going far beyond Aristotelian metaphysics (participation is not a theme dear to Aristotle) and is working out a personal explanation of the analogous character of the various levels of reality by incorporating into his own thought certain elements of Platonism. The result is something that goes beyond the wisdom of the Greeks. That he was fully aware of what he was doing in his search for a new wisdom is evident from the beginning of his introduction to this *Commentary*. Quoting Ecclesiasticus 32:15–16, "Be first to run home to thy house, and there withdraw thyself, and there take thy play, and do what thou hast a mind," Thomas says this:

> The desire for wisdom has this privileged character: in the course of its fulfilment it becomes more sufficient unto itself. In fact, a man needs the help of many others, in his external activities, but in the contemplation of wisdom, the more a person remains in solitude with himself the more efficacious is his work. Thus the Author of Wisdom, in the text just quoted, recalls man to himself, saying: "Be first to run to thy house," that is, solicitously turn back to your own mind from external matters, before becoming occupied with something else whose concern is but an occasion for distraction. Thus, Wisdom, 8:16, says: "When I go into my house, I shall repose myself with her," that is, with wisdom.
>
> Just as the contemplation of wisdom requires that a person preoccupy himself with his own mind, in order that he may fill his whole house with the contemplation of wisdom, so too, must he be wholly internalized in his thinking, lest his attention be distracted to various other matters. So it is added: "and there withdraw thyself," that is, gather in your whole mental attention there. And so, when that interior house has been completely cleared out, and a man is completely present in it in his thinking, what must be done is explained, in the next clause, "and there take thy play." In this text, we should observe that the contemplation of wisdom is fittingly compared to a game by reason of two features that are found in a game. First, a game is enjoyable for itself and the contemplation of wisdom provides the greatest enjoyment. Thus, Ecclesiasticus 24:27, says from the mouth of wisdom: "For my spirit is sweet above honey." Second, the activities of a game are not directed toward some other objective but are cherished for their own sake. This same feature is present in the delights of wisdom.[48]

Thomas Aquinas had discovered in his early thirties that thinking about ultimate questions cannot be made a group activity. Wisdom is not the product of a committee meeting but of private and personal effort. He learned in his own way the truth of St. Augustine's dictum: "Do not go outside, go back into thyself; truth dwells in the inner man."[49]

---

[48] *In B. de Hebdomadibus, Prologo* (ed. Parm., XVII, 339).

[49] S. Augustini, *De vera religione*, 39, 72: "noli foras ire, in teipsum redi; in interiore homine habitat veritas."

CHAPTER ELEVEN

Preacher General in Italy

ALMOST a decade (1259–1268) was spent by Thomas Aquinas in various Dominican houses of study in the vicinity of Rome. During this same period he took a leading part in many meetings of his Order and province, was consulted by many personages in the Church on doctrinal and practical matters; yet, busy as he was, he managed to do a good deal of writing. He was now a key figure in his province, in the Order, and in the Church at large. Yet, here again, the early biographers have left us a rather confused and spotty picture of his detailed activities. However, there is perhaps more indirect documentary information for these years than for any other period in St. Thomas' life.

Bartholomew of Lucca says that Thomas returned to Italy from Paris, for "well-determined reasons," at the command of Pope Urban IV. The same historian adds, obviously but vaguely, that in Italy Thomas "did and wrote many things."[1] From other documents, as we shall see shortly, it is known that Aquinas was back in the Papal States before the beginning of the pontificate of Urban IV, who became pope in May, 1261. The reasons for his return to his own province have been much discussed. Six possibilities are suggested: Thomas was removed from Paris because of the continued friction with the secular masters at the university; Thomas' superiors wished to have him in his own province for special duties; his services were required at the papal court; Cardinal Hugh of St. Cher felt that Thomas might be made a cardinal or given some other ecclesiastical preference; and it was desirable to turn over his chair of theology at Paris to a new Dominican professor.[2] As a matter of fact, several of these

[1] *Hist. Eccles.*, XXIII, c. 21 et 24. [2] *Walz-Novarina (1962)*, pp. 115–116.

reasons may have been operative but the last one was quite enough: the usual term for a Dominican professor of theology at Paris was three years and Thomas had finished his triennium by 1259.[3]

Thomas arrived at the Dominican monastery at Anagni (a few miles southeast of Rome, on the road to Cassino) in the late summer of 1259.[4] Because of difficulties in Rome, Pope Alexander IV moved his residence to Anagni. Apparently, Thomas began to teach courses in theology, as *Lector* in the Dominican house at Anagni, from 1259 to 1261. There is no documentary evidence that he held any official position at the papal court. Several of his students in these years are known: Tommaso de' Fuscis who became a preacher general in 1273, Tomasello of Perugia, and possibly Ranieri Maturo of Pisa.[5]

The first Provincial Chapter that Thomas now attended was held in Naples, in 1260. There, as the province records have it: "In the year 1260, the Provincial Chapter was celebrated at Naples. . . . In this Chapter, several Preachers General were made; among them was Brother Thomas de Aquino who had returned from Paris as a Master in Theology."[6] What this meant was that Aquinas was given a special status in his Order. Then, as now, only a few outstanding men in the Order of Preachers are raised to this dignity. A preacher general was somewhat independent of the jurisdiction of his prior; he was allowed "complete liberty of initiative and action in his ministry";[7] he was permitted to use a personal seal[8] (whether St. Thomas had such a seal, we do not know); and he was expected to devote himself, at times, to the affairs of the Order as a whole. It is quite possible that Thomas Aquinas was raised to this dignity with a view to his continued attendance at the annual chapters.[9] Apart from the general chapters, those of the Roman Province required Thomas to travel to many different parts of Italy, as the following list indicates:

---

[3] An old French life (A. Touron, O.P., *La Vie de saint Thomas d'Aquin* [Paris: Gissey et Bordelet, 1740], p. 164) points this out — and then maintains that Thomas stayed for two more years in his first professorate!

[4] P. Mandonnet, "Thomas d'Aquin lecteur à la Curie Romaine," *Xenia Thomistica* (Rome, 1925), III, 9–40, is still a useful study of this period.

[5] Mandonnet, "Novice prêcheur," *Rev. Thom.*, VII (1924), 374; *Walz-Novarina* (*1962*), p. 117; M. Grabmann, "Die persönlichen Beziehungen des hl. Thomas v. Aq.," *Hist. Jahrbuch*, LVII (1937), 310.

[6] *Fontes*, VI, 582.

[7] Mandonnet, *et al.*, *Saint Dominique*, p. 205.

[8] Douais, *L'Organisation des études*, p. 14.

[9] *Walz-Novarina* (*1962*), pp. 117–118.

1260, September, at Naples
1261, September 14, at Orvieto
1262, July 6, at Perugia
1263, September (?), at Rome
1264, September 29, at Viterbo
1265, September 8, at Anagni
1266, August 5, at Todi
1267, July (?), at Lucca
1268, May 27, at Viterbo.

On September 14, 1261, Thomas was assigned as *lector* in the Dominican monastery at Orvieto.[10] This is a small town lying to the north of Rome, a little beyond Viterbo. Pope Urban IV (1261–1264) had taken up his residence there and, for the next four or five years (until the summer of 1265), Orvieto became the center of a great deal of scholarly activity. As Bartholomew of Lucca reports the situation:

> At this time [speaking of the pontificate of Urban IV] Brother Thomas, while teaching at Rome, commented and redacted in the form of glosses or commentaries almost the entire philosophy of Aristotle, both natural and moral, but especially the *Ethics* and *Metaphysics,* and he used a method of exposition that was remarkable and new.[11]

This report involves certain chronological discrepancies. Thomas was not teaching in Rome during the pontificate of Urban IV; his work in Rome began in 1265. Grabmann interprets this account to mean that, "Aquinas started his commentaries on Aristotle at the court of Urban IV in Orvieto and continued them later, during his residence in Rome."[12]

Actually, Pope Urban IV was an active patron of philosophical and scientific studies.[13] He had as physician to the papal court a famous Italian mathematician, Giovanni Campano di Novara. This man edited Euclid's *Elements of Geometry,* commented on the mathematical treatises of Leonardo da Pisa, and wrote several scientific works of his own. Dedicating one of his treatises (*Theotica Planetarum*) to Pope Urban, Giovanni Campano acknowledged his own debt and added that Urban enjoyed

---

[10] *Fontes,* VI, 582: "Assignamus fr. Thomam de Aquino pro lectore in conventu Urbevetano in remissionem suorum peccatorum."

[11] *Hist. Eccles.,* XXIII, c. 24.

[12] M. Grabmann, *Guglielmo di Moerbeke, O.P., il traduttore delle opere di Aristotele* (Roma: Università Gregoriana, 1946), p. 63.

[13] *Ibid.,* p. 43: "il Papa Urbano IV è stato un grande amico e promotore degli studi filosofici."

having many important philosophers with him.[14] As further evidence of Urban's reputation as a patron of philosophy, there is a Latin poem (*De statu Curiae Romanae*) by Magister Henricus of Würzburg, written at Orvieto in 1263–1264. In six lines of this poem,[15] quoted by Grabmann, there is mention of a "great philosopher" who came to Urban's court. This was taken by the original editor (H. von Grauert) as a reference to Thomas Aquinas. Grabmann shows, however, that this personage "who armed the papal residence with all the arts" (*omnibus armata est artibus illa domus*) was Albert the Great.[16]

The fact is that both Albert and Thomas were working at Orvieto in the year 1262. Albert had retired from his See at Ratisbon and was now resident at the papal court for the entire year.[17] As if this were not a sufficient gathering of Dominican scholarship, William of Moerbeke, O.P., already a well-known translator of philosophic and scientific works from the Greek, was recalled from the missions and stationed at Orvieto.[18] There is little question that, as several early documents say, William of Moerbeke now began to translate and revise existing versions of most of the philosophical writings of Aristotle, at the request (*ad instantiam*) of Thomas Aquinas.[19]

As we shall see in our next chapter, Thomas now undertook a very important work in the service of his Church and of Western scholarship. With papal approval and support, he undertook to review all of Aristotle's philosophy and to determine how and to what extent it might be used in Christian schools. Much of this decade in the Papal States was devoted to this significant activity. As Pierre Mandonnet has said:

---

[14] G. Tiraboschi, *Storia della letteratura italiana* (Milano, 1833), VII, 257–259, gives a portion of the Latin dedication, translated into Italian, in which one clause reads: "Urbano godeva di aver seco alla mensa molti valorosi Filosofi."

[15] Grabmann, *op. cit.*, pp. 45–46, cites the edition of H. von Grauert, *Magister Heinrich der Poet in Würzburg und die römische Curie* (München: Abhandl. d. Bayer. Akademie, 1912).

[16] M. Grabmann, "Ist das philosophische Universalgenie bei Magister Heinrich dem Poeten Thomas von Aquin?" *Hist. Jahrbuch,* XXXVIII (1917), 315–320.

[17] F. Pelster, *Kritische Studien* (Freiburg, 1920), p. 86.

[18] Grabmann, *G. di Moerbeke,* pp. 41–48, gives the evidence for this chronology.

[19] "Fr. Wilhelmus Brabantinus, Corinthiensis [William became Bishop of Corinth in 1278] transtulit omnes libros naturalis et moralis philosophiae de greco in latinum ad instantiam fratris Thomae." G. Meerssemann, O.P., *Laurenti Pignon Catalogi et Chronica* (Romae, 1936), p. 62; for several other texts to the same effect, see Grabmann, *G. di Moerbeke,* pp. 62–67.

Thomas Aquinas, disciple of Albert, undertook on a new level the work of his teacher. The Roman Church, which was ever facing this inevitable problem of the spreading of Aristotle's writings, was no stranger to the enterprise. If she did not first conceive the project, she certainly encouraged it to the full. It could not have been, indeed, by virtue of fortuitous circumstance that William of Moerbeke, the new translator of Aristotle, and Thomas Aquinas, the new commentator, were found simultaneously at the pontifical court at the moment of carrying out their double work. Urban IV, who had brought them together at the very time that he was renewing the old prohibition of the teaching of the books of the Stagirite (1263), had obviously committed this work to them.[20]

Aquinas' published expositions of the various works of Aristotle are usually dated from the late 1260's, and some are thought to have been written after his return to Paris in 1269. We do not yet know the whole story of how he produced these impressive commentaries. There is no doubt that the written expositions incorporate material from Greek commentaries which became available to him only in the late 1260's. However, he may have delivered *oral* lectures on the main works during his stay at various Dominican houses in the Papal States, and then, after the lapse of some time, *edited* and supervised the making of fair copies in his later years at Paris and Naples.[21]

There is an interesting possibility that Thomas made a long sea trip during 1263. In a sixteenth-century chronicle, Sebastian d'Olmeda reports that Aquinas was sent in this year to the General Chapter of the Order, held in London, at which Humbert de Romans was reluctantly permitted to resign from his office as Master General. Sebastian wrote:

> He [Humbert de Romans] insisted with great emphasis, at the Chapter in London, England, and he was absolved from the responsibility of Master General on the last day of the Chapter, with Brother Thomas, the one from Aquino, acting as *definitor* for Italy and Bartholomew of Tours as *definitor* for France.[22]

Few biographers take this testimony seriously. The trip is not noted in the early documents but, then, few actual incidents in Thomas' life are. In the old French *Life of St. Thomas* by Touron, it is carefully recorded

[20] Mandonnet, *Siger de Brabant*, 2me éd., I, 39.

[21] Pelster advanced this suggestion in "Die Uebersetzungen der aristotelischen Metaphysik in den Werken des hl. Thomas," *Gregorianum*, XVII (1936), 382. Grabmann, *G. di Moerbeke*, p. 76, admits that the chronology of these expositions demands more study.

[22] *Chronica Ordinis Praedicatorum*, ed. M. Canal Gomez (Rome, 1936), p. 46; the Latin text is quoted in *Fontes*, VI, 582.

with the remark that some historians (Echard and Leander are cited) think that Thomas did go to England.[23] Angelus Walz mentions it with considerable skepticism.[24]

It is also recorded in various early biographies and chronicles that Pope Urban commissioned Thomas Aquinas to compose, in 1264, the Office for the feast of Corpus Christi. Bartholomew of Lucca, a good historian writing between 1312 and 1317, reports it this way.

> He [Thomas] also made the Office of Corpus Christi at the command of Urban. Now this was completed, both the *lectiones* and the whole Office for the day and the night, even the Mass and whatever is sung on that day.[25]

Some modern liturgical scholars are inclined to doubt that Thomas Aquinas did this. They point out that the feast had been celebrated as early as 1246, at Fosses in Belgium, and that several of the hymns antedate the period of St. Thomas. The text of a so-called "primitive" liturgy has been edited.[26] Perhaps the whole historical problem would not have arisen, if people had read William of Tocco carefully. As he said:

> [Thomas] wrote the Office of Corpus Christi at the command of Pope Urban, in which he expounded all the ancient forms of this Sacrament [*omnes veteres figuras exposuit*] and compiled [*compilavit*] the truths that pertain to the new grace.[27]

Tocco speaks of Thomas' literary work as a compilation; there is no suggestion that it was an entirely original piece of work. It is quite clear that Thomas did an editorial job, at the direction of the Pope, and that he is entitled to credit for this work.[28] The liturgical text used in present-day celebrations of the feast is not identical with what Thomas compiled. A fifteenth-century Roman liturgy with many interpolations modified the work of St. Thomas.

Various other hymns and prayers are traditionally attributed to Thomas Aquinas. Mandonnet printed the hymn, *Adoro te devote,* along with ten prayers (including the well-known prayer before Communion: "Almighty, eternal God, behold I go"), under the heading of "scarcely doubtful"

---

[23] A. Touron, *Vie de saint Thomas d'Aquin,* pp. 183–184.

[24] Walz, *San Tommaso (1945),* p. 130.

[25] *Hist. Eccles.,* XXII, c. 24.

[26] C. Lambot and I. Fransen, *L'Office de la Fête-Dieu primitive* (Textes et mélodies retrouvés) (Maredsous: Editions de Maredsous, 1946); see the review by Dom A. Strittmatter in *Traditio,* V (1947), 396–398.

[27] Tocco, *Vita,* c. 17 (*Fontes,* II, 88).

[28] Grabmann, *Die Werke,* pp. 365–367, reviews all the historical data available.

works.[29] Dom A. Wilmart has edited what appears to be the original text of the hymn (it actually begins: *Ave devote, latens veritas*) and it differs greatly from the version now in use. Wilmart is unable to decide whether Thomas composed it.[30] As far as the prayers are concerned, there is a strange lack of evidence for their authenticity.[31]

Thomas' brother, Aymo of Aquino, was still alive in 1264 and lived on the property at Montesangiovanni, in the Papal States. He was now a loyal supporter of Pope Urban. While Thomas Aquinas was never personally involved, to our knowledge, in political events of this period, he could hardly have been completely unaware of them. When Frederick II died in 1250, the power of the Hohenstaufen dynasty declined in Italy. Conrad, Frederick's eldest son, died within four years and the successor was a baby boy. Another son of Frederick, Manfred, tried to seize power, fighting rather successfully against weak papal armies for the next seven years. Then the French Popes, Urban and Clement, sought the assistance of the famous King Louis IX of France. In 1265, Charles of Anjou, the brother of Louis IX, was sent to Italy. He defeated and killed Manfred at the gory battle of Benevento (January 20, 1266). Charles of Anjou now began to rule the Sicilian empire with a heavy hand. No strangers to plotting and chicanery, the rebellious south Italians brought in a grandson of Frederick II, Conradin, and installed him as their king. However, at Tagliacozzo (August 23, 1268), Conradin was defeated and brought to Naples where Charles executed him.

Some indication of the continuing influence of the Aquino family is given by three papal documents of the year 1264. There is first a letter to the Bishop-Elect of Capua, Marino d'Eboli.[32] In it, Pope Urban directs the Bishop-Elect to install clerics of Aymo's selection in two churches in the vicinity of Montesangiovanni. Obviously, Aymo is now in the good graces of the papal government. The second document is a sort of *aide-mémoire* from Pope Urban, ordering the Count of Acerra (Thomas II d'Aquino) to prevent Manfred's forces from entering the territory about Montesangiovanni. The fact that there were at least two men named Thomas d'Aquino may explain why some fourteenth-century writers

---

[29] *Opuscula Omnia* (Paris: Lethielleux, 1927), IV, 536–545.

[30] A. Wilmart, "La tradition littéraire et textuelle de l'Adoro te devote," *Recherches de Théol. anc. et méd.*, I (1929), 21–40, 149–176; see also his *Auteurs spirituels et textes dévots* (Paris, 1932), p. 393.

[31] Grabmann, *Die Werke*, p. 372.

[32] *Fontes*, VI, 566.

thought that St. Thomas was involved in the affairs of Charles of Anjou, as we shall see in Chapter Seventeen. In any case, Pope Urban mentions "his beloved son, Aymo d'Aquino, who is persevering in his devotion to this Church," and then includes Aymo under the general injunction to stop Manfred, under the pain of loss of rights.[33] The third document is a letter to the same effect, written directly to Aymo and his supporters at the castle of Montesangiovanni. Evidently, Aymo performed satisfactorily, for he is mentioned in two royal documents from the court of Charles of Anjou (1266) which show that he is serving as justiciar in the Kingdom of Sicily. Aymo eventually secured under Angevin patronage a position similar to the one that his father had held in the Hohenstaufen period. There is never the slightest reference to events of this sort in the writings of St. Thomas.

As an example of Thomas' letters, we will give here the full text of an answer that he wrote in 1262 to a query from the Dominican *lector* at Florence, James of Viterbo.[34] It illustrates the very strict views then current on usury, the charging of interest on a loan, particularly if one charged for the use of the money because of the length of time elapsing before repayment.[35]

> To his very dear Brother in Christ, James of Viterbo, Lector in Florence, Brother Thomas of Aquino sends greetings:
>
> I have received your letter concerning certain moral problems on which you have asked the judgment of the Bishop-Elect of Capua [Marino d'Eboli] and myself. After conferring with the same Bishop of Capua, and later with Cardinal Hugh [of St. Cher], I am required to answer the first problem as follows.
>
> Supposing that this custom of deferring payment for three months, as described, is for the common good of the merchants, that is, to facilitate the work of the merchants or their transactions, and not for fraudulent usury, then it seems that we must make a distinction. For, either the seller sells his merchandise, on the basis of deferred payment, for an amount exceeding the just price, or for an amount in accord with the just price. If the first alternative is so, there is no doubt that the contract is usury, since the lapse of time enters into the price. Nor can this be an excuse, that

---

[33] *Ibid.*, 567–568.

[34] Cardinal Hugh of St. Cher is mentioned in the letter as still living; he died at Orvieto, March 19, 1263; cf. Walz, *I Cardinali domenicani* (Firenze-Roma, 1940), p. 15.

[35] *Responsio super materia venditionis, Opusc. Theol.*, (Turin: Marietti, 1954), I, 185; for a better text see: A. O'Rahilly, "Notes on St. Thomas on Credit," *Irish Ecclesiastical Record,* XXXI (1928), 359–364. My present translation is a revision of the version in *Pocket Aquinas,* pp. 223–225.

the second seller is an agent of the first, because there is never any legitimate reason why the price may be increased on the basis of the time involved in waiting for payment. However, if the second alternative is so, there is no usury. That he might sell for less if the payment were made immediately makes no difference, as can be seen from a comparison with other debts. If an amount due to a person is payable after a certain date, even though he might remit part of the debt if it were paid sooner, such a person is entirely free from the charge of usury. Although it does suggest usury to take more than is owed because of deferred payment, still to take less so that payment will be made earlier is not suggestive of usury, particularly on the part of the person who takes less. However, on the part of the one who pays less by virtue of prompt payment there might seem to be some degree of usury, since he is selling an interval of time. Consequently, in the problem under consideration, there would be more fear of usury on the side of the buyer who, in paying less before the three months, buys the cloth for less than the just value, than there is on the side of the seller who asks for less so that he may be paid more promptly.

From this, what we should answer or say about the second problem is clear. If the Tuscan merchants bringing cloth from the Fair at Lagny sell the cloth for more than it is worth in the general market, because they defer payment until Easter, there is no question that this is usury. However, if they sell, not for more than its worth but for more than they would get if they were paid promptly, then this is not usury.

In the third problem, a similar answer is evident. If those who accept money on the basis of a charge for a loan, with the intention of recovering it by selling the cloth at more than its worth because of the aforementioned waiting for payment, then there is no doubt that this is usury, for time is obviously being sold. Nor are they excused on the argument that they wish to protect themselves from loss, for no one should protect himself from loss by committing a mortal sin. And although they may legitimately recover in their sale other lawfully incurred expenses, such as the cost of transporting the cloth, they may not recover the excessive charges that they paid, since this was an unjust payment. Especially so, since in paying excessive charges they sinned by providing the usurers with an occasion for sin. For the need that is asserted, their desire to live more respectably and to do more business, is not so compelling as to provide a reason for excusing the sin under consideration. This is clear by comparison, for a person could not in selling cloth recover expenses that he had carelessly and imprudently contracted.

The inquiry on the fourth problem also becomes clear from what has been said concerning the preceding cases. If a man who owes a debt payable on a certain date pays before that date provided a part of the debt is remitted, he apparently commits usury, for he is evidently selling the time involved in the payment. Hence he is required to make restitution. He is not excused by the fact that he is inconvenienced by making the payment ahead of time, or by the fact that he is induced to do this by someone else, since all usurers could be excused by such reasoning.

This is the firm and definite judgment of myself and the aforementioned Bishop-Elect of Capua and Cardinal Hugh concerning these cases. Farewell.

It is probable that Thomas wrote this letter from Rome. On the eighth of September, 1265, the Provincial Chapter at Anagni had given him a new assignment.

> We enjoin Brother Thomas of Aquino, under remission of sins, to take charge of the house of studies in Rome; and we desire that the brothers stationed with him be provided for, in regard to necessary clothing, by the convents from which they originated. Moreover, if these students are found negligent in their studies, we give Brother Thomas the authority to send them back to their convents.[36]

So, Thomas became the regent of the theology course at the Roman monastery of Santa Sabina. Besides teaching theology there from the fall of 1265 to the spring of 1267, he continued his study of Aristotle. Pope Urban died in 1265 and was succeeded by Clement IV. Like Urban, Clement was a Frenchman who was well acquainted in the world of scholarship. He is the man whom Roger Bacon had known in Paris as Guy de Foulques, a canon lawyer. To Clement, Roger sent (1267–1268) those grandiose treatises on the proposed reformation of Christian learning, the *Opus Majus, Opus Minus,* and *Opus Tertium.*[37] Pope Clement did nothing to discourage Thomas Aquinas' Aristotelian studies but, even now, no official position was held by Thomas at the papal court. His main duties remained those of director and teacher in the Dominican school of theology in Rome.

A clear indication of the considerable authority exercised by Aquinas in the Roman *studium* is given in a papal document.[38] A member of the Order of Preachers, Walter of Calabria, had been consecrated Bishop of Dschibleh in Syria. Pope Clement sent the following letter, on July 14, 1267, from his residence in Viterbo.

> To Our beloved son, Brother Thomas of Aquino, of the Order of Friars Preachers:
>
> Since it is a good thing for friars to live equably and cheerfully in community, and since every being enjoys another like unto itself, We, motivated by benevolence, command by apostolic document that Our venerable Brother . . . designated for the bishopric of Dschibleh, be provided with brothers from his Order, in whose company he may find relaxation. You are to assign to him at your discretion, for whatever time is necessary, two brothers from your Order, one a cleric and the other a lay brother. They are to accompany him, to obey and have regard for him, exception being made for obedience to their superiors in the Order.
>
> Given at Viterbo, II Ides of July, in the third year [of Our pontificate].

---

[36] *Fontes,* VI, 583.

[37] Cf. Gilson, *Hist. of Christ. Philos.,* 294–295.

[38] *Fontes,* VI, 570.

At least as early as the beginning of his residence in the Papal States (1259), Thomas Aquinas had been provided with the services of his own *socius,* Reginald of Piperno. This fellow Italian was his constant companion for the rest of Thomas' life. Brother Reginald was a priest in the Order of Preachers; he heard Thomas' confessions and they regularly served each other's Masses.[39] Reginald appears to have held no academic degree but he was doubtless an able scholar, for he assisted Thomas in writing his works and this help went beyond that of a mere clerk. Several transcripts (*reportationes*) of Aquinas' lectures are due to the industry of Reginald. He will figure prominently in the later career of Thomas Aquinas.

Reginald is the source of an account of the healing of a hemorrhaging woman, while Thomas was preaching during Holy Week in Rome. In the canonization testimony of Leonard of Gaeta, the event is reported as taking place at the Church of St. Mary Major;[40] William of Tocco thought it had occurred in St. Peter's Cathedral.[41] In any case, they both cite Reginald who said that the woman decided, while listening to Thomas preaching, that she might be cured of her ailment if she touched his habit. After he finished his sermon, she went up and put her hand on the edge of his robe. She was immediately healed.

Possibly during this residency in Rome, Thomas was invited to spend the Christmas season at the country home of Richard Cardinal Hannibaldi.[42] The Cardinal had an estate called Molaria (today it is a farm[43]) which probably had been inherited from his family. What happened there is told by Bartholomew of Capua, at the Naples inquiry before Aquinas was canonized.

> Lord Richard, Cardinal deacon of S. Angelo, arranged to have the same Thomas of Aquino, beloved of God, (whom the Cardinal much liked and treated as if he were of his own family) invited to Molaria. The Cardinal asked him to celebrate the feast of the Nativity with him. When Brother Thomas arrived, he found that two Roman Jews were guests of the Cardinal. Father and son, they were well versed in Hebrew, very rich and special friends of the Cardinal. While these men were present, the Cardinal said: "Brother Thomas, say a few of your good and holy words to these stubborn Jews!"

[39] Tocco, *Vita,* cc. 27 et 63 (*Fontes,* II, 101, 136).

[40] *Proc. Can. Neap.,* LXXV (*Fontes,* IV, 369).

[41] Tocco, *Vita,* c. 53 (*Fontes,* II, 126–127).

[42] De Groot, *Het Leven van den H. Thomas,* p. 229; *Walz-Novarina* (*1962*), p. 136; both suggest the year 1265.

[43] Cf. M.-H. Laurent, *Fontes,* IV, 389, note (b).

Brother Thomas replied that he would gladly say whatever good things he could, provided they desired to listen. Eventually, Brother Thomas and the Jews withdrew to a private room in the chapel of the castle of Molaria. They remained together for a long time, discussing and arguing among themselves. Brother Thomas satisfied their difficulties. Eventually, observing that the Jews seemed to be in complete agreement with his explanations, Brother Thomas said to them: "Go and think it over. Come back to this room tomorrow and frankly tell me all your difficulties."

On the following day, Christmas eve, the Jews came and spent some time with Brother Thomas in the same church. They had lunch with Brother Thomas in this chapel and afterwards the voices of Brother Thomas and his companion were heard singing the hymn, *Te Deum laudamus.* Hearing this chanting, the Cardinal (who suffered from gout and was unable to walk about) had himself carried to the church. With his chaplains and other members of his household, he joined in singing the remaining verses of the hymn, there in the church. The Jews were baptized.

Then the Cardinal summoned many noblemen from the city, along with distinguished men from the countryside, to give praise and rejoice at Molaria. As a result of this sudden conversion, they celebrated a great feast on the estate at Molaria. Moreover, the Jews told the Cardinal that they had been unconvinced when they entered the chapel with Brother Thomas but, when they heard him talking, their attitude was completely changed and they could hardly advance any argument or objection to his words.[44]

Thomas spent two years teaching in Rome. Apparently, the new Emperor, Charles of Anjou, wished to have a general house of studies (*studium generale*) established in the Eternal City but political disturbances and the lack of money prevented this plan from fulfillment. Some think that Thomas was stationed at Santa Sabina in order to develop more advanced studies there.[45] However, it did not achieve the status of a university course in theology during the regency of Aquinas. He did conduct disputations in Rome, possibly in 1266–1267, out of which came the edited versions of the *Disputed Questions on the Power of God.*[46] It is even possible that parts of his *Questions on the Soul* and *on Evil* were orally disputed in Rome.[47]

At some point during these years, the Master General asked Thomas to give his judgment on the orthodoxy of the theological teaching of his Dominican colleague, Peter of Tarentaise. Some anonymous person had

---

[44] *Proc. Can. Neap.*, LXXXVI (*Fontes,* IV, 389–391); much the same story is in Tocco, *Vita,* c. 22 (*Fontes,* II, 96); Calo, *Vita,* c. 14 (*Fontes,* I, 33).

[45] Castagnoli, "Regesta Thomistica," *Divus Thomas, Piacenza,* XXXII (1929), 449–450.

[46] On the Italian origin of the *Q. D. de potentia Dei,* see Eschmann, "Catalogue," p. 391; Grabmann, *Die Werke,* p. 306.

[47] Eschmann, "Catalogue," p. 391.

selected one hundred and eight propositions from Peter's lectures on the *Sentences* and sent this list to John of Vercelli with the accusation of unorthodoxy. The result was a memorandum from Aquinas to the Master General, now known under the title: *Response to Brother John of Vercelli concerning One Hundred and Eight Articles from the Work of Peter of Tarentaise.*[48] The whole affair must have been a matter of considerable embarrassment, both to the Master General and to Aquinas. Peter of Tarentaise was a distinguished Dominican scholar who had served with Thomas on the Valenciennes commission in 1259. His lectures on the *Sentences* were probably delivered during the period of Thomas' first Paris professorate. In Stephen of Salanhac's list of Dominican masters in theology at Paris, Peter is the third man mentioned after Thomas Aquinas.[49] At the time of his denunciation by an anonymous detractor, Peter was provincial of the French Province.[50] As evidence of his eventual stature in the Church, we have the fact that Peter became archbishop of Lyons in 1272 and pope (Innocent V) in 1276.

Peter's theological views were not identical with those of Thomas Aquinas. On many points he was closer to the more conservative thinking of St. Bonaventure.[51] However, Thomas' comments on the allegedly erroneous teachings are models of judicious restraint. The anonymous critic's first assertion, for instance, is that wisdom and goodness are quite distinct items in God and that Peter is wrong in saying that they differ only in their *rationes*. To this, Thomas quietly answers by explaining what *ratio* means (this explanation is still worth reading) and then he bluntly says that the objector's charge against Peter is sheer calumny. Throughout, Thomas defends Peter's views; occasionally he admits that some passages, taken out of context, may sound improper. A few of Peter's statements are judged to be simply wrong. Thus the sentence, "Although in the creation of the soul, new matter is created from the point of view of

---

[48] *Responsio ad fr. Joannem Vercellensem de articulis CVIII ex opere Petri de Tarentasia,* in *Opusc. Theol.* (Turin: Marietti, 1954), I, 223. Cf. R. Martin, "Notes critiques au sujet de l'Opuscule IX de s. Thomas d'Aquin," *Mélanges A. Pelzer* (Louvain, 1947), pp. 303–323.

[49] Douais, *L'Organisation des études,* p. 164.

[50] Grabmann, *Die Werke,* p. 376.

[51] Cf. B. M. Smeraldo, O.P., *Intorno all'opuscolo IX di S. Tommaso d'Aquino. Pietro da Tarantasia ha errato in teologia?* (Roma, 1945), decides that Peter was not an unorthodox theologian. Peter's *Commentary on the Sentences* is dated *ca.* 1257–1259.

esse, yet essentially it is united and joined to pre-existing matter, as a point to a point," is bluntly condemned by Thomas as neither well expressed nor intelligible.[52] Generally, Aquinas tells the Master General that the anonymous critic is a stupid person who is interested in causing trouble. We do not know what formal action was taken by John of Vercelli, but it is evident that Peter's reputation was not seriously affected by these charges.

Thomas attended the General Chapter of his Order, in July, 1267, at Bologna. He is mentioned in the chronicle of Galvano della Fiamma as *definitor* for the Roman Province at this meeting. However, he was not named to this position at his own Provincial Chapter. It has been suggested that the Master General required Thomas' presence at the Bologna General Chapter for some other purpose.[53] In any event, it may have been on this occasion that an incident occurred which is recorded by Tocco as a mark of Thomas' humility. It could easily be taken as evidence of his good humor.

> When the aforesaid Doctor was visiting the convent at Bologna, he was walking about in the cloister wrapped in contemplation, as was his custom. A certain Brother from another monastery, who did not know the Doctor, had received permission from the Prior to take the first brother that he met as a companion for a business trip to the city. He encountered Thomas and said: "Good Brother, the Prior has ordered you to accompany me."
>
> Immediately, Thomas nodded his assent and followed him. Unable to walk as fast as his companion, Thomas was often scolded by the friar. He humbly apologized. Now, some of the citizens who knew Thomas were amazed to see so famous a Doctor walking behind a friar of modest estate, a man in fact whom he should have preceded. Thinking that this must have happened because of a mistake, they informed the friar who this man was that he was leading about. Turning to Brother Thomas, he asked to be excused for his offense, because of his ignorance. The citizens looked toward the Master with respect and asked him to explain this example of great humility. Thomas answered that all religious life finds its perfection in obedience, whereby a man subjects himself to another man for God's sake, just as God had obeyed man for man's sake.[54]

Pope Clement IV had taken up his residence at Viterbo and Thomas was sent to work there, at the Dominican monastery, during the last years that he spent in the Papal States.[55] Precisely why he was stationed at

[52] *Declaratio centum et octo Dubiorum,* q. CVI, as printed in *Opusc. Omnia,* ed. Mandonnet, III, 244.

[53] *Walz-Novarina (1962),* p. 146.

[54] Tocco, *Vita,* c. 25 (*Fontes,* II, 98).

[55] *Walz-Novarina (1962),* pp. 147–148.

convents in the same towns where the popes lived is not known. There is no extant evidence that he held any office in the papal court. Some modern authorities think that Thomas disputed his *Questions on Spiritual Creatures* in Viterbo.[56]

At some time during the school year 1268–1269, Thomas received the news that his superiors had again appointed him to teach theology at the University of Paris. It was somewhat unusual for a Dominican in the thirteenth century to be given a second professorate at Paris. The only other known cases are those of Peter of Tarentaise and William of Alton.[57] There is little doubt that the Dominicans needed one of their best scholars at Paris in what promised to be a period of controversy and doctrinal strife. John of Vercelli had asked Albert the Great to go, but Albert had declined.[58]

It is actually very difficult to establish the precise time at which Thomas now left Italy for Paris. We know that he was back in Paris in the spring of 1269; he is mentioned as present at the general Chapter of Paris, in May of 1269. One Paris manuscript contains the following introduction to a work in which Aquinas was involved:

> The Questions that follow were proposed at the General Chapter held at Paris in the year of Our Lord MCCLXIX, in the presence of the Masters of the Order and the Definitors, among whom were seven Lectors and one Master; also before several Masters assembled at that time, namely, Brother Thomas of Aquino, Brother Bonhomme, Brother Peter of Tarentaise, Brother Bartholomew, Brother Balduin and Brother Gilbert, all of whom answered unanimously as follows.[59]

However, it is now generally agreed that Aquinas had come to Paris early in 1269, and quite possibly he started the school year there in the fall of 1268.[60] The chronicle of Galvano della Fiamma says that Thomas "determined certain questions in 1268."[61] Mandonnet took this to mean that Thomas held Quodlibets at Paris, in the Christmas season of 1268.[62]

---

[56] Eschmann, "Catalogue," p. 391; Grabmann, *Die Werke,* pp. 304–306.

[57] P. Glorieux, *Repértoire des Maîtres,* I, 107, 113.

[58] H. D. Scheeben, *Albert der Grosse. Zur Chronologie seines Lebens* (Vechta-Leipzig, 1931), pp. 90–92.

[59] This incipit of *De Secreto* is from *MS Par. Bibl. Nat., lat.,* 14546 (anc. Vict. 635), fol. 255ᵛ. This manuscript is early fourteenth century; see Grabmann, *Die Werke,* pp. 188–191.

[60] Mandonnet, "Thomas d'Aquin lecteur," in *Xenia Thomistica,* III, 26; *Walz-Novarina (1962),* p. 148.

[61] *Chronica Ord. Praed., MOPH,* II, 100.

[62] *Siger de Brabant,* 2me éd., I, 88.

Although the point is not settled, the likelihood is that Thomas left Viterbo in the summer of 1268 and made his way on foot to Paris. There is good possibility that he stopped at the Dominican monasteries along the route, at Bologna and Milan.[63] In a manuscript in the Ambrosian Library, Milan, there is a group of three *Sermons* attributed to Brother Thomas of Aquino.[64] One of these is entitled: "Sermon of Brother Thomas of Aquino, preached on the same Sunday (it follows another Sermon preached in Paris on the first Sunday of Advent) in the House of the Preachers at Bologna, in the presence of the University."[65] As Mandonnet reconstructed the trip, then, Thomas preached at Bologna on the first Sunday of Advent, 1268, and at Milan on one of the later Sundays in Advent.[66]

Thomas Aquinas was on his way to spend three of the most controversial and busy years of his life in the intellectual hub of Christendom, at the University of Paris.

---

[63] Cf. Mandonnet, "Thomas d'Aquin lecteur," pp. 31–38.
[64] For a description, see Eschmann, "Catalogue," p. 427, n. 81.
[65] Latin text in *Opera Omnia* (Paris: Vivès), XXXII, p. 693.
[66] *Walz-Novarina* (*1962*), p. 151.

CHAPTER TWELVE

Growth in Wisdom

THE works that Thomas Aquinas wrote during the 1260's show how his intellectual genius flowered as he matured in age. Somewhat freed from the academic formalities of university teaching, he could now work at his own pace with adequate assistance from other scholars and secretaries. Of course, he taught courses in the various Dominican houses in which he resided and he was busy with the affairs of the Roman Province of the Order of Preachers and with the queries of many correspondents, ecclesiastical and lay. Yet in this decade of residence at various towns in the Papal States, Thomas was able to produce a wide variety of writings.

He had begun to write the *Summa contra Gentiles* in Paris.[1] Testimony at the canonization proceedings indicates that one of his Dominican students, Nicholas of Marsilliac, saw Thomas writing this *Summa* on scraps of paper while in the Paris monastery.[2] The probable occasion for the writing of this work was a request from St. Raymond of Penafort for a treatise that would help with the training of missionaries to the Mohammedans. This is explained in an early fourteenth-century chronicle by Peter Marsilio:

> Furthermore, strongly desiring the conversion of unbelievers, Raymond asked an outstanding Doctor of Sacred Scripture, a Master in Theology, Brother Thomas of Aquino of the same Order, who among all the clerics

[1] The full title in the manuscripts is *Summa de veritate fidei Catholicae contra Gentiles.* It is critically edited in ed. Leon., Vols. XIII–XV (Roma, 1918–1930). English: *On the Truth of the Catholic Faith,* trans. A. C. Pegis, J. F. Anderson, V. J. Bourke, and C. J. O'Neil (New York: Doubleday, 1955–1956), 5 vols.

[2] So reported by Brother Antonius de Brixia, *Proc. Can. Neap.*, LXVI (*Fontes,* IV, 355).

of the world was considered in philosophy to be, next to Brother Albert, the greatest, to compose a work against the errors of unbelievers by which both the cloud of darkness might be dispelled and the teaching of the true Sun might be made manifest to those who refuse to believe. The renowned Master accomplished what the humility of so great a father asked, and composed a work called the *Summa contra Gentiles,* held to be without equal in its field.[3]

As a matter of fact, St. Thomas makes his purpose in composing the *Summa contra Gentiles* rather clear in the opening chapters of the work. Here again, he undertakes to speak about the man of wisdom. Some men, he says, are skilled in special arts that govern other minor or auxiliary arts. The master of the art of government, or of medicine, or of navigation, is recognized as a wise man in his own field. However, this is a qualified, limited meaning of wisdom. He who is wise, without qualification, is the man who thinks in terms of the "highest causes." Then Thomas states one of his favorite themes: "Of all the pursuits open to men, the search for wisdom is more perfect, more sublime, more profitable, and more full of joy." After quoting some biblical texts to this effect, he proceeds to speak more personally than is his wont:

So, as a result of my confidence in divine compassion, I have taken as my function in life [*officium*] the search for wisdom. Even though it exceeds my personal powers, my intended purpose is to show, within the limits of my capacity, the truth that the Catholic faith professes, by means of the refutation of the errors opposed to it.[4]

Thomas proceeds to explain who the "Gentiles" are: simply all people who do not accept the Catholic faith. Some are Jews, he says, and in addressing them he will use the Old Testament; some are heretical Christians, and in their case he will cite the New Testament. Still others are Mohammedans and pagans who do not accept either part of the Bible, so with them "it is necessary to have recourse to natural reason, to which all men must give assent."[5] His program, then, is rather clear. He is undertaking, in the *Summa contra Gentiles,* a defense of his beliefs, using all the means at his disposal. His argument throughout is both theological and philosophical. It is important to stress this point, for in some centuries of Thomistic scholarship men commonly referred to this work as a *Summa*

[3] Cited in ed. Leon., XIII (1918), *Praefatio,* p. VI; English trans. by A. C. Pegis, *On the Truth of the Catholic Faith,* I, 20–21.

[4] *Summa c. Gentiles,* I, c. 2.

[5] *Ibid.,* c. 2, ad fin.

Philosophica,[6] as if it contrasted with the *Summa Theologiae*. Actually, there is no philosophical *Summa* among the works of St. Thomas. His *Summa contra Gentiles* uses much philosophical reasoning in its first three books (I: "On God's Existence and Perfections"; II: "On Creation and Man as a Creature"; III: "On the Ordering of Creatures under Divine Providence") but the fourth book ("On the Trinity, Incarnation and the End of Creatures") relies on the testimony of Sacred Scripture.[7]

Just how much of this major essay in Thomistic wisdom was finished before Aquinas left Paris is not known. Some think that he had written up to Book III, Chapter 45, before his return to the Papal States. The main reason for this conjecture is the fact that in one group of manuscripts the text terminates at this point.[8] The autograph manuscript (*Vat. Lat.*, 9850, fol. 2ʳ–89ᵛ) contains most of the text of the first three books. Other writers suggest that he had not written more than the first fifty-three chapters of Book I in Paris.[9] In any case, he finished the *Summa contra Gentiles* at Orvieto in 1264.[10]

Another work that was completed during the pontificate of Urban IV (1261–1264) was a *Commentary on the Book of Job*.[11] Some Thomistic scholars place this Scripture commentary in the years 1269–1272, because it is evidently the work of a mature scholar.[12] However, Bartholomew of Lucca dates this work in the pontificate of Urban IV.[13] The *Exposition of Job* is very philosophical in character and utilizes many quotations from Aristotle. In particular, the citations of the Aristotelian treatises *De Animalibus* use the Arabic-Latin versions of the *Historia Animalium*

[6] This unwarranted title was used on many printings: Naples, 1846; Paris, 1853, 1855; Parma, 1855; Paris: Lethielleux, 1877, 1906.

[7] *Summa c. Gentiles*, IV, c. 1: "erit hic modus servandus ut ea quae in sermonibus Sacrae Scripturae sunt tradita quasi principia sumantur."

[8] See Chenu, *Introduction*, p. 251, note 1; cf. Dondaine, *Secrétaires*, p. 92, note 25: "le *Contra Gentiles* fut rédigé à Paris au moins jusqu'au livre III, ch. 45."

[9] *Walz-Novarina* (*1962*), p. 223; following A. Gauthier, *Contra Gentiles, livre premier* (Paris: Lethielleux, 1961), pp. 20–59.

[10] Eschmann, "Catalogue," pp. 385–386; Grabmann, *Die Werke*, pp. 290–294.

[11] *Expositio in Job ad litteram*, ed. Parma, XIV, 1–147; ed. Leon., XVII, 1962. There is no English version.

[12] *Walz-Novarina* (*1962*), p. 221; Eschmann, "Catalogue," pp. 393–394, dates the commentary, 1261–1264.

[13] *Hist. Eccles.*, XXII, c. 24 (in Foster, *Life*, p. 131): "The *Contra Gentiles* and the *Questions de Anima* also belong to the period of Urban's pontificate, besides the *Commentary on Job* and various other minor works."

which indicates that it was definitely written before the Greek-Latin version was used by Thomas.[14]

Aquinas' explanation of the Book of Job is very "medieval" in its style. In some ways the commentary is like an Italian "Green Pastures." The Hebrew Patriarch carries on an academic disputation with his friends concerning his tribulations and the order of Divine Providence. At times, the "Lord" intervenes as the *Determinator* of the disputation. Thus, where the text says (Job 38:1–2): "Then the Lord answered Job out of a whirlwind, and said, Who is this that wrappeth up sentences in unskillful words?" Aquinas interprets it as if it were a discussion at the University of Paris!

> In the foregoing disputation of Job and his friends concerning divine providence, for a time Elihu took his place as the *determinator,* arguing against Job on some points and against his friends on other matters. But since human wisdom is not adequate to the comprehension of the truth of divine providence, it became necessary for the foregoing disputation to be determined by divine authority. Since Job was generally right in his view of divine providence but had greatly gone to excess in his way of speaking, with the result that scandal might arise for those who were evil in their hearts, thinking that he [Job] was not showing proper reverence for God, the Lord entered the argument as a *Determinator* of the question, correcting Job's friends for their views which were not right, Job himself for the lack of order in his manner of speaking, and Elihu for the impropriety of his determination. . . . And so, having criticized Elihu's determination, the Lord Himself began to give the determination to the disputation. First of all He aroused Job's attention, saying: "Gird up thy loins like a man." This has a metaphorical meaning, for men are accustomed to gird up their loins so that they may be ready for a trip, or for some kind of activity. So the Lord wanted him to be ready to think about what He was going to tell him. . . .[15]

Thomas proceeds to write out the contents of these chapters (38–41) as if they were the *corpus* of a Disputed Question.

Modern readers and Scripture scholars may be amazed at the way in which Thomas uses philosophical writings in this commentary. As Eschmann describes it, "Aristotle, Plato, Cicero, Pliny, Porphyry, Avicenna, Averroës and others are quoted abundantly in the elucidation of this scriptural work."[16] Though such a juxtaposition of pagan and Mohammedan

---

[14] William of Moerbeke had translated the *Historia Animalium,* at the end of 1260 (see Grabmann, *G. di Moerbeke,* pp. 119–126) but Aquinas may not have seen this version (made at Thebes) for some time.

[15] *Expositio in Job,* 38, lectio 1; Parma, XIV, 126.

[16] "Catalogue," p. 393, n. 17.

"authorities" with the text of the Bible may be initially disconcerting, it illustrates very well the diversified sources of the new wisdom which Aquinas was developing. He did not keep his learning in airtight compartments, now writing as a historian of philosophy, and again as a commentator on Scripture. He was very conscious of the gradual movement of all mankind toward a better understanding of the facts of reality and human life. As he explained this, in his introduction to the commentary,[17] the older Greek philosophers were inclined to attribute a great deal to chance. But the philosophers who came after them came to realize that physical phenomena are not fortuitous, that they are reasonably regulated, that they occur according to the order of Divine Providence. However, the philosophers were not so clearly aware of the regulation of human activities by the same Providence. So Aquinas uses the Book of Job to show how even human events, like the afflictions of Job, have a reasonable explanation and a definite order under the guidance of a providential divinity. Students of the practical wisdom of Aquinas will find much that is rewarding in his meditations on Job.

Also little read, today, is another scriptural work which Thomas began at the request of Pope Urban IV but did not complete until several years after this Pope's death. This is the *Gloss on Matthew, Mark, Luke and John,* which is called the *Golden Chain* (*Catena Aurea*) in later Thomistic bibliography.[18] Actually, this great work was *edited* by Aquinas, for it consists of many selections from the Fathers of the Church, explaining the four Gospels.[19] This compilation has been fully translated into English by several of the leaders of the "Oxford Movement," including J. H. Newman, but this version has become rare and many bibliographers of St. Thomas do not know of its existence.[20]

In the *Dedicatory Epistle* which prefaces the exposition of St. Matthew's

---

[17] *Exp. in Job, Prologo;* Parma, XIV, 1.

[18] *Glossa continua in Mathaeum, Marcum, Lucam, Joannem,* ed. A. Guarienti, 2 vols. (Turin: Marietti, 1953).

[19] Bartholomew of Lucca, *Hist. Eccles.,* XXII, c. 24: "When, for definite reasons, Brother Thomas had to be recalled from Paris, he did a great deal of literary work for Pope Urban . . . he wrote an exposition of the Gospels, combining passages from diverse authorities in such a way that they all seemed the work of one author — a task requiring considerable skill on the compiler's part" (translation from Foster, *Life,* p. 131). Compare, Tocco, *Vita,* c. 17 (*Fontes,* II, 87).

[20] Thomas Aquinas, *Catena Aurea. Commentary on the Four Gospels, collected out of the Works of the Fathers,* edited by E. B. Pusey, J. H. Newman, J. Keble and C. Marriott, 4 vols. in octavo (Oxford, 1841–1845).

Gospel, Aquinas himself mentions the fact that Pope Urban had directed him to undertake this work.[21] It is evident, then, that he was able to finish the commentary on Matthew by 1264. However, the dedication of the exposition of St. Mark (to Cardinal Hannibaldus) shows that the compilation of the Commentaries on the other three Gospels postdated Pope Urban's death. As Thomas wrote to his former student and colleague:

> As a matter of fact, when the supreme Pontiff [he has just mentioned that he was ordered by Urban IV to make this compilation] was removed from this life, three Gospels, Mark, Luke and John remained to be explained. Lest the work that obedience had begun might remain incomplete by negligence, I diligently took care to complete it with much labor, so that I might finish the exposition of the four Gospels, keeping in all the same style of quoting the texts of the Saints [i.e., the Fathers of the Church] and putting their names before the passages. Also, so that the exposition might be integral and [historically] continuous, I had certain expositions by the Greek Fathers translated, and interspersed various commentaries by the Latins with these, prefixing the names of the writers.[22]

This last point should be stressed: "Because of this research into Greek theological sources, the *Catena* marks a turning point in the development of Aquinas's theology as well as in the history of Catholic dogma."[23] The *Catena Aurea* is St. Thomas' noteworthy contribution to positive theology.

It was not negligence that prevented Thomas from finishing the gospel commentaries before Pope Urban died; he was busy with many other writings. Most probably he was already working on his exposition of a notoriously difficult treatise, that *On the Divine Names*. We still do not know the full story on its obscure author who is now called Dionysius the Pseudo-Areopagite. From the sixth century onward, Christian learning had known a group of five literary works whose author gave the impression that he had been in Athens in Apostolic times, had known St. Paul and witnessed some events connected with the earliest days of Christianity. These works came to be called the *Corpus Areopagiticum* and their author St. Dionysius.[24] Today scholarly opinion considers that these Christian writings could not have been written before the fifth century A.D. (because they utilize the writings of Proclus, A.D. 410–485); their author is still unidentified but is now called the "Pseudo-Areopagite."

The treatise *On the Divine Names* is the longest and most important of

---

[21] *Epistola Dedicatoria,* ad Urbanum IV, Pont. Max., ed. Parm., XI, 1.

[22] *Catena super Marci Evangelium, Epistola Dedicatoria,* ed. Parm., XI, 335.

[23] Eschmann, "Catalogue," p. 397.

[24] Gilson, *Hist. of Christ. Philos.*, pp. 81–85, 597.

these writings.[25] It takes up the problem of how God may be called Good, Being, Life, Wisdom, Beauty, Perfect, One, and so on. God is good, of course (the initial *affirmation*), but not in the limited way that sensible things are good. So, in a second predication (the moment of *negation*), one should say that God is not good. Now since both of the preceding judgments have some validity, one should proceed to combine them in a third (that of *eminence*), saying: God is *Super-Good.* In other words, God transcends all ordinary modes of human knowing, yet it is possible to speak of Him by using some sort of remote and vague analogy.

Thomas Aquinas, following in the tradition of many other earlier thirteenth-century authors (Thomas Gallus, Robert Grosseteste, St. Albert) undertook to explain this obscure combination of Christian beliefs and Neoplatonic philosophy. His *Exposition of Dionysius on The Divine Names* was written in Italy before 1268.[26] This was the year in which Proclus' basic metaphysical work was put into Latin by William of Moerbeke[27] and Aquinas did not have Proclus when he commented on Dionysius.

The commentary is literal in style, expounding the text of Dionysius phrase by phrase. It represents one of Aquinas' most important contacts with Platonic metaphysics. Introducing his *Exposition,* he reviews the content of Dionysius' main theological writings (some of which are nonextant, both for Thomas and for us) and then he says this:

> We should keep in mind the fact that blessed Dionysius used an obscure style in all his books; this he did, not because of lack of learning but deliberately, in order that he might conceal sacred and divine teachings from the ridicule of unbelievers. Difficulty occurs in his books for many reasons. First, he often uses the style and manner of speaking that the Platonists employed but which is not customary among modern writers. Wishing to reduce all composite or material things to simple principles, the Platonists posited Forms that were separated from things; they said that there is "man" apart from matter, and likewise "horse," and so on for the other Forms of natural things. They asserted that this singular or sensible man is not what "man" is in himself. Rather, he is called man by virtue of participation in this separated "man." Hence, something (such as individual matter and other similar characteristics) is found in this sensible man which does not belong to the specific form of humanity; but in the separated "man" there is nothing that does not belong to the form of humanity. Hence he called the separated "man" the "man-in-himself" (*per se hominem*),

[25] Dionysius, *On the Divine Names and the Mystical Theology,* trans. C. E. Rolt (London: S.P.C.K., 1920).

[26] *In librum B. Dionysii de divinis nominibus,* ed. C. Pera (Turin: Marietti, 1956). Chapter 4, lect. 5–6, are translated in my *Pocket Aquinas,* pp. 269–278.

[27] Cf. Grabmann, *G. di Moerbeke,* p. 147.

because he possesses nothing that does not pertain to humanity; and man in the primary sense (*principaliter*), since humanity comes to men in the sense world by derivation from the separate "man," according to the mode of participation. So too, one may say that the separated "man" is superior to men in the plural, and that the separated "man" is the humanity of all men in the order of sensible realities, in the sense that human nature, without admixture, belongs to the separated "man" and comes from him to men in the sense world by derivation. Nor did the Platonists take this position only with regard to the ultimate specific forms of bodily things in nature but also in regard to those most general characteristics, to the good, one and being. They took the position that there is a Primary One, the very essence of goodness, and unity, and existing being (*esse*), what we call God; and that all other things are called good, or one, or beings, by derivation from the First. Hence, they named this First, the Good Itself, or the Good through Itself, or the principal Good, or the Super-Good, or even the Goodness of all goods, or essential and substantial Goodness, in the sense that has been used in explaining the separated "man."

Now, this Platonic position is not in agreement with the faith nor with the truth, in regard to what it includes concerning the separated Forms of things in nature; however, in regard to what they say about the first principle of real things, their opinion is very true and in agreement with Christian faith. On this basis, Dionysius at various times calls God the Good Itself, or Super-Good, or Principal Good, or the Goodness of all goods. And likewise, he calls Him Super-Life, Super-Substance, and the Godhead which is "thearchic," that is the Principal Godhead — for even in the case of certain creatures the name of divinity is received according to some sort of participation.

A second difficulty occurs in his statements, due to his frequent use of efficacious arguments to prove his point, many times couched in a few words, or even implying them in but one word.

A third difficulty arises from the frequent use of a multiplicity of words, which though they may seem superfluous are found to contain great profundity of meaning when they are carefully considered.[28]

Notice how St. Thomas treats Platonic metaphysics as a *positio,* a theory which merits serious consideration but which is not necessarily true in all its aspects.[29] Here in prefacing his explanations of Dionysius, Aquinas rejects the Platonic theory of Ideal Forms but vigorously supports that part of their view which asserts that all corporeal and limited types of being derive from one, supreme source of reality. Whether this "Platonism" is the historical view of Plato himself is beside the point. Actually, we do not know that Thomas Aquinas ever read any of the *Dialogues.* What is important is the fact that he is now in possession of another significant non-Christian metaphysics which is quite different from Aristotelianism.

[28] *Expos. in librum de divinis nominibus, Prologo.*

[29] R. J. Henle, "Saint Thomas' Methodology in the Treatment of *Positiones,*" *Gregorianum,* XXXVI (1955), 391–409.

One other feature of this *Prologue* is the stress on participation. That "the many" share in the perfection of "the One," is a standard teaching of the whole tradition of Platonism and Neoplatonism. The theme of participation is not prominent in Aristotle. In Thomistic metaphysics it plays a key role in his theory of analogy and causality.[30] The effort to incorporate certain features of Platonism into his personal explanation of reality will continue during the second Paris professorate, as we shall see later.

During the years in which Thomas Aquinas was working in the Papal States, he devoted some of his time to *Disputed Questions.* Here again, we should recall that Bartholomew of Capua records that he disputed the *Questions on the Power of God,* and others in Italy.[31] There is much disagreement among modern Thomistic scholars concerning the chronology of the *Disputed Questions.*[32] There is little doubt that Thomas wrote or disputed *On the Power of God* while he was regent of studies at St. Sabina, Rome, in 1265–1267. This collection of questions is one of his best theological works and it is also an important source of information on his metaphysics.[33]

In the *De Potentia Dei* there are ten major questions: I, On God's power; II, On generative power in the divine (Persons); III, On creation; IV, On the creation of unformed matter; V, On the conservation of things in existence by God; VI, On miracles; VII, On the simplicity of the divine essence; VIII, On the relations predicated of God from eternity; IX, On the divine Persons; X, On the procession of the divine Persons. These topics parallel, in part, certain questions that will be written later in the better known *Summa of Theology.*[34] A comparison shows that most of the corresponding sections in the *Summa of Theology* are actually condensations and abridgments of the relevant questions in the *Disputed*

---

[30] Cf. C. Fabro, *Participation et causalité selon s. Thomas d'Aquin* (Lovain-Paris: Nauwelaerts, 1961); G. P. Klubertanz, *St. Thomas on Analogy* (Chicago: Loyola U. Press, 1960), pp. 55–64.

[31] *Proc. Can. Neap.,* LXXXV (*Fontes,* IV, 388).

[32] Grabmann, *Die Werke,* pp. 301–308, surveys the chronologies suggested by Mandonnet, Glorieux, Pelster, and several others. Eschmann, "Catalogue," p. 391, dates *Q. D. de Potentia* 1259–1268, Italy.

[33] A standard text is: *Quaestiones Disputatae* (Turin: Marietti, 1953). English: *On the Power of God,* trans, L. Shapcote (Westminster, Md.: Newman, 1952).

[34] Compare, for instance, *Pars Prima,* q. 25, De potentia Dei; q. 27, De processione personarum q. 45, De creatione; q. 3, De simplicitate Dei; q. 28, De relationibus divinis; and qq. 29–43, an extended treatise on the Divine Persons.

Questions On the Power of God. Take the initial article in each work: both have the same statement of the problem: "Whether there is power (*potentia*) in God." To deal with this in the *Disputed Questions,*[35] Aquinas uses eighteen objections, three statements to the contrary, a general response of about forty printed lines, and replies to the eighteen objections. In the corresponding article in the *Summa of Theology,*[36] we find four objections, one *Sed contra,* twenty lines in the general answer, and brief replies to the four objections. This is usually the case: the *Disputed Questions* are frequently much more ample in their discussion of a given problem than the *Summa of Theology.*

However, it is obvious that the *Summa of Theology* follows a different plan, or order, for presenting the discussion of God's power and its consequences. One may wonder where St. Thomas found the principle of organization for a large work such as the *Questions on the Power of God.* A rather convincing argument has been made that he structured these *Questions* so that they might constitute a Christian reply to the emanationism of Avicenna.[37] To put the point very briefly, this great Mohammedan theologian had described the origin of the manifold beings of the created world as the *necessary* outpouring of the richness and goodness of divine Being. There is no question of divine freedom in the Avicennian emanationism. God's "only 'contribution' to the production of things consists in a passive acquiescence to an emanation which would proceed from His essence anyway."[38] Obviously, the problem of the "procession" of the divine Persons will not be given formal treatment in Mohammedanism (which is non-Trinitarian) but, even if it did, there would be little difference between procession and creation for Avicenna.

In opposition to this metaphysics of necessary essences, Aquinas builds an explanation based on the primacy of the act of existing. The *Questions on the Power of God* constitute an important statement of the existentialism of Thomistic metaphysics.[39]

Quite possibly two other *Disputed Questions* stem from oral exercises

---

[35] *Q. D. de potentia Dei,* I, 1.

[36] *S.T.,* I, q. 25, art. 1.

[37] See Beatrice H. Zedler, "Saint Thomas and Avicenna in the 'De Potentia Dei,'" *Traditio,* VI (1948), 105–159; "The Inner Unity of the *De Potentia,*" *The Modern Schoolman,* XXV (1948), 91–106.

[38] Zedler, in *Traditio,* VI, 122.

[39] See G. B. Phelan, "The Existentialism of St. Thomas," *Proc. Amer. Cath. Philos. Assoc.,* XXI (1946), 25–40.

conducted by Aquinas in the ensuing years in Italy. The *Question on Spiritual Creatures* is, according to some early manuscripts, a result of a disputation held in Italy. It probably dates from 1267–1268.[40] Similarly, the *Question on the Soul* may have been disputed in Italy, though written up later in Paris.[41] These *Questions* deal with the nature and powers of human souls and angels.

We have now to note what was undoubtedly one of the great formative influences on the mature thought of Aquinas: the reading and exposition of the major philosophical works of Aristotle. Speaking of the pontificate of Urban IV (1261–1264), Bartholomew of Lucca says:

> And at this time Thomas — now directing the house of studies at Rome — also wrote commentaries covering the whole field of philosophy, both moral and natural, but with particular attention to ethics and mathematics [possibly an error for "metaphysics"], which he treated in a very striking and original way.[42]

These *Commentaries* can only refer to the expositions of Aristotle which we now have among the works of St. Thomas. We need not take Bartholomew's chronological indications without modification, for there is internal evidence that the final versions of these expositions were written only in the late 1260's and, indeed, some of them in the second Paris professorate and at Naples. However, there is little doubt that St. Thomas began the close study of the text of Aristotle in 1265, if not earlier.[43] Some of the resultant expositions are *reportationes* (e.g., the commentary on the first book of Aristotle's *De Anima*) which means that they are, at least in part, transcripts of lectures delivered by Thomas and revised later for publication. Many of the expositions are unfinished, interrupted by various incidents in a life which is not known in detail. Certainly these breaks do not mean that Thomas was working on all of the incomplete commentaries just before his death. Other events, particularly changes of residence from town to town and country to country, would explain the unfinished character of many of these writings.

Possibly the best plan to follow in surveying these expositions of Aris-

[40] *Q. D. de Spiritualibus Creaturis,* ed. L. W. Keeler (Roma: Gregorianum, 1946). English: *On Spiritual Creatures,* trans. J. Wellmuth and M. Fitzpatrick (Milwaukee: Marquette U. Press, 1949). For the date: Eschmann, "Catalogue," p. 391; *Walz-Novarina (1962)*, p. 223.

[41] *Q. D. de Anima,* in *Quaest. Disp.* (Turin: Marietti, 1953). English: *The Soul,* trans. J. P. Rowan (St. Louis: Herder, 1949).

[42] *Hist. Eccles.,* XXII, c. 24 (in Foster, *Life,* p. 131).

[43] Eschmann, "Catalogue," pp. 400–405.

totle is to treat them according to the classifications used in Aristotelian scholarship. Among the logical treatises, Thomas commented on two: the treatise *On Interpretation* and that called the *Posterior Analytics.*[44] Toward the end of the second book of the *Posterior Analytics* (c.19, 199b18–200b5) Aristotle had described how the first indemonstrable premises come to be known in the human intellect. How does a medical doctor first realize that a certain drug is a specific remedy for a given disease, for instance? Aristotle's explanation is that such universal judgments arise out of sense experience: many sense perceptions of individual instances are retained in memory, many memories are combined in experience, and out of the manifold of experience there arises a universal. Commenting on this sensory induction, Aquinas adds the following.

> Indeed, the universal is said to be lying at rest in the mind, in the sense that it is considered apart from the singulars in which motion occurs. Furthermore, the fact that he [Aristotle] speaks of it as one apart from the many does not mean in real existence but in the consideration of the intellect which thinks of any nature, say that of man, without relating it to Socrates and Plato. Though, on the basis of intellectual consideration, it is one apart from many, nevertheless it is one and the same in all singulars — not numerically so, as if there were the same numerical humanity for all men, but according to the specific rational character. For, just as this white thing is the same as that white thing, in whiteness, but not in the sense that one numerical whiteness is existing in both, so also is Socrates like Plato, in humanity, but not in the sense that one numerical humanity is existing in both.[45]

This is important to the understanding of St. Thomas' theory of first principles of the arts and sciences; he is not saying that they result in the mind from some ungrounded intuition but that these starting points in the life of the intellect are based on insight into the unified meaning of the presentations of sensory experience. There is an almost naturalistic empiricism at work here. To make it clear that he is not thinking of something like Platonic "forms" residing in the members of a given class of sense things (as treeness would be present in many trees), Thomas even puts his explanation in terms of *negative* differences.

---

[44] *Expositio in libros peri Hermeneias* (the commentary ends in Bk. II, lect. 2, at 19b26); edited in Volume I of the Leonine ed. (1882) (reprinted: Turin: Marietti, 1955). English: *Aristotle On Interpretation — Commentary by St. Thomas and Cajetan,* trans. Jean Oesterle (Milwaukee: Marquette U. Press, 1962). *Expositio in libros posteriorum analyticorum,* also in Leon. I, and same volume of Marietti. English: trans. P. Conway (Québec: M. Doyon, 1956).

[45] *In II Post. Anal.,* lect. 20; trans. from *Pocket Aquinas,* p. 33.

> If many singulars are taken and they are not different in regard to some one item existing in them, this one item according to which they do not differ, when received in the mind, is the first universal, whatever it may be, whether it pertains to the essence of the singulars or not. Because we find Socrates and Plato, and many others, to be not different in regard to whiteness, we take this one item, namely *white,* as the universal; and in this case it is an accident. Similarly, because we find that Socrates and Plato and others are not different in regard to rationality, we take this one item in which they do not differ, namely the *rational,* as a universal; and this is a specific character.[46]

This is more than a theory of formal logic. In commenting on the *Posterior Analytics,* Aquinas suggests a good deal of his general understanding of how reality comes to be grasped in the initial phases of reasoning.

A second group of Aristotelian treatises comprises the various physical works. In this category, Aquinas produced expositions of the *Physics, Meteorology, On the Heavens and Earth,* and *On Generation and Corruption.*[47] Of these, the explanation of the eight books of the *Physics* is the most extensive and important. It is thought to have been written between 1268 and 1271[48] but this does not preclude the possibility that he lectured on the *Physics,* during the 1260's in the Papal States. Both Grabmann and Mansion regarded the doctrine of this exposition as prior to that of the first Part of the *Summa of Theology.*[49]

Evidently, Thomas Aquinas made a long and thorough study of Aristotle's philosophy of corporeal nature and did this well before he went to Paris for his second teaching period. While this investigation provided a solid basis for Aquinas' speculative philosophy, it also conditioned his thinking to certain factual and interpretive views in the range of physical science which were inaccurate and sometimes misleading. He accepted the

---

[46] *Ibid.,* p. 34.

[47] *Exp. in VIII libros Physicorum,* ed. Leon., II (1884). English: *Commentary on Aristotle's Physics,* trans. R. J. Blackwell, R. J. Spath, and W. E. Thirkel (London: Routledge & Kegan Paul; New Haven: Yale U. Press, 1963). *Exp. in libros Meteorologicorum,* ed. Leon., III (1886); this commentary terminates in Bk. II, c. 5, 363a20. No English version. *Exp. in libros de Caelo et Mundo,* ed. Leon., III (1886); this ends in Bk. III, lect. 8, at 302b9. No English version. *Exp. in libros de Generatione et Corruptione,* ed. Leon., III (1886); this ends in Bk. I, c. 5, 321b34. No English version.

[48] Eschmann, "Catalogue," pp. 401–402; see my "Introduction," to the English translation, pp. XVIII–XXI, for the suggestion that the oral commentary stems from Italy.

[49] Eschmann, "Catalogue," pp. 401–402, summarizes the views of Grabmann and A. Mansion in English.

old theory that there are four basic elements, earth, air, fire, and water, and that these combine in various ways to make the various substances in the material world. He thought that these elements had their "proper places" in the spherical universe which centered about the earth. This picture of a universe of concentric spheres dominated Aquinas' views on space and time. He was, of course, unable to rise above the limitations of the natural science which was current in the thirteenth century. As a result, many of the examples used in the speculative philosophy of Aquinas are taken from a physical science which is, in good part, outmoded in the twentieth century. This is why modern Thomists, with a few notable exceptions, are least successful in this particular branch of philosophy.

Thomas Aquinas produced no expositions of the works of Aristotle dealing with the animal world but he showed much interest in the psychological treatises. His commentary on the three books *On the Soul* is the main work in this area, but he also explained the short treatises, *On Sense and Its Object* and *On Memory and Recollection.*[50] The first book *On the Soul* is commented in the form of a *lectura* (lecture course) recorded by Reginald of Piperno. Most scholars now think that this course was delivered by Thomas before he left Italy.[51] The written expositions of the last two books stem from the second Paris professorate. Aristotelian views on the nature, powers, and functions of man are important factors in the total psychology of Thomism, but Aquinas developed a more profound treatment of the subject in his other works. It has been forcefully demonstrated in recent studies that Augustine's psychology is very influential in this area of Thomistic thought.[52]

One of the longest and most influential of Aquinas' commentaries in his *Exposition of Twelve Books of the Metaphysics of Aristotle.*[53] It is very probable that this work occupied a good deal of his time during his years in the Papal States. This is one commentary which may have to

[50] *Exp. in III libros de Anima,* ed. A. Pirotta (Turin: Marietti, 1949); English: *Aristotle's De Anima with the Commentary of St. Thomas Aquinas,* trans. K. Foster and S. Humphries (London: Routledge & Kegan Paul; New Haven: Yale U. Press, 1951).

[51] *Walz-Novarina* (*1962*), p. 222, dates the *Lectura* on Bk. I, in 1268.

[52] Cf. A. C. Pegis, *At the Origins of the Thomistic Notion of Man* (New York: Macmillan, 1963).

[53] *Exp. in XII libros Metaphysicorum,* ed. Spiazzi (Turin: Marietti, 1950). The commentary stops at the end of Bk. Lambda, at 1076a4. English: *Commentary on the Metaphysics of Aristotle,* trans. J. P. Rowan, 2 vols. (Chicago: Regnery, 1961).

be edited eventually according to the method proposed by Antoine Dondaine.[54] Apparently Thomas did not start his explanation with the first book and continue in order to the twelfth. There is a Naples manuscript[55] which contains two portions of the *Commentary on the Metaphysics* (the second and third books and a good part of the fifth to the seventh books). These passages seem to have been dictated by St. Thomas to two secretaries. When Thomas began his commentary he does not seem to have had a translation of Book *Kappa,* consequently he referred to the next book (*Lambda*) as Book XI, until William of Moerbeke translated *Kappa.* After Thomas received this translation of *Kappa,* he referred to Book *Lambda* as Book XII. It is usually maintained that Moerbeke's translation of *Kappa* was first known by Aquinas at the end of 1270 or the beginning of 1271.[56] This so-called *Lambda* criterion could obviously be helpful not only in dating the parts of the *Commentary on the Metaphysics* but the many other works in which St. Thomas cites the later books of Aristotle's *Metaphysics.* Presumably, if he cites Book *Lambda* as XI, this would occur before 1270, if he cites it as XII, this would place the reference after 1270. The only real difficulty is that we do not really know when William of Moerbeke translated Book *Kappa.* It is perfectly clear that Grabmann, in the study published in 1946, did his best to date all of Moerbeke's translations of Aristotle.[57] However, Grabmann was unable to find independent evidence for the dating of Moerbeke's translation of Book *Kappa.* Thus the *Lambda* test is useful in providing a relative criterion for distinguishing earlier and later works of St. Thomas, but it does not offer us an absolute point of demarcation. It is quite possible, then, that many of Aquinas' writings which are now crowded into the second Paris professorate (1269–1272) were actually written, at least in part, earlier. In any case, the *Lambda* criterion offers some evidence that Thomas commented on Books V–VII of the *Metaphysics* before he explained Books II–III.[58] Probably he dictated, or lectured on, or wrote,

---

[54] Dondaine (*Secrétaires,* p. 207) recognizes this dictated quality of the Exposition.

[55] *Napoli Bibliot. Nazionale,* VIII, F. 16 (see T. Kaeppeli, in *Angelicum,* X, 1933, 111–125; and J. J. Duin, "Nouvelles précisions sur la chronologie du 'Commentum in Metaphysicum' de s. Thomas," *Revue Philos. de Louvain,* 53, 1955, 511–524).

[56] Eschmann, "Catalogue," p. 387.

[57] Grabmann, *G. di Moerbeke,* pp. 85–127; for the translation of the *Metaphysics,* pp. 96–103.

[58] Eschmann, "Catalogue," p. 404.

expositions of various sections of the *Metaphysics* at different times (and not following the numerical order of the books) during the 1260's. He may not have revised the whole until around 1270.[59]

Naturally one cannot summarize a work like St. Thomas' explanation of Aristotle's *Metaphysics*. It does represent a step in the development of Thomistic wisdom. This is most clearly evident in the thoughtful *Prologue*.[60] He has no hesitation in asserting that metaphysics is a type of wisdom.

> All sciences and arts are directed in an orderly way toward one thing, that is, to the perfection of man which is his happiness. That is why one of them must be the ruler of all the others. It is justified in taking the name *wisdom;* for it is the function of the wise to rule others.[61]

Thomas proceeds to show that metaphysics is the highest of the philosophical sciences: because it treats of the highest causes of reality, because its objects are the most universal principles of being, because it is the most general of the sciences, and because its objects are most separated from the obscurity of matter. He concludes by explaining why such a study has three names.

> It is called *divine science* or [natural] *theology*, because it deals with the separated substances [i.e., those which exist apart from matter]. It is called *metaphysics*, because it considers being and its properties. These properties that transcend physical classifications are discovered in the process of analysis, in which the more general comes after the less general. Again, it is called *first philosophy*, because it deals with the primary causes of things.[62]

Of the practical philosophical works of Aristotle, Thomas prepared commentaries on the *Nicomachean Ethics* and a portion of the *Politics*.[63] It is particularly important to note that the commentary on the last five books of the *Politics*, printed as a supplement in the usual editions of St. Thomas, is written by Peter of Auvergne who was a man with different views from Thomas Aquinas.[64] It will be recalled that, as a student, St.

---

[59] See Rowan, "Introduction," pp. XI–XXIII.

[60] For this *Prologue* in English, see Rowan, pp. 1–2; or *Pocket Aquinas*, pp. 145–148.

[61] *Pocket Aquinas*, p. 145.

[62] *Ibid.*, pp. 147–148.

[63] *Exp. in X libros Ethicorum*, ed. Spiazzi (Turin: Marietti, 1949). English: a translation by C. I. Litzinger is announced, from Henry Regnery of Chicago.

[64] *Exp. in libros Politicorum*, ed. Spiazzi, as in note 63. Thomas commented only to Bk. III, c. 6, 1280a6. No English version.

Thomas attended and recorded Albert the Great's lectures on the *Nicomachean Ethics.* Apart from the works on logic and natural science which he probably knew as a university student at Naples, the *Ethics* was the first great work of Aristotle with which he was familiar as a young man. Even in his first Paris teaching period, he cites this treatise abundantly. It influences many parts of the lengthy third book of the *Summa contra Gentiles.* Quite possibly he lectured on the *Nicomachean Ethics* at one or the other of the Dominican houses of study in the vicinity of Rome, during the 1260's. The edited version of this commentary on the *Ethics* is now placed in the second Paris professorate.[65] One can be quite sure, however, that it was impossible for Aquinas to have produced all these Aristotelian commentaries during these last few years in Paris. The whole chronology of these works should remain open for further discussion.

The Aristotelian commentaries have their own value as sources for the study of the progress of Aquinas' thought. Somehow the notion has developed among some Thomistic scholars that they are not as important, for the student of Thomism, as the great theological writings. It is sometimes implied that they do not represent the personal thinking of St. Thomas. This attitude must be regarded with a grain of salt. Thomas Aquinas spent a good part of his time as a mature scholar in trying to explain what Aristotle said. Obviously he does not always agree with this pagan Greek philosopher, but he must have felt that it was useful to expound his philosophy. As far as we know, it was by personal choice that Thomas did these expositions — no rule of his Order, or regulation of the schools in which he taught, required such extended studies of Aristotle. Indeed, as a teaching theologian, Thomas may have had at times to justify to his superiors the time and energy that he was devoting to nontheological work. Yet even in his last years at Naples, he continued to study Aristotle. The exposition of the treatise *On Generation and Corruption* was one of his last writings.[66] It would be a mistake, then, to disregard the Aristotelian commentaries.

However, even granting what is evident, i.e., that Thomas Aquinas was a professional theologian, it still remains true that his strictly theological works incorporate a great deal of Aristotelian learning into the context of

---

[65] Eschmann, "Catalogue," p. 405, suggests 1271–1272.

[66] Tocco testified (*Proc. Can. Neap.*, LVIII, *Fontes,* IV, 345) that he saw Thomas writing on the *De Generatione,* and "that he believed that it was his last work in philosophy." This, of course, was in the Naples monastery.

his Christian wisdom. We have noticed earlier how, in commenting on the Book of Job, he cites Aristotle throughout. Not only the ethical and political views of this pagan writer are used to build out the meaning of Scripture — the *Physics, Metaphysics,* and psychology of Aristotle make their contribution. Even more obvious is the presence of Aristotelian notions, arguments, and examples on almost every page of the *Disputed Questions* and the *Summa of Theology.* It used to be fashionable to say that Thomas Aquinas "baptized Aristotle." That is not quite true. He completely rethought Aristotelianism and adapted it to a new kind of wisdom which went far beyond the horizons of Greek thought.

Already during his years in Rome, at the convent of Santa Sabina, Aquinas was planning and perhaps beginning to write a new type of work which would be a final statement of his wisdom. This was to be arranged according to a plan of presentation that suited Thomas, rather than according to the scheme of textbooks such as Lombard's *Sentences.* The *Summa of Theology* was begun in the 1260's and it occupied many of St. Thomas' later years. We will return to it in a subsequent chapter.

CHAPTER THIRTEEN

Second Paris Professorate

SINCE there were signs of new difficulties for the Dominicans at the university, Thomas Aquinas must have returned to Paris in the fall of 1268 with mixed feelings. There is little doubt that he loved the city, enjoyed his work as a university teacher, and had many friends there. An incident which may have occurred in this period throws a little light on his appreciation of the city.[1] Thomas was returning one day from a trip to Saint-Denis, then a village to the north of Paris, where the famous abbey held the tomb of the patron saint of France. As Tocco introduces the story: "He had gone there with his students to visit the monastery and to see the relics of the saints."[2] When Thomas and the young Brothers came near the city, they stopped for a short rest in full view of Paris. One youth said to Thomas:

> "Father, what a beautiful city is this Paris!"
> Thomas replied, "Indeed it is beautiful."
> "I wish it belonged to you," the Brother continued.
> "What would I do with it?" asked Thomas.
> "You might sell it to the King of France and with the money you could build places for all the Friars Preachers," the Brother said.
> "As a matter of fact," Thomas replied, "I would much prefer to have Chrysostom's *Commentary* on St. Matthew."[3]

Since Thomas cites St. John Chrysostom's *Homilies on Matthew* as

[1] *Walz-Novarina* (*1962*), p. 170.

[2] Tocco, *Vita,* c. 42 (*Fontes,* II, 115).

[3] This is the version of the conversation that is given in the testimony of Bartholomew of Capua, *Proc. Can. Neap.,* LXXVIII (*Fontes,* IV, 376). For other variants, see *Fontes,* IV, 356, and Tocco, *Vita, loc. cit.*

early as the first Paris professorate and certainly during the 1260's,[4] it is probable that the "commentary" which he desired was actually Chrysostom's *Opus imperfectum in Mathaeum.*[5] However, Aquinas may simply have needed a better translation of Chrysostom, since he complains about the bad translation in his *Catena Aurea* (A.D. 1261–1264).[6]

In Tocco's version of the story, Thomas added: "If this city belonged to me, it would disrupt my thinking on divine matters, because of the problem of ruling it, and that would interfere with my peace of mind."

The story is told, of course, to show Aquinas' humility and lack of concern for material possessions. Perhaps it is more important to us as a slight break in the veil of impersonality that surrounds Thomas Aquinas in the early documents. It suggests that he did relax at times from his studies and that he was ready for a bit of repartee with his students. Incidentally, although we do not know when the incident occurred, this story is one of the most solidly attested facts in the personal life of Aquinas.

One friend with whom he renewed contact in Paris was Adenolf of Anagni who had become provost of Saint-Omer in 1264. Adenolf attended Thomas' theology lectures from 1269 to 1272 and was a good friend during this period of theological controversy. He gave positive evidence of his friendship by now paying the expenses of making fair copies of Reginald of Piperno's record of Thomas' *Exposition of the Gospel of St. John.* It gives us some idea of the cost of publication procedures in the thirteenth century to note that this was considered an act of considerable generosity.[7]

Yet Thomas knew that he had enemies, or at least unfriendly critics, in Paris. Some remembered and kept alive the old antagonism of the secular clergy toward the Dominican and Franciscan teachers. Others felt strongly that Thomas Aquinas was ruining Catholic theology with his philosophical novelties. Still others regarded Thomas as not Aristotelian enough. The result was that he soon found his theological teaching and studies interrupted by bitter controversies. On all sides he faced criticism: the tradi-

[4] See *In Matt. Evang. Exp.*, Chaps. 1 and 4; the *Catena Aurea* (written 1262–1267) cites St. John Chrysostom's *Homilies on Matthew* frequently.

[5] Cf. G. Morin, "Quelques aperçus nouveaux sur l'Opus imperfectum in Mathaeum," *Revue Bénédictine,* 37 (1925), 239.

[6] See the dedication of the *Catena super Mathaeum:* "interdum etiam sensum posui, verba dimisi, praecipue in Homiliario Chrysostomi, propter hoc quod translatio est vitiosa" (ed. Parm., XI, 2a).

[7] M. Grabmann, "Adenulf von Anagni, Propst von Saint-Omer," *Traditio,* V (1947), 269–283.

tional Augustinian theologians questioned his religious orthodoxy; the masters in the arts faculty felt that he was baptizing Aristotle; and some of his fellow professors actively campaigned against his actual right to teach. We shall see more about these unfortunate disputes in the following chapter.

Of course, Thomas was now a comparatively famous man in the Church and in academic circles. There is, for instance, a record dated December 17, 1269, of permission being granted to the Dominicans to build a convent at San Germano, within the domain of the Abbey of Montecassino. In the document, the Benedictine Abbot, Bernard I Ayglerio, makes it clear that this permit is given out of friendship for Brother Thomas of Aquino.[8] Again, in March of 1272, the Archbishop of Salerno, Matthew della Porta, gave to the Order of Preachers the Church of St. Paul plus some adjacent buildings and land in Salerno, with the understanding that they would build a monastery there. Here, also, one of the reasons for the gift is friendship for Brother Thomas of Aquino. The Bishop even calls Thomas "Our father and teacher" (*patrem et magistrum nostrum*).[9] Since Matthew became bishop in 1263, it is not too likely that he had actually been a student under Aquinas.

Near the beginning of his second residence in Paris, Thomas was consulted on a curious dispute between two Dominican scholars concerning the authorship of a commentary on the *Sentences*. The quarrel came to a head at the General Chapter on May 12, 1269, in Paris.[10] Thomas was present at this meeting. There were two Dominicans with identical Latin names, *Johannes de Colonia*. One was an Italian, John of Colonia San Faustino (near Viterbo); the other was a German, John of Cologne. Both claimed to have written a work called the *Johannina de Colonia!* This peculiar situation is described in a note found in a Viterbo manuscript;[11] this record is obviously partisan to the cause of the Italian.

---

[8] The document (*Fontes,* VI, 571–572) reads in part: "Consequently, for the honor of God and of the venerable man, Brother Thomas of Aquino, and of the religious Brother Troianus of the same Order of Preachers, Our very dear friends in well deserved affection, We freely grant permission for the building of a house and church in Our City of San Germano. . . ."

[9] *Fontes,* VI, 573–574.

[10] Quétif-Echard, *Scriptores Ordinis Praedicatorum* (Paris, 1719–1721), I, p. XVII.

[11] Edited in Masetti, P. T., *Monumenta et Antiquitates veteris disciplinae Ordinis Praedicatorum* (Romae, 1864), I, 363; reprinted in Mandonnet, *Siger de Brabant,* 2me éd., I, 83–84.

> At this time John the Jurist of Colonia San Faustino completed his work on the *Sentences* which he entitled the *Johannina de Colonia*. Then there was a great quarrel at the General Chapter of Paris because his friend, named John of Cologne, had stolen it while they were both studying at Bologna. Now, when our Brother from Viterbo presented the work for correction at the Chapter, the other Brother, John of Cologne, said it was his. Neither an order made out against the German, nor a written record under the seal of confession, was of any avail for the Italian against the German.
>
> The most distinguished Masters were assigned to it, among them Brother Thomas de Aquino on the Italian side and Peter of Tarentaise, later a Pope, with five others for the German side. Questions were put as to whether it was possible to force each man to testify under command [of his superior]. No conclusion was reached except that the title of the work should stand, without naming the country, Italy or Germany, and that it should be called the *Johannina* by Brother John of Colonia, for this is true and does injury to no one.

Independently of this admittedly biased report, we know that the Dominican commission appointed to decide this literary dispute and its consequent problems included six men: Thomas Aquinas, Peter of Tarentaise, and Brothers Bonhomme, Bartholomew, Balduin, and Gilibert. They are named at the beginning of a Paris manuscript containing the decisions of the group, under the title: *Concerning a Secret.*[12] Six questions were considered: (1) If one Brother accused another of a secret sin, could the religious superior command the accused to give a true answer in public? To this, the committee answered that the superior could not. (2) Could the superior command that an answer be given privately? Again, the answer was negative. (3) Could the accuser be commanded to tell the truth, or the accused be required to confess in public? The committee's reply was negative. (4) Could the superior command that an act committed secretly by a subordinate be revealed? The committee answered that the superior could, provided the publication of the secret act would prevent grave consequences, such as general harm to the community. (5) This question was lengthy (and the printed text appears to be corrupted) but essentially it was asked: If a man told in the confessional about some evil act harmful to another and gave permission to the confessor to tell his superior, provided the name of the person confessing were not revealed, could the superior command that the secret be revealed? The question was further complicated by the circumstance (which appears to have applied

[12] See the "incipit" of *De Secreto* (from *MS Paris, Bibl. Nat.*, Lat. 14546, formerly *Saint-Victor 635*) as printed in Mandonnet, *Opuscula Omnia*, IV, 497; or *Opusc. Theol.* (Turin: Marietti, 1954), I, 447.

in the case of John of Colonia) that the penitent had sent a letter concerning the case to his confessor, outside the confessional but under a promise of secrecy. In any event, the committee answered that the superior did not have the authority to require that such a secret be revealed.

Now it was to this complicated last question that Thomas Aquinas entered a minority report, definitely disagreeing with the other Dominican consultants.

> However, Brother Thomas said that, if proper judicial procedure were used, that is, if the accuser stated that he would be available for proof or would accept the obligation to make restitution, then the superior could inquire by commanding an answer. And the accuser was obliged to obey and tell the truth, just as he would to a judge — because wherever a secular judge could demand an answer under oath, a religious superior could do the same under precept.[13]

The other commission members objected to Thomas' view, claiming that no man can be a judge of secret matters, and that only God was competent to judge such things. They further argued that, when a man is legally obliged to tell the truth under oath, this obligation does not extend to secret information which could not be established by public proof. Neither a judge nor a superior could force a man to reveal such information, they maintained. As the record duly states: "On this judgment, he [Thomas] was not in agreement with the decision of the other Masters."

There was a sixth and last question: suppose some evil deed is done but it is not known who did it, for example, a theft occurs or a house is burned, can a superior inquire by commanding that he be answered, and is the culprit required to reveal himself? Aquinas' answer to this is first recorded. "Brother Thomas said that the superior could issue a general command like this: I command that whoever did this, or whoever knows about it, is required to speak up." The document closes with this sentence: "On this answer, the other Masters disagreed with Brother Thomas of Aquino."[14]

From the foregoing summary, it should be clear that the *De Secreto* is not a work written personally by Aquinas, although it is now customary to print it among his shorter writings. Rather, it is a record of an inquiry in which he participated in the spring of 1269.[15] However, the document is important in the biography of Thomas Aquinas for three reasons. It

---

[13] *De Secreto,* ed. Mandonnet, IV, 500.

[14] *Ibid.,* p. 501.

[15] See Eschmann's comment, "Catalogue," n. 60, p. 417.

shows that he was in Paris by the spring of this year. It indicates that he was inclined to grant more authority to a religious superior (at least on this question) than were his colleagues. We also learn from it, what has never been doubted, that he had a mind of his own. Apparently he was the only Italian member of the group, as the Viterbo manuscript suggests.

During most of Aquinas' life, there was but one King of France, the saintly Louis IX (1226–1270). Very little is known of the personal relations between Thomas and King Louis. However, William of Tocco tells a famous story which probably has reference to this second period that he spent in Paris. This dating used to be questioned, because the story refers to Manichaeism and it was thought that Thomas was not much concerned with this heresy between 1269 and 1272. But we now know that he was; both the *Treatise on Separate Substances* (c. 16) and the *Disputed Questions on Evil* (q. XVI, 1) treat of Manichaeism. Moreover, the only other time that Thomas was in Paris was during the 1250's, and he was not working on the *Summa of Theology* then.

> One time, St. Louis of France invited him [Thomas] to his table. He humbly asked to be excused because of his work on the *Summa of Theology* which he was dictating at this time. Considering the King's invitation and the Paris Prior's order that the humble Master abandon the heights of contemplation, he put aside his work along with the thoughts he had in mind while in his cell and went to the King, at the express command of King and Prior.
>
> While at the royal table, he was suddenly inspired by a truth of the faith. He struck his fist on the table and cried out: "Now, that's the answer to the Manichean heresy!"
>
> Nudging him the Prior said: "Pay attention, Master, you are at the table of the King of France." Then he jerked his cowl forcibly to withdraw him from his thoughts. Somewhat returning to his senses, he bowed to the holy King and asked his pardon for his distraction at the royal table.
>
> At this, the King was much astonished and edified by the Master, for, although he was of the nobility and well able to enjoy the hospitality of such a king and able to relax from contemplation, such concentration prevailed in his mind that when a thought occurred to him he did not put aside its significance in the course of the conversation. Now the holy King arranged that this meditation which was powerful enough to distract the Doctor's attention would not happen to be lost. Calling his scribe, he commanded him to put into writing in his presence the thoughts that the Doctor had in mind. Of course, nothing that the divine Spirit internally impressed on the Doctor's memory was lost or failed to be preserved.[16]

In point of fact, King Louis must have had other things on his mind, too. On July 11, 1270, Louis was to leave on the eighth crusade, so this

[16] Tocco, *Vita*, c. 43 (*Fontes*, II, 117).

story must have reference to the year running from the summer of 1269 to that of 1270. The crusading King reached North Africa during the heat of the late summer and his forces were stopped by the Berbers near Tunis. Cholera struck the crusaders. Louis himself contracted the disease and died there on August 25, 1270.[17]

These doleful events are mentioned here because this crusade indirectly occasioned another consultation of Thomas Aquinas. During the preparations for the disastrous expedition, the Dominican Master General, John of Vercelli, had appointed Brother Bartholomew of Tours, O.P., as vicar-general of the friars who were to accompany the crusaders.[18] Bartholomew then made out his last will and testament, an act contrary to the regulations of his Order and in defiance of the Master General. When reprimanded, Bartholomew brought countercharges against John of Vercelli. The latter sought the advice of three Dominican scholars: Robert (Kilwardy, apparently), Latinus de Malabranca, and Thomas Aquinas. Later, Brothers Michael of Neuvirelle and Lambert of Liège were brought into consultation. Bartholomew of Tours was quite a prominent Dominican scholar but he was found guilty of grave misconduct. The General Chapter of Milan (June 1270) issued an order putting him on twelve days of bread and water, requiring him to say a penance of six Psalters, depriving him of his seal as a preacher general and of all public participation in the affairs of the Order, and forbidding him to serve as a Dominican superior. Of course, Bartholomew was removed from his position as vicar of the Dominicans on crusade.[19] As far as we know, Aquinas concurred in the findings of the other consultors.

During the early part of the following year (1271), Thomas was consulted several times concerning a set of curious questions. Since several of his short works developed out of these consultations, and since the matter must have occupied a good deal of his time, it is useful to explain how these questions originated. The whole story is not yet fully investigated but several recent discoveries and studies enable us to reconstruct the general outlines of the affair.

In the school year 1269–1270, at the Dominican monastery of Santa Sabina in Rome, some unknown master conducted a Quodlibetal Disputation; several tricky problems were raised concerning the possible influence

[17] Henri Daniel-Rops, *Cathedral and Crusade* (London: Dent, 1957), pp. 476–479.

[18] A. Mortier, *Histoire des Maîtres Généraux de l'Ordre des Frères Prêcheurs* (Paris, 1903–1920), II, 72–75.

[19] *Fontes,* VI, 572–573; cf. Glorieux *Répertoire des Maîtres,* I, 105–106.

of angels on the motions of celestial bodies and on terrestrial events.[20] In Aristotelian physics and astronomy, the existence of certain "intelligences," or minds existing apart from matter, was postulated. These intelligences were assigned, by Aristotle, the function of moving the stars or planets in the outer spheres of the universe. It was only natural for some Christian readers in the thirteenth century to wonder: Are these incorporeal intelligences of Aristotle identical with the angels? Some people did make this identification and thus there arose various problems concerning the angels as higher causes of the motions of things celestial and terrestrial. We have, as yet, no record of this original Quodlibet in Rome but there is sufficient evidence that it did take place.

Some of the questions must have been hotly debated there, for the whole matter came to the attention of the Master General, who eventually decided to seek the advice of the most learned men in the Order of Preachers on the philosophical and theological implications of the whole problem. These same questions also had repercussions in the Dominican house of studies at Venice, probably in 1270. There, a Dominican teacher, Brother Baxianus of Lodi, seems to have become involved in a discussion of the questions with his students. He becomes known in the literature as the Lector of Venice. By March, 1271, Baxianus had sent to Thomas Aquinas in Paris a group of thirty questions, of which at least fifteen more or less center on the problem of angelic "movers." Other questions from the Lector of Venice are concerned with miracles, the soul and body of Christ, and the distance from the surface of the earth to its center.

The first documentary evidence that we now have on all this commotion is a letter which Aquinas wrote to Brother Baxianus at Venice in March, 1271. This contains the first set of answers given by Thomas to these questions and it was only identified as such in 1930.[21] In his terse reply, Thomas asserts that the fact that the angels do move the celestial bodies is not only proved many times by the philosophers but is also clearly stated by Christian teachers (*a sacris doctoribus*). The other questions from the Lector of Venice are answered in the light of this positive position which Aquinas took. Some of these questions have little to do with the angels

[20] On this *Quodlibetum,* see J. Destrez, "La Lettre de saint Thomas d'Aquin dite lettre au Lecteur de Venise," *Mélanges Mandonnet* (Paris: Vrin, 1930), I, 128–132.

[21] The editor, J. Destrez, calls it "Text A" of the *Letter to the Lector of Venice;* the text is printed as *Appendice* II to Destrenz's *art. cit.,* pp. 155–161. Text A begins: "Incipit epistola sancti thomae de Aquino, ordinis praedicatorum, ad fratrem Baxianum, lectorem Venetum super quibusdam articulis numero XXX."

but are of real scientific interest. For instance, Question 14 asks whether it is possible to determine the distance from the surface of the earth to its center. Aquinas answers that it is possible to calculate this distance but he does not indicate how.[22]

We now know quite exactly the next development concerning these strange problems. During the celebration of the solemn Mass on the Wednesday of Holy Week (April 1, 1271), Thomas received the news that a special letter had come to him from the Master General, John of Vercelli.[23] The matter was evidently urgent and Thomas read the Master General's letter immediately. He found that it posed forty-three questions, of which thirty-six are identical, or very closely connected, with the problems raised by Brother Baxianus from Venice. John of Vercelli ordered Thomas to answer these questions promptly, indicating: (1) whether the Fathers of the Church (the *Sancti*) favored the view expressed in the respective articles; (2) whether Thomas himself held the view expressed in each of these articles; and (3) if Thomas as consultor did not hold this view, could it be tolerated as not contrary to the faith?[24] It is clear that the Master General now regards the problems as theological difficulties and he is concerned with them by virtue of his obligations as head of the Order.

Thomas immediately suspended his participation in the services of Holy Week and quickly wrote his answers, completing them on the following day which was Holy Thursday.[25] Evidently, both he and his superiors in Paris regarded the Master General's commission as a matter of extreme urgency. The replies that he sent to John of Vercelli (called *Response to John of Vercelli concerning Forty-Two Articles*) are very similar to most of the answers that he had written for the Lector of Venice. Twenty-three of the "articles" in the General's letter are practically identical in subject matter with the same number of questions in Baxianus' inquiry.[26] In John of Vercelli's letter, two articles were very similar, so their number is reduced from forty-three to forty-two in Thomas' *Response*. Considering

---

[22] *Ed. cit.*, p. 160: [14] "Ad 14 dico quod potest."

[23] This is known from the opening lines of Thomas' reply, *Responsio ad fr. Joannem Vercellensem de articulis XLII*, in Mandonnet, *Opus. Omnia*, III, 196; and *Opus. Theol.* (Turin: Marietti, 1954), I, 211–218.

[24] *Ibid.*

[25] "Quibus articulis statim sequenti die secundum formam a vobis traditam, praetermissis aliis occupationibus secundum quod mihi occurrit, respondere curavi." *Ibid.*

[26] Cf. Destrez, *art. cit.*, p. 123.

the third article, Aquinas assures the Master General that the Fathers do teach that God moves celestial bodies by means of spiritual creatures; Augustine is cited to this effect. Thomas adds that he cannot recall that any Father of the Church, or philosopher, has ever denied this.[27] Then, answering Article 7, Aquinas adds: "To speak briefly, all of the preceding questions have little or nothing to do with the teaching of the faith; rather, they are questions of natural philosophy." After giving his opinion on certain questions (see Number 15, for example), Thomas says that, of course, a contrary view may be tolerated. In considering the twenty-third article, which is concerned with Aristotle's embryological teaching, Thomas gives Averroës' (the standard commentator) interpretation and then adds pungently: "I fail to see what this has to do with the teaching of the faith, however the words of the Philosopher [Aristotle] are explained!"

These answers of Thomas Aquinas show, better than anything else that he wrote, how clearly he separated the work of philosophy from that of the theologian. As far as he was concerned, Thomas felt that nothing that Aristotle had said directly affected a single belief of the Christian faith. Moreover, he thought that this distinction worked the other way: there was no point in trying to modify the philosophical conclusions of Aristotle, simply because some theologian felt that Aristotelianism was not in accord with Christian doctrine. In fact, we shall see that Thomas' view of the autonomy of both theology and philosophy was not shared by his colleagues.

From recent historical research, we now know that John of Vercelli sought the advice of two other Dominican scholars concerning these problems, apparently at much the same time that he wrote to Aquinas. Some light is thrown on the independence of Thomas' mind by looking at the corresponding judgments of his fellow consultors.

In 1930, Father Chenu published an informative study, in which he edited the replies of Robert Kilwardby, O.P., to the Master General's query about the same articles.[28] It may clear the air to say right at the

---

[27] "Sed caelestia corpora a spirituali creatura moveri, a nemine Sanctorum vel philosophorum negatum legisse me memini." *Responsio art. XLII,* art. 3; Mandonnet has *legatum* for *negatum,* a misprint.

[28] M. D. Chenu, "Les Réponses de s. Thomas et de Kilwardby à la consultation de Jean de Verceil (1271)," *Mélanges Mandonnet,* I, 191–222. Kilwardby's *Responsiones* are printed on pp. 193–211, with some elisions by the editor. Chenu further discussed and emended the Kilwardby text in: "Aux origines de la 'Science Moderne,'" *Revue des Sciences Philos. et Théol.,* XXIX (1940), 206–217.

start that Robert Kilwardby was an English Dominican who never cared for the philosophy or theology of Thomas Aquinas. He became one of the most outspoken critics of Thomism in the Order. When Robert later became archbishop of Canterbury, he condemned (on March 18, 1277) thirty philosophical propositions, of which at least seven were basic tenets in Aquinas' philosophy of nature.[29] The twenty-sixth "error" condemned by Kilwardby was: "that the vegetative, sensitive and intellective are one simple form." In other words, Kilwardby was a man who did not see that philosophy is a subject that is distinct from theology, for he here established the doctrine of the plurality of substantial forms in the human being, *by episcopal edict.* As we shall see in our final chapter Kilwardby ordered the dismissal of any Master who disagreed with him on these points of philosophy from his teaching position at Oxford University.

It comes with no surprise, then, to discover that Robert Kilwardby differed greatly from Aquinas in his answers to the Master General. Indeed, Kilwardby is so flatly in contradiction with Thomas that Father Mandonnet has argued that the English Dominican (in 1270 Kilwardby was provincial in England) first read Aquinas' *Responsio* before writing his own.[30] Kilwardby certainly took more time than Aquinas in answering the Master General and it is possible that he secured some sort of copy of Thomas' replies, even though such documents addressed to the head of the Order on consultation were usually kept in confidence. An indication of this is found in Kilwardby's judgment on the second article.[31] He says that the angels do not, and cannot, move the celestial bodies. Sarcastically Kilwardby states that, if angels are understood properly "as we Catholics speak of them" (*sicut nos catholici loquimur*), then they cannot be taken as celestial movers. He further claims that the view that celestial bodies are moved by angels "is not philosophical and I cannot remember that it has been approved as true and certain by any of the Fathers."[32] The language used by Kilwardby is an echo of Aquinas' judgment — but in blunt contradiction to it.

Answering the third article, Kilwardby says that there are two opinions:

[29] See the Document in *Fontes,* VI, 615–617.

[30] P. Mandonnet, *Bulletin Thomiste,* III (1930), 139.

[31] Chenu text, Quaestio II [III], *art. cit.,* p. 197.

[32] *Ibid.,* "nec est philosophica, nec memini eam esse ab aliquo sanctorum approbatum tamquam veram et certam." Compare this wording with the sentence from St. Thomas, in note 27 *supra.*

(1) that celestial bodies are not moved by spirits, and (2) that they are moved by spirits. Then he repeats his own view in ironical language which definitely appears to refer to Thomas Aquinas:

> Now, facing this difference of opinion, I greatly commend the first opinion and think very little of the second. And I should say this without prejudice to brighter intellects; nor is it proper in the case of such doubtful matters to assert something contentiously, as if such an opinion were to be held so that the Catholic truth would be forever safe.[33]

Concerning the fourth question (Is it infallibly demonstrated that the angels are the movers of the celestial bodies?), Thomas Aquinas had answered that both the Platonic and the Aristotelian philosophers thought that they had proved this point efficaciously. Their arguments rested on the order of reality, in which God rules lower things by means of higher ones, "as the Holy Doctors also teach." To say that the celestial bodies are merely moved by their natures, as heavy and light bodies are on earth, is, in the view of Aquinas, "altogether impossible."[34] To this same query, Kilwardby replies as follows:

> No. When there are different reasonable opinions on the same point, none of which, perhaps, can be perfectly demonstrated, then none can be infallibly proved. [He then offers his review of the teaching of Plato and Aristotle, and adds:] However, since the Catholic position is placed contrary to their positions, I do not regard their proofs as infallible.[35]

Robert's irony is showing. It is hard to believe that he had not seen Thomas' answers. Kilwardby, in fact, proceeds to argue that the celestial bodies *are* moved by their natures, and that any other manner of movement (even by angels) would involve violent, or nonnatural, motion. On this point, let us in all fairness note that Kilwardby was probably right, from the point of view of modern science.[36] However, we may well wonder whether Kilwardby's answers were of real assistance to the Master General. As Father Chenu remarks, in comparing the replies of Thomas and Robert: "Kilwardby remains on the level of physics, on the level of motion, we could almost say on the level of experience. The Angelic Doctor has nothing to do with this."[37]

---

[33] *Ibid.*, p. 198.

[34] S. Thomae, *Responsio ad XLII art.*, art. 5; ed. Mandonnet, III, 199.

[35] Chenu text of Kilwardby *Responsiones, art. cit.*, p. 198.

[36] Chenu, "Aux origines, etc.," pp. 206–217. Cf. D. E. Sharp, "The *De Ortu Scientiarum* of R. Kilwardby," *New Scholasticism*, VII (1934), 1–30.

[37] Chenu, "Les Réponses de s. Thomas et de Kilwardby," pp. 220–221.

Still another Dominican was consulted by the Master General. This became clear in 1960, with the publication of two research articles arising out of the discovery, in St. Paul's Cathedral Library, London, of a third set of replies to the queries sent out by John of Vercelli.[38] The third consultor was Albert the Great. There seems to be no doubt that the newly discovered treatise is Albert's work: Weisheipl has marshaled the evidence quite convincingly and Callus is in agreement on this attribution.[39]

It may surprise some readers to learn that Albert's answers are very different from those of his pupil, Thomas Aquinas, but we have earlier suggested that their ways of thinking are diverse. In general, the work by Albert is much more lengthy and pretentious. He did not write it in one day.[40] It is a *determinatio,* in the full medieval sense of the word: Albert lays down the definitive answers in full, like a Dutch uncle! As did Kilwardby, Albert goes into great detail on the scientific and philosophic aspects of the questions. He evidently thinks that there must be not only a Catholic philosophy but even a Christian astronomy. (It should be made clear that precisely the same forty-three questions are considered by the three Dominican consultors, a fact which provides an excellent opportunity to compare Thomas Aquinas' position with those of two of his most distinguished Dominican contemporaries.) Albert cites all kinds of weird authorities — the *Liber de Causis,* Eudoxus, Alpetragius, Hermes Trismegistus, Apuleius, Avicenna, Algazel, Isaac Israeli, Moses Maimonides, Philo Judaeus, Dionysius the Pseudo-Areopagite, and dozens of others. German *Wissenschaftslehre* was no stranger to St. Albert.

Doctrinally, on the major issue of the angels as movers of celestial bodies, Albert is much closer to the position of Kilwardby than to that of Aquinas. He makes it abundantly clear that he does not identify the angels of Christian tradition with the "intelligences" of Aristotelian philosophy. Rather pontifically, Albert informs the Master General that he has already explained the whole thing in his *Commentary on the Liber de Causis.*[41] Of course, this commentary is an authentic work of Albert's and his reference to it is an important testimony to his authorship of the

---

[38] D. A. Callus, "Une oeuvre récemment découverte de saint Albert le Grand: *De XLIII problematibus ad Magistrum Ordinis* (1271)," *Rev. des Sc. Philos. et Théol.,* 44 (1960), 243–261; and J. A. Weisheipl, "The Problemata Determinata XLIII ascribed to Albertus Magnus," *Mediaeval Studies,* XXII (1960), 303–354.

[39] Weisheipl, *art. cit.,* pp. 307–311.

[40] Weisheipl's paleographical edition is in *ibid.,* pp. 316–354.

[41] Weisheipl ed., p. 327.

Problemata Determinata XLIII. Moreover, he is more than a little impatient with the Master General for taking up Albert's time, and for not having thoroughly digested Albert's other important writings. As Albert determines the key question, Number 3:

> All these things are proved in philosophy; and the proofs of the philosophers have been diligently explained by Us [as a retired bishop, he uses the honorific plural] in the book *On Causes*. Therefore, it is obvious that an angel is not an intelligence; and if it were, it still would not be the proximate mover of any celestial sphere. And if that is so, which is most certainly proved, then the angels do not move the celestial bodies ministerially; and so it follows, further, that no other lower bodies are moved by them.
>
> If someone says that it does move the celestial spheres at the command of God, this motion will be a motion of obedience and non-natural. And nothing can be determined philosophically on this point, because the principles of philosophy, which are self-evident axioms, are inadequate on this level. Hence, a person who says such things does not deserve to be addressed as a philosopher, for he does not adhere to the principles of philosophy. Indeed, Aristotle says that a geometer need not talk with non-geometers.
>
> Thus the determination of the third question is evident, for the angels are not the movers of the celestial bodies, according to philosophy, as has been shown already with necessity.[42]

Albert is little concerned with the theological or ecclesiastical aspects of these questions. He rarely mentions the views of the Fathers (*Sancti*). Albert does say that the eight questions starting with Number 25 are matters of theology but he then proceeds to indicate how ridiculous these questions seem to him. His language becomes rather violent: one article (No. 26) is called the statement of a madman; another (No. 30) seems to him to be crazy (*videtur mihi esse deliramentum*); another (No. 31) is laughable and useless; and a question (No. 33) about the origin of Christ's soul is fatuous (*questio fatua est*). The ill-tempered character of his remarks may be merited by some of the queries, but Albert's tone of disrespect contrasts throughout with Aquinas' courtesy and sober regard for the Master General.[43]

The final paragraph of Albert's response may be quoted, so that the reader may judge for himself. While superficially respectful, Albert's conclusion chides the Master General for bothering a great man with such nonsense. There is also a suggestion of other problems concerning mental health and his personal relations with the administration of the Order, even at this time.

---

[42] *Ibid.*

[43] See Callus' comments, *art. cit.*, pp. 252–255.

And so, [Albert concludes], We who are becoming blind before our old age [*cecutientes pre senectute*] have studiously given, because of Our love and reverence for Your Paternity, these answers to Your questions. We would have preferred to turn our attention to prayers concerning something else, rather than to the answering of curious questions. May Your Paternity be well forever, and may God hear my prayers for You to bring Your [the manuscript has *vestrum*] Order back to the primitive purity of conscience and of religion.[44]

This was an odd way for a Dominican (even one who has the status of a bishop) to write to his Master General.

For Thomas Aquinas, the affair was not yet over. In April, 1271, he received another communication from Venice. This one was from some of the students of the Lector Baxianus and it requested a further explanation of some of the same questions.[45] Busy though he was, Thomas again went to work and wrote a second, and longer, *Letter to the Lector of Venice concerning Thirty-Six Articles*. This reply is Text B, in the nomenclature of Destrez, and it is the version that is printed in the present editions of Thomas' *Opuscula*.[46] Since this version of the response to Baxianus was written after Thomas had learned of the Master General's interest in the problems, it is longer and gives more Patristic references. However, Thomas' position is doctrinally the same; he keeps to the theological issues and avoids philosophical discussions.

It is even possible that there is some connection between the foregoing disputes about the possibility that angels move the celestial bodies and a very significant metaphysical treatise produced at this time by Aquinas. This is the *Treatise on Separate Substances, or on the Nature of the Angels*, dedicated to his beloved *socius*, Brother Reginald. The work is not complete (possibly due to Thomas' departure from Paris in 1272) but what we have of it shows that Aquinas now undertook to review all the teachings of the philosophers on immaterial beings, and also the Christian doctrine on the angels. We now have a critical edition of the Latin text which will provide an accurate basis for further study of this work.[47] Though some chronologies place this treatise in the Naples period (on the basis that its

---

[44] Weisheipl ed., p. 327.

[45] The *Articuli . . . iterum remissi sibi a quibusdam scolaribus* are printed with Thomas' answers, *Opera Omnia* (Paris: Vivès), Vol. XXXII, 832.

[46] For Text B, see Destrez, "La Lettre de s. Thomas," *Mélanges Mandonnet*, I, 162–172; or *Opus. Theol.* (Turin: Marietti, 1954), I, 193.

[47] S. Thomae Aquinatis, *Tractatus de Substantiis Separatis*, ed. F. J. Lescoe (West Hartford, Conn.: St. Joseph's College, 1962). Father Lescoe printed an English version: *Treatise on Separate Substances* (*id.*, 1960).

incompleteness was due to his death), the best present estimate is that the work *On Separate Substances* was written in Paris, between 1270 and 1272.[48] One might tentatively suggest that it is Aquinas' major effort to explain the metaphysical status of the angels in the order of creation, and that it was occasioned by his growing awareness in the early 1270's that there was considerable disagreement among Catholic theologians on the whole question of the relation between the Aristotelian intelligences and the Christian angels. Throughout the *Treatise on Separate Substances,* Thomas leaves no doubt that he still identifies them, though he does not confuse the speculations of the philosophers with the theological conclusions on the angels. He is at great pains to point out that, in Christian teaching, the angels are all created by God, that they are not limited in number to the number of the celestial spheres or bodies, and that they are not in any sense the "souls" of the heavenly bodies.[49] In view of these points of emphasis, it seems likely that Aquinas was writing *On Separate Substances* in the last year of his second Paris professorate (1271–1272) and that his writing was interrupted, not by his death as Mandonnet supposed,[50] but by the termination of his residence in Paris.

That Thomas did take some time to relax, during the summer vacations, is evident from one of his few extant *Letters.*[51] A certain gentleman, James de Burgo, wrote to Aquinas in Paris and asked what he thought about fortune-telling. Thomas replied that he had put aside his studies for a while during the vacation period but that he could not refuse the request of a friend. Hence he proceeded to write for this layman a little treatise on the uses and abuses of various ways of foretelling future events. The letter is not short; it occupies about twenty-five pages in a modern printing. Thomas learnedly reviews the various kinds of events that people try to foretell and the many devices used to make such prophecies. Basically, his advice to Sir James is to have nothing to do with forecasters of the future, except in the case of weather forecasting and similar things.[52] He

[48] See Lescoe, *Treatise on Separate Substances,* "Introd." pp. 3–7; cf. Eschmann, "Catalogue," n. 54, p. 412.

[49] In Chapter XVII (p. 97, in Lescoe's English version) Thomas begins to contrast what the philosophers say about immaterial substances with what the Christians say about angels.

[50] "Introduction," to S. Thomae, *Opuscula Omnia* (Paris, 1927), I, 52.

[51] See "Prologue" to *De Sortibus ad Dominum Jacobum de Burgo, Opus. Theol.* (Turin: Marietti, 1954), I, 159.

[52] *De Sortibus,* c. 5: "Si quis astrologum consulat utrum sit aestas futura pluviosa vel sicca: non est nugatoria consultatio."

warns James against thinking that the stars influence human thinking or willing. At the end, Thomas points out that canon law forbids the use of various superstitious and harmful devices for determining future events. He indicates that even games of chance are not without some element of vicious superficiality. This letter was probably written during the years 1269–1272.[53]

Associated in subject matter are two other letters written by Aquinas. Both are addressed to a layman who is called "A Certain Knight beyond the Alps." This man does not appear to be identical with the Sir James mentioned above but one of these letters, *On the Use of Astrology,* covers very briefly the same points that are treated in *De Sortibus.*[54] The other letter is entitled *On the Occult Workings of Nature,* and seems to be directed to the same gentleman (whose qualification as "Ultramontane" may simply mean that he lived in the Papal States). This letter deals with the widespread superstition that certain objects, natural or artificial, possess hidden and magic powers. Thomas says that the whole matter pertains to the realm of superstition.[55] Some chronologies assign these letters to the 1270 period but we do not really know when, or where, they were written.

One rather important treatise which is very difficult to date may have been begun in the second Paris period: the *Compendium of Theology.*[56] It was intended as a summary of Thomas' views on faith, hope, and charity, but the *Compendium* breaks off in the midst of the discussion of hope (*Pars II,* c. 10). Scholars have long thought that it was interrupted by Thomas' death and hence that he was working on it in Naples, but the truth is that we do not know precisely when this treatise was started.

Throughout this second period of teaching in Paris, Thomas was occu-

---

[53] Eschmann, "Catalogue," pp. 422–423, n. 73, where by a misprint the addressee is called "Sir John." The last name of this correspondent is spelled in a variety of ways in different manuscripts.

[54] *De judiciis astrorum,* in *Opus. Philos.* (Turin: Marietti, 1954), p. 155. The address: *ad fratrem Raynaldum,* included in some printings of the title is nonsense; cf. Eschmann, "Catalogue," p. 423, n. 75.

[55] "Hae enim actiones . . . sunt ad superstitionem pertinentes." *De occultis operationibus naturae, ad quemdam militem ultramontanum,* ad fin., in *Opus. Philos.* (Turin: 1954), p. 159. See J. B. McAllister, *The Letter of St. Thomas Aquinas De Occultis Operibus Naturae* (Washington, D. C.: Cath. U. Press, 1938), for an English version.

[56] *Compendium Theologiae ad fratrem Reginaldem socium suum carissimum,* in *Opus. Theol.* (Turin, 1954), I, 13–170. English: C. Vollert (St. Louis: Herder, 1947). For the indefinite chronology, Eschmann, "Catalogue," pp. 411–412; P. Glorieux has recently argued (*Sciences Ecclésiastiques,* XIII, 1961, 7–34) for the date 1270.

pied with his regular teaching of theology at the Dominican house, and with the task of revising and writing many of his major works. It was a very productive time for him. We leave the discussion of his main literary activities to the next chapter.

By the end of 1271, the University of Paris had become a very disturbed institution. The organization of the university was disrupted by a quarrel between two factions in the faculty of arts concerning the office of rector. One large group supported the claims of Master Albericus of Rheims; another smaller faction defended the election of Siger of Brabant as rector. This was the state of affairs early in the spring of 1272.[57] Roger Bacon also reports that "many theologians" were sent away from the university and from Paris at this time because of public complaints against their immoralities.[58] The Bishop of Paris, Etienne Tempier, had to intervene when the university suspended its classes and academic activities during Lent, 1272. By June of that year, Tempier had succeeded in securing the resumption of classes in all faculties, with the exception of law.[59]

Aquinas may have departed from Paris during the Lenten interruption of teaching, or after conducting his Easter *Quodlibets*.[60] In any case, he was at the General Chapter in Florence, on June 12, 1272. The provincial meeting of the Roman Province was also held there.[61] As a preacher general, Thomas participated in these chapters and received his assignment for the coming years.[62]

> We assign the general house of studies [at Naples] to Brother Thomas of Aquino, with full powers as to place, personnel, and the number of students.

Thomas Aquinas was now to begin his last teaching assignment as regent of studies at the place where he had entered the Order some twenty years earlier.

---

[57] For details see: *C.U.P.*, I, 521–530.

[58] *Compendium studii philosophiae*, ed. J. S. Brewer (London, 1859), III, 412.

[59] Mandonnet, *Siger de Brabant*, 2me éd., I, 202.

[60] Glorieux, *Répertoire des Maîtres*, I, 97.

[61] Walz, *Thomas von Aquin* (1953), p. 109.

[62] *Fontes*, VI, 583.

CHAPTER FOURTEEN

Thomism Faces Attack

WHAT Thomas Aquinas was doing to develop a new type of Christian intellectualism was not unknown in Paris during the 1260's. Of course, his writings were not yet used as academic texts, and some of his greatest works were not yet written, but he already had a reputation at the university. This reputation was doubtless one reason why his superiors sent him back to Paris. Almost as soon as he arrived there, in the early months of 1269, Thomas found that powerful forces were aligned against him. Criticism came from three different sources. His interpretation of Aristotelian philosophy was challenged by a group of teachers in the arts faculty, led by a Belgian scholar, Siger de Brabant. Thomas' theological and philosophical innovations aroused the opposition of a second faction which included some of the leading figures in the faculty of theology and in the diocese of Paris. And finally, Aquinas' way of life, as a religious devoting himself to scholarship and teaching, came under further attack by some of the diocesan clergy.

As far as we now know, no Paris professor of liberal arts directly attacked Thomas Aquinas. What happened in this first area of controversy was much more subtle and indirect. Some of the priests who taught philosophy at the University of Paris during the 1260's carried on much the same sort of literal study of the text of Aristotle that Aquinas had been pursuing in the same period while resident in the Papal States. They regarded Aristotle as "The Philosopher," just as St. Thomas did. They soon saw (and in this they were sound textual scholars) that the original philosophy of Aristotle necessarily leads to some conclusions which contradict Christian teachings. In drawing these conclusions, the arts teachers were influenced by other philosophers in the non-Christian tradition — by Averroës,

Avicenna, Proclus, and the anonymous compilers of certain Neoplatonic metaphysical treatises, such as the *Book of Causes.*[1]

These philosophical conclusions may be reduced to three, insofar as they affected the reputation of Aquinas. First, it was claimed that there is but one properly intellectual soul for all men; that this is an immaterial substance, the lowest of the separate Intelligences that Aristotle had talked about; and that this contains both the agent and possible intellects described in the third book of Aristotle's *On the Soul.* In this interpretation, individual men are not equipped at birth with any truly intellectual powers; they have, as their highest cognitive potencies, the various powers of internal sensation, including capacities to store up and concretely interpret sense experience and even to turn upward to the higher intellectual soul and to share, momentarily, in something of its understanding of the universal meanings of reality. This is monopsychism. As an interpretation of Aristotle, it goes beyond what was actually said in the treatise *De Anima,* but it was supported by the views of "The Commentator," Averroës. This first conclusion, then, could certainly be called Averroistic.

Monopsychism is not, however, compatible with the Christian faith and theology — and these arts professors said that it was not. Where they differed from Thomas Aquinas was in their implied view that this theory of human intelligence was the only conclusion that a philosopher, as such, could reach. They never said that monopsychism is the truth (for they were Catholic priests and knew that this teaching undermines the spiritual character of the individual human soul, the personal immortality of man, and the Catholic teaching that every man is morally capable of being raised to the beatific vision in heaven). Rather, these arts teachers continually affirmed that the teaching of Catholic theology (that each person is equipped with his own intellectual powers) is true. To the unsophisticated listener or reader, however, it would appear that these teachers were saying that one conclusion is true in rational philosophy while its contradictory is true in Catholic theology. Thus they were soon to be accused by the Bishop of Paris of teaching a theory of "double truth."[2]

[1] For one account of the growth of this "heterodox Aristotelianism," see Van Steenberghen, *Aristotle in the West,* pp. 198–229; for a different evaluation of "Latin Averroism," see Gilson, *Hist. of Christian Philos.,* pp. 387–402.

[2] In Bishop Tempier's condemnation of March 7, 1277 (Doc. XXXVIII, *Fontes,* VI, 596) the prologue speaks of "nonnulli Parisius studentes in artibus" who have been teaching obvious errors. "Dicunt enim ea esse vera secundum philosophiam, sed non secundum fidem catholicam, quasi sint due contrarie veritates. . . ."

A second conclusion which these teachers found in Aristotle's physics, astronomy, and metaphysics was that this physical world had no beginning or termination. To speak loosely, it is eternal. Historically and textually, it is correct to say that Aristotle conceived of the physical universe as without beginning. Clearly, however, this is opposed to Christian belief — and the arts professors said so. On this point, Thomas Aquinas partly agreed and partly disagreed with these teachers. He thought that Aristotelian philosophy is unable to demonstrate that the world did not always exist, and so the Christian teaching that it had a beginning is based on faith alone and is not demonstrable.[3] In fact, Thomas felt that rational arguments intended to show that the world had a beginning are so weak that their use might tend to bring ridicule on Christianity.[4] However, there were important theologians at this time who claimed that it is possible rationally to prove that the world did not always exist. In his *Commentary on the Sentences,* St. Bonaventure had bluntly asserted:

> To say that the world is eternal or eternally produced, maintaining that all things are produced from nothing, is completely against truth and reason, as my last argument proves. It is so contrary to reason that I believe that no philosopher, however small his understanding, has maintained this view.[5]

Bonaventure is not saying that there are theological arguments opposing the view that the world could have been created without a durational beginning; he asserts that his arguments are based on propositions that are self-evident, "according to reason and philosophy." A similar position had been taken in the Franciscan *Summa of Theology* compiled in honor of Alexander of Hales, during the 1240's.[6] Even Albert the Great taught that at least probable arguments could be given against the theory that the world was eternally created.[7]

---

[3] *S. T.*, I, 46, 2, c: "Dicendum quod mundum non semper fuisse, sola fide tenetur, et demonstrative probari non potest; sicut et supra de mysterio Trinitatis dictum est. . . . Unde mundum incoepisse est credibile, non autem demonstrabile vel scibile."

[4] *Ibid.*, c. ad fin.; see *S.C.G.*, II, c. 32–38, where there is a fuller statement of St. Thomas' position.

[5] S. Bonaventurae, *In II Sententiarum,* d. 1, p. 1, a. 1, q. 2, Resp. (editio minor, Quaracchi: Collegium S. Bonaventurae, 1938, II, 15). He has just given six arguments to prove that it is wrong to assert that the world was produced from eternity, beginning with this sentence "Sed ad oppositum sunt rationes ex propositionibus per se notis secundum rationem et philosophiam."

[6] *Summa Fratris Alexandri,* p. 1, n. 64 (ed. Quaracchi, 1924, I, 95).

[7] Alberti Magni, *In VIII Physicorum,* tr. I, c. 13 (ed. Borgnet, III, 552).

Now this is a good example of how these arts professors made difficulties for Thomas Aquinas. His position on the question of philosophy and the eternity of the created universe appeared to the more conservative theologians to be little different from the Aristotelianism of the teachers in the arts faculty. Eventually Aquinas will have to write (in 1271) a note explaining his own view on the question, for those who are complaining about it.[8] We shall examine this controversial writing later in this chapter.

A third view held by Siger and his associates was that the human will is a passive potency that is actuated in its volitions by intellectual judgments concerning good and evil.[9] To many contemporary theologians, this was tantamount to a denial of free will.[10] Now, without intending perhaps to compromise the Thomistic theory of volition, these arts professors did, in fact, attract unfavorable attention and criticism to Aquinas' explanation of the working of human will. Thomas did not think that the will is a wholly active power; he described it, in his *Disputed Questions on the Virtues in General* (from Paris, 1269–1272), as a power capable of being perfected by habits of justice and charity. Hence the human will, as he sees it, is partly active and partly passive. Some of his contemporaries thought that Thomas was teaching a sort of intellectual determinism, that he was denying freedom to the human will, as some of the arts teachers may have done on the level of Aristotelian philosophy. In other words, by offering an extreme caricature of something like Thomas' explanation of willing, these teachers made his position appear vulnerable to criticism from more conservative theologians.

Until comparatively recently, we have known very little about these philosophers in the arts faculty at Paris. Up to the mid-nineteenth century, Siger of Brabant was simply a name known to Dante scholars. In the *Divine Comedy,* Dante reaches the fourth heaven where he sees a luminous circle of twelve distinguished souls.[11] Thomas Aquinas is one of them and

---

[8] S. Thomae, *De aeternitate mundi contra murmurantes,* in *Opuscula Philosophica* (Turin: Marietti, 1954), p. 105.

[9] For this and the two preceding positions (monopsychism and the eternity of the world), see the summary of Siger de Brabant's teachings in F. Van Steenberghen, *Le Mouvement* (1951), pp. 273–275. Siger also had certain metaphysical views (including a denial of the real distinction between essence and *esse*) which I do not include here, because these views did *not* make trouble for St. Thomas.

[10] Thus, the third proposition in Tempier's 1270 condemnation was: "Quod voluntas hominis ex necessitate vult vel eligit." I, p. 486.

[11] *Paradiso,* X, 133–138; the passage is merely summarized in Dante Alighieri,

he introduces Dante to Albert, to himself (Aquinas), and then to Gratian, Peter Lombard, Solomon, Dionysius the Pseudo-Areopagite, Orosius, Boethius, Isidore of Seville, Venerable Bede, Richard of St. Victor, and lastly, to Siger of Brabant. In comment on the last of these men of wisdom, Dante's "Thomas of Aquino" says:

> This figure which your eyes encounter as they return towards me is the light of a spirit who, wrapt in grave thoughts, found death slow in coming. This is the eternal light of Siger who, when he taught in the Street of Straw [Paris], established invidious truths.

Little more attention was paid to Siger until Ernest Renan wrote a book in the nineteenth century which maintained that this Siger of Brabant was the leader of a school of freethinkers in thirteenth-century Paris.[12] Renan called them "Latin Averroists." Later, the Dominican historian, Pierre Mandonnet, opened up the study of Siger, in an important but pioneering work which endeavored to discover the personality and thought of this philosopher.[13] Still somewhat influenced by the imaginative constructions of Renan, Mandonnet laid the groundwork for more scholarly studies of the works of Siger. Martin Grabmann, Fernand Van Steenberghen, Bruno Nardi, Etienne Gilson, Philippe Delhaye, C. A. Graiff, and others, have now uncovered, edited, and interpreted Siger's writings.[14] In effect, we now know that Siger was born about 1240 in the southern part of what is now Belgium. He became a canon of the Church of Saint-Martin in Liège, went to Paris to study liberal arts, and eventually became a prominent master in arts at the university some time before 1265.[15] The first solid date in his life is August 27, 1266, when Siger was embroiled in a struggle between two factions vying for control of the arts faculty.[16] He taught in the liberal arts division from 1265 to 1277.

On March 7, 1277, Bishop Etienne Tempier issued his sweeping condemnation of 219 erroneous teachings.[17] Since many of these approximated

The Divine Comedy, trans. T. G. Bergin (New York: Appleton-Century-Crofts, 1955), pp. 28–30 of the *Paradise.*

12 *Averroès et l'averroisme* (Paris: Calmann-Lévy, 1852).

13 *Siger de Brabant et l'averroisme latin au XIIIe siècle,* 2me éd., 2 vols. (Louvain: Institut Supérieur de Philosophie, 1908–1911).

14 Cf. A. Maurer, "The State of Historical Research in Siger of Brabant," *Speculum,* XXXI (1956), 49–56; F. Van Steenberghen, "Siger of Brabant," *The Modern Schoolman,* XXIX (1951), 11–27.

15 Van Steenberghen, *Le Mouvement,* p. 266.

16 *C.U.P.,* I, 455–456.

17 *Ibid.,* 543–555; also printed as *Doc.* XXXVIII (*Fontes,* VI, 596–614).

the views of Siger, and since he was summoned in the fall of 1277 to appear before the French Inquisitor, Simon du Val, Siger then abandoned his teaching career and fled from Paris. Submitting an appeal of the charge of heresy to the Roman Curia, he went to the papal court at Orvieto to plead his cause. There Siger was absolved of formal heresy but was ordered to remain in Orvieto, so that he would stir up no more trouble in France. According to most accounts, Siger was stabbed by his demented secretary and died in Orvieto, during the pontificate of Pope Martin IV (1281–1285).[18]

Siger of Brabant, then, was the leading figure among the Aristotelian philosophers at the University of Paris, when Thomas returned in the first months of 1269. There were others with similar views. Boethius of Sweden, Martin of Denmark, James of Douai, Giles of Orleans, Anthony of Parma, and Bernier of Nivelles are gradually coming to be better known for their association with the movement known as Latin Averroism.[19] Van Steenberghen would prefer to call them heterodox Aristotelians.

In any case, it was to refute the monopsychism of Siger that Thomas Aquinas wrote his treatise, *On the Unity of the Intellect against the Averroists.*[20] He probably finished it before Bishop Tempier's first condemnation (December 10, 1270), because there is no reference to this ecclesiastical censure in Thomas' work. The opening lines clearly state what Aquinas is opposing and how he proposed to develop his criticism. He does not name Siger of Brabant, but it is evident that this priest in the arts faculty is his chief opponent.[21] The *Prologue* also indicates the depth of Aquinas' feeling on the subject.

---

[18] Van Steenberghen, *Le Mouvement,* p. 268. In a *Letter* to the University of Oxford, dated November 10, 1284, John Peckham apparently refers to Siger's death (see *Fontes,* VI, 629). Bishop Peckham (a Franciscan) speaks of certain errors which he does not accuse the Dominicans of teaching, and adds: "Nor do We think that they originated with persons in the religious Orders but rather with some seculars; two of their principal defenders, or rather discoverers, are said to have ended their days in a wretched manner in transalpine regions, even though they were not natives of those parts."

[19] Gilson, *Hist. of Christian Philos.,* pp. 725–726, provides references to the texts and studies of some in this group.

[20] *De unitate intellectus, contra Averroistas,* ed. L. W. Keeler (Rome: Gregorianum, 1936). English: *The Unicity of the Intellect,* trans. Sr. R. E. Brennan (St. Louis: Herder, 1946).

[21] Cf. Keeler, *op. cit., Introd.* pp. XIX–XX; two early fourteenth-century manuscripts (*Oxford, Corpus Christi,* 225, and *Munich, Lat.,* 8001) name Siger as the primary object of criticism. The Oxford manuscript concludes the text: "contra

> Recently an error concerning the intellect, taking its origin from statements of Averroës, has developed among many men who try to claim that the intellect which Aristotle calls the possible (though he used the unsuitable name "material") is some sort of substance separated in its existence from body and not in any way capable of being united with it as form; and further, that this possible intellect is one for all men. We have already written several refutations of this view but, since these mistaken people in their rashness will not stop attacking the truth, our deliberate intention is to write a criticism of this error, whereby this error may be plainly refuted.
>
> Nor do we propose to do this by showing that this position is erroneous because it is opposed to the truth of the Catholic faith. This should be sufficiently clear to anyone, immediately. If we take away from men the diversity of intellect, which is the only part of the soul that is evidently incorruptible and immortal, the result will be that nothing in the souls of men endures, except this unique intellectual substance. On this assumption, the sanction of rewards and punishments would be destroyed and so would the distinction of these sanctions.
>
> Rather, we propose to show that this view is no less opposed to the principles of philosophy than it is to the evidence of our faith. Moreover, since some of these people reportedly have little regard for the texts of Latin writers on this topic, but say that they are followers of the writings of the Peripatetics (whose books dealing with this subject they have never seen, except for Aristotle who was the founder of the Peripatetic school), we shall first show that this position is completely opposed to his writings and thought.[22]

Aquinas proceeds to argue that Aristotle did not say that the intellective soul is a substance distinct from the body of the individual man. Reviewing the pertinent texts of the *Physics,* the *De Anima, Metaphysics,* and the *Generation of Animals,* Thomas interprets them all to mean that the intellective soul is the substantial form of the individual human body. At the conclusion of his first chapter, he says:

> So then, having carefully considered nearly all of Aristotle's statements about the human intellect, it is apparent that he was of the opinion that the human soul is the act of the body, and that a part or power of it is the possible intellect.[23]

In the second chapter, the interpretations of three noted Greek commentators, Themistius, Theophrastus, and Alexander of Aphrodisias, are examined. According to Thomas, Themistius taught that both agent and

---

magistrum Sigerum de Barbantia [sic] et alios plurimos Parisius regentes anno D.ni M.CC.70." (See Keeler, p. XXI.)

[22] *De unitate intellectus, Proemium;* ed. Keeler, pp. 1–3.

[23] *Ibid.,* c. 1; ed. Keeler, p. 33. (W. D. Ross, *Aristotle* [London: Methuen and Co., 1923], pp. 148–153, seems to agree.)

possible intellects are powers intrinsic to each individual human soul; Theophrastus and Alexander held that each man possesses his own possible intellect. Next, the Arabic commentators, Avicenna and Algazel, are presented as teaching that at least the power of the possible intellect is present in each human soul. Ending this chapter, Aquinas suggests that the only Arabic philosopher found to support the notion that there is but one possible intellect for all men is Averroës.

Chapters Three to Five are designed to show that Aristotle's text is misinterpreted by Averroës and that the whole force of the Aristotelian philosophy of nature requires acceptance of the theory that each human soul is possessed of its own intellectual power. Though himself convinced that each soul also has its own agent intellect, Thomas does not try to prove that this is so in Aristotle. It is sufficient to his purpose to demonstrate the plurality of possible intellects.[24] The treatise *On the Unity of the Intellect* shows a mature Thomas Aquinas operating strictly as a philosopher, aware of the importance of the subject to Christian belief but using purely rational and philosophical argument. It ends with one of the most emotional and personal statements that he ever wrote in the heat of controversy.

> These, then, are the arguments that we have brought together in writing to destroy the aforementioned error, not based on proofs from faith but on the reasonings and statements of the philosophers themselves. Now, if any person trying to achieve glory through pseudo-science wishes to say something against what we have written, let him not do his talking on street-corners or before boys who are unable to make a judgment on matters of such difficulty. Instead, let him write a reply to this, if he dares. He will find that not only I (one of the least among others) but many other zealous supporters of the truth can oppose his error or advise his ignorance.[25]

Apparently Siger accepted the challenge and wrote in reply, *On the Intellective Soul,* to restate his position.

In a sermon thought to have been preached on Sunday, July 20, 1270, before the masters and students of the University of Paris, Thomas treated the same general theme, this time from the viewpoint of the theologian.[26]

---

[24] *Ibid.,* c. 4; *ed. cit.,* pp. 54–55: "Forte enim de agente hoc dicere aliquam rationem haberet, et multi philosophi hoc posuerunt. Nihil enim inconveniens videtur, si ab uno agente multa perficiantur . . . quamvis hoc non sit secundum intentionem Aristotelis."

[25] *Ibid.,* c. 5; *ed. cit.,* p. 80.

[26] *Sermo in tertia dominica post festum Apostolorum Petri et Pauli. Attendite a*

> Some people are found who study philosophy and say things that are not true according to the faith; and when they make these statements opposed to the faith, they assert that the Philosopher says this but they are not giving it as their own opinion but are only reporting the Philosopher's words. Such a man is a false prophet, or a false teacher, for it is the same thing to bring forward a difficulty and not solve it as it is to concede it. This is the meaning of Exodus [21:33] where it is said that: "if a man open a pit, and open a well and cover it not, and an ox comes near it and falls into the well, then he who has opened up the well may be held responsible for restitution."
>
> He who brings up a difficulty concerning matters of faith opens up a well. He fails to cover the well, when he does not answer the difficulty, even though he himself may have a sound and clear understanding of the matter and may not be deceived. Another person who does not have such clear understanding is certainly deceived, and he who presents the difficulty is responsible for restitution, because he is responsible for the other man falling into the pit.
>
> See now: there have been many pagan philosophers and they have made many statements on points connected with the faith, and you will hardly find two of them agreeing on one judgment. Whenever one of them has said something true, he has not said it without some admixture of falsity. In fact, one old woman knows more about matters of faith than all the philosophers of yore. We read that Pythagoras was originally a wrestler, that he heard a teacher discussing the immortality of the soul and maintaining that the soul is immortal. He was so much taken by this that he put aside everything else and devoted himself to the study of philosophy. But what old woman today does not know that the soul is immortal? The faith can do much more than philosophy: so, if philosophy is contrary to the faith, it should not be accepted.

This is St. Thomas putting philosophy in its place in the economy of Christian learning. Actually, we find a very similar sermon, also preached before the University of Paris, by St. Bonaventure.[27] This antedates Aquinas' sermon by almost three years and uses the same text of Scripture (Exodus 21:33) to point out the same moral. People who teach false philosophical conclusions, says Bonaventure, are digging a well into which others may fall. The ironical thing about Bonaventure's sermon, however, is that he states one of these false conclusions and it is precisely the teaching that, according to philosophy, the world may have been created from eternity. This, as we have seen, was a contention of Thomas Aquinas! Here is the significant portion of Bonaventure's talk:

---

falsis prophetis. Ed. Parm., XXIV, 226–228; reprinted in part in Mandonnet, *Siger de Brabant,* 2me éd., I, 109.

[27] *Sermo II* (third Sunday in Advent, 1267; ed. Quaracchi, IX, 62–63). For the date, see J. G. Bougerol, *Introduction à l'étude de s. Bonaventure* (Paris: Desclée, 1961), p. 243.

> Those who study philosophy should, then, take care. . . . If you think that the world is eternal, you will try to prove it. Actually you are not a believer. Listen to Scripture: "when a man opens a pit without covering it, and an ox or an ass falls into it, he will have to make restitution." Do you think the Holy Spirit is merely talking about a material pit? Certainly not; He is talking mainly about the pit of error. The pit is opened when you, by your rational arguments, make some error appear believable.[28]

We do not know whom Bonaventure had in mind in saying these words but we do know that he was critical of several Thomistic notions during these years.

Actually, Thomas Aquinas was not the first critic of the teachers of Peripatetic philosophy at the University of Paris. Bonaventure had begun his more sweeping opposition by the year 1267. He continued to criticize this "rationalism" until well into 1273.[29] And it was not simply Siger and his arts colleagues that Bonaventure was worried about. He considered Thomas Aquinas to be the source of dangerous teachings. Thus the sophisticated Thomistic position that the eternity of the world cannot be refuted by purely philosophical reasoning was precisely the sort of thing that Bonaventure distrusted.[30] A second teaching of Aquinas, the real distinction between the human soul and its operative potencies, was openly attacked by the Franciscan Master General.[31] There were other points of disagreement: Bonaventure insisted on the activity of human will much more than did Thomas; and certainly Bonaventure felt that there must be more than one substantial form in each human being, while Thomas opposed any plurality of such forms in one substantial being.

This brings us to the second area of doctrinal attack which Aquinas met in his second Paris professorate. More and more he became an object of suspicion to the more traditional theologians in the Orders, both Dominican and Franciscan, and to the diocesan authorities. This carried Thomas into further controversy in the early 1270's.

There is little doubt, for instance, that Thomas Aquinas was vigorously criticized at a disputation in the University of Paris by the Franciscan Regent Master, John Peckham. Neither the exact date, nor the content of the discussion, nor the outcome, is entirely clear from the scanty records

---

[28] This portion of Bonaventure's sermon is printed in French, by Bougerol, *op. cit.*, p. 210.

[29] Bonaventurae, *Collationes in Hexaemeron,* (a set of university sermons, dated April 9 to May 28, 1273, by Bougerol, *op. cit.*, p. 245).

[30] *Collationes,* 4, n. 13; ed. Quaracchi, V, 262.

[31] *Collationes,* 2, n. 26; ed. Quaracchi, V, 220. Cf. Bougerol, *op. cit.*, p. 186.

that are now available. The dispute occurred at some time during the years 1270 to 1272. William of Tocco gives a somewhat confused account of the incident.[32] He reports that a certain "religious" was being examined for the magistrate at Paris and that this candidate defended an opinion contrary to the truth, as Brother Thomas had determined it in his classes. In his humility, continues Tocco, Thomas refrained from correcting the student and quietly returned to his monastery.

> However, his students and secretary could not bear this injustice to their Master, so they said: "Master, we have suffered a serious personal attack, for this scholar should not have spoken against your view and you should not have had to put up with this injury to the truth before all the Parisian masters."
>
> The undisturbed Master answered them, more in his thoughts than in words, "Sons, it seemed to me that the new master should be spared at his inaugural lecture, lest he be embarrassed before all the teachers. I have no doubts about my own teaching, as a result of contradiction by any teacher, for I have established it with God's help on the standard texts of the Fathers and on reasons of truth. However, if the Brothers think otherwise, I shall be able to take care of my omission tomorrow."
>
> On the following day, when Brother Thomas gathered with the students in the Bishop's hall and the same questions and answers were repeated by the candidate without any correction, Brother Thomas said in all moderation, "Master, this opinion of yours, save the truth, cannot be held. It is against a certain Council. So, you ought to speak differently, if you wish to avoid disagreement with a Council."
>
> Then the candidate did begin to make a different statement but he did not change his opinion on the judgment. Again taking up the argument against him and citing the Council, Thomas compelled him to confess his error and humbly to ask the aforesaid Doctor (Thomas) to explain the truth more fully. Then Thomas said, "Now you are talking properly," and he taught him what should be held as the truth.

Some scholars think that this religious candidate was the Franciscan, John Peckham.[33] However, this identification is not established clearly.[34] Certainly there were features to the encounter that escaped William of Tocco. Bartholomew of Capua may be referring to the same incident in the following testimony at the canonization proceedings:

> The same witness [Bartholomew] said that he had heard from many Friars Preachers, worthy of belief, that when Brother Thomas was on one

[32] Tocco, *Vita,* c. 26 (*Fontes,* II, 99).

[33] D. Prümmer, O.P., editor of Tocco, *Vita,* says in a footnote (*Fontes,* II, 99, note 1): "Iste Religiosus videtur esse Johannes Peckham."

[34] P. Glorieux, *Répertoire des Maîtres en théologie à Paris,* III, 87, indicates that Peckham held the Franciscan chair of theology at Paris from 1269 to 1271 but does not say when he took the magistrate.

occasion carrying on a disputation at Paris, where Brother John Peckham, O.F.M., who later became Archbishop of Canterbury, was present, although this Brother John had irritated Brother Thomas with bombastic and pompous language yet Brother Thomas never lost control of his own humble speech and continued to answer gently and humanely. Brother Thomas similarly conducted himself in every disputation, no matter how sharp or artful.[35]

From Franciscan records, one gets a different notion of the encounter. Writing about 1282, Roger Marston, O.F.M., describes what seems to be the same event mentioned by Tocco and supplies a new identity for the actual candidate.

> I was in Paris and I heard it with my own bodily ears, at the inception of the Precentor of Péronne before Master Gerard of Abbeville, in the presence of Brother Thomas of Aquino, Brother John Peckham, and about twenty-four other doctors in sacred theology, when this opinion was solemnly excommunicated as contrary to the teaching of the Saints, particularly of Augustine and Anselm, as was made manifest by the opposition.[36]

A marginal note in one of the manuscripts of Roger's work adds that the censured teaching was Thomas' teaching in his *Commentary on the Sentences,*[37] that the divine Word is expressed in an essential manner (*essentialiter*). This would imply that the disagreement between Thomas and John Peckham was concerned with a theological question. Moreover, the suggestion is that Aquinas' personal view was condemned by his colleagues in the faculty of theology at Paris!

Several remarks by John Peckham himself serve to reinforce this interpretation. John remembers the incident as an occasion when he had to help Thomas Aquinas in trouble, before a group of Parisian masters of theology! But Peckham claims that the argument hinged on the quite different problem of the number of substantial forms in one substance! In one letter,[38] dated January 1, 1285, Archbishop Peckham complains of the philosophical errors that are still being taught at Oxford University. He singles out as most pernicious "that only one form is present in man." Then Peckham adds:

> Indeed, this was the opinion of Brother Thomas of Aquino, of holy memory; however, on these and other similar matters he humbly declared

[35] *Proc. Can. Neap.*, LXXVII (*Fontes,* IV, 374).

[36] *Doc.* XLIV (*Fontes,* VI, 625) citing Marston's *Quaestiones Disputatae,* ed. Quaracchi, 1932, pp. 116–117.

[37] *In I Sent.,* d. 27, q. 1, a. 1; for the marginal note, see *Fontes,* VI, 625–626.

[38] *Fontes,* VI, 637.

> his innocence at Paris, in the assembly of the masters of theology, submitting all his views of this kind to the judgment and correction of the Parisian masters. Of this, We are witness to its accuracy by Our own ears.[39]

In the same year, writing to Bishop Oliver Sutton,[40] Peckham asserts that he is still being accused of attacking the dead Thomas Aquinas, concerning his mistaken opinion on substantial forms, when it is really Thomas' obstinate followers that he is correcting. Peckham again reverts to the Paris incident:

> It is said that We continue to persecute this opinion on the unity of forms, by arguments and the testimony of the Saints, against the dead. [Aquinas has been dead for more than ten years.] This is false. On the contrary, he of whom we speak was wisely censured for this opinion by the Bishop of Paris, and by the masters of theology, and even by his own Brothers. We alone stood by him, defending him as well as we could without offending the truth, until as a humble teacher he was able to submit all his views that demanded correction to the judgment of the Parisian masters.[41]

We shall see in our final chapter that Archbishop Peckham used his episcopal powers to the full, in order to censure and stop the teaching of Aquinas' philosophical views. It is quite unlikely that Peckham "stood by" Thomas Aquinas, as he blandly asserts, at Paris. Indeed, with all due consideration for faulty memories and the complexity of the incident, one wonders about the veracity of the various reports on this encounter. It is possible that Peckham and Thomas disagreed at more than one disputation in Paris.

In any event, John Peckham was not alone in his opposition to Thomism. In the letter just cited, there is a remark about the condemnation by the Bishop of Paris of Thomas' view on the question of plural substantial forms. That there was such a condemnation is true. On December 10, 1270, Bishop Etienne Tempier issued a list of thirteen theses, all of which he forbade to be taught in his diocese which, of course, included the University of Paris. The condemnation was mainly directed against Siger and his philosophical associates. Included under the episcopal censure were views such as the unity of the intellectual soul for all men, the eternity of the created world, and the passivity of the human will.

Earlier in 1270, a Paris Dominican (probably Giles of Lessines) had

---

[39] *Ibid.*, 637–638.

[40] *Ibid.*, 643.

[41] This long letter to Oliver Sutton (*Fontes*, VI, 639–646) deals with the friction between the Franciscan and Dominican Orders on questions of philosophy.

sent a letter to Albert the Great, warning him that fifteen theses in philosophy were about to be condemned by the Bishop of Paris. Albert was still a vigorous defender of the study of philosophy. His reply has been discovered and edited.[42] From it we learn that the fourteenth and fifteenth suspected theses involved Aquinas' teaching on the unity of the substantial form and the simplicity of angelic being.[43] What other steps Albert took in the matter, we do not know, but these last two theses were not condemned by Tempier in 1270. Obviously, these views of Thomas came close to being censured at that time.[44]

There is no question, however, that some of the philosophical teachings of Aquinas were already under attack from other sources than Bonaventure and John Peckham. Giles of Rome was probably a student under Thomas during the early years of the second Paris professorate but Giles bluntly branded as an error the notion that there is but one substantial form in one body.[45] Though Giles of Rome (not to be confused with Giles of Lessines) accepted some of the teachings of Aquinas, he was far from being the simple "Thomist" that some of the older histories of philosophy call him. As another example of such opposition, we have the British Dominican, Robert Kilwardby. He fully agreed with John Peckham that Thomas was in error. As successor to Peckham in the See of Canterbury, Kilwardby forbade anyone at Oxford to teach the Thomistic doctrine on substantial forms.[46] We shall see more about this in our last chapter.

In response to some of this criticism, Thomas wrote (1270–1271) one of his most controversial works, *On the Eternity of the World, Against the Complainers.*[47] This was a reply to contemporary theologians who felt that

---

[42] Mandonnet, *Siger de Brabant,* II, 29–52.

[43] Cf. Mandonnet, *Siger de Brabant,* I, 105–107, for a discussion of these fifteen theses in reference to Thomas Aquinas. Fabro, "Tommaso d'Aquino," *Enc. Catt.,* XII (1954), col. 282, says: "gli ultimi due proposti per la condanna ma non condonnati, riguardavano le dottrine tomiste dell'unita della forma nei corpori e della semplicità degli angeli." See also: F. Van Steenberghen, "Le 'De quindecim problematibus' d'Albert le Grand," in *Mélanges A. Pelzer* (Louvain: Nauwelaerts, 1947), pp. 415–439, where Albert's little treatise is dated 1273–1276.

[44] Glorieux, *Répertoire des Maîtres,* III, 293.

[45] Giles of Rome, *Errores Philosophorum,* ed. J. Koch, trans. J. O. Riedl (Milwaukee: Marquette U. Press), c. 1, n. 11, p. 8: "quod sit in composito una forma tantum, falsum est."

[46] For the text of the "errors" condemned in 1277 by Kilwardby, see *Fontes,* VI, 615–617; note especially item 26, on p. 616.

[47] *De aeternitate mundi contra murmurantes,* see note 8, *supra;* practically the same text is in ed. Parm., XVI, 318–320.

Aquinas' views on the subject were heretical. We have seen that Bonaventure was a central figure among these critics.[48] As a matter of historical fact, Bonaventure had forcefully argued in his lectures on the *Sentences* (about 1250) that the notion of an everlasting but created world is opposed both to truth and reason. It was of this view that Bonaventure punned: "This error has both a bad beginning and a worse end!"[49] Into the 1270's Bonaventure continued to attack this notion as a dangerous error.

With this background in mind, we are better able to appreciate the significance of the opening lines of Aquinas' brief work, *On the Eternity of the World.*

> Taking it on the basis of the Catholic faith that the world has not existed (as some mistaken philosophers have claimed) from eternity but that the world (as Sacred Scripture testifies) had a beginning for its duration, the problem arises: whether it could have existed always. In order to explain the truth of this problem, we must first distinguish the point on which we agree with those who take a contrary position, from the point on which we differ from them.
>
> If the statement, that something apart from God could have existed always, be understood to mean that there could be something apart from Him, as not made by Him — then this is an abominable error, not only on the basis of faith but also among the philosophers, who assert and prove that everything that exists in any way whatever could not exist unless caused by Him Who has existence (*esse*) in the greatest and truest manner. However, if it be taken to mean that something always existed yet was caused by God according to the entirety of what is in it, then we should examine whether this could stand.
>
> Now, if this were called impossible, such a statement would be made, either because God was not able to make something that existed forever, or because such a thing could not be made even if God were able to make it. Concerning the first alternative, all are agreed, namely, on the point that God could have made something that always existed, keeping in mind His infinite power. So, the question remains for us to examine: whether it is possible for something that has always existed to be made.[50]

It is advisable to note carefully what Thomas is saying here. He believes

---

[48] See above, notes 29 and 30; cf. Chenu, *Introduction,* p. 289, note 3, where Bonaventure is identified as an adversary.

[49] S. Bonaventurae, *In II Sent.*, I, 1, 1, 2 (ed. minor, Quaracchi, 1938, II, 12–16): "Unde iste error et malum habet initium et pessimum habet finem." This is the closing sentence of Bonaventure's *Responsio.* In his reply to the sixth objection (p. 17), Bonaventure mentions that the "Philosophers" think that God in creating must have moved from idleness to activity — and he comments: "So it appears that their argument is stupid."

[50] S. Thomae, *De aeternitate mundi, init.* (ed. Parm., XVI, 318a).

that the world is not eternal; this is from faith. Having stated this, he asks: Could God have created it so that it would have been eternal? To this hypothetical question, Thomas answers affirmatively. As he further explains the problem: "The whole question consists in this: whether an actual being created by God in its whole substance — and the fact that it does not have a beginning of its duration — are mutually incompatible, or not."[51] Thomas proceeds to argue that it was quite possible for God to have made an eternal world, since a cause which produces its effect without motion does not have to precede this effect in duration. Why some people do not see this is explained, with gentle irony, by Thomas.

> Since men are accustomed to think about acts of production of the type that involve physical change, they do not readily grasp the fact that an agent cause need not precede its effect in duration. As a result, inexperienced men who reflect on few matters may easily express their views on many things.[52]

He then shows that there is nothing intellectually repugnant in a created universe that has always existed. His argument embodies several quotations from the *Sancti,* that is, from writers in the early theological tradition of the Church: St. Augustine, Boethius, and St. Anselm. The portion of his argument which examines the character of created being, as contrasted with that of the Creator, is a most important statement of Aquinas' metaphysics. Thomas indicates that, while creatures are indeed different because *de facto* they exist in time, the more profound nature of creatureliness is found in the fact that every created being gets its act of existing from another Being.[53] Even if there were an everlasting creature, it would be utterly different, metaphysically, from God.

In a sense, St. Thomas is saying that Siger of Brabant was not wholly wrong.[54] There are some things that must be accepted as true, on the basis of belief alone; not all truth is open to rational demonstration. However, Thomas' argument in this treatise, *On the Eternity of the World,* is not based on Aristotle (who is only once mentioned and never cited) but on the reasoning of Christian theology. But it is a speculative theology.

[51] *Ibid.,* "In hoc ergo tota consistit quaestio, utrum esse creatum a Deo secundum totam substantiam, et non habere durationis principium, repugnent ad invicem, vel non."

[52] *Ibid.,* 319a.

[53] *Ibid.,* 319b: "Esse autem non habet creatura nisi ab alio; sibi autem relicta, in se considerata, nihil est." Compare Chenu's comment, *Introduction,* p. 289.

[54] See W. J. Dwyer (ed.), *L'Opuscule de Siger de Brabant "De aeternitate mundi"* (Louvain: Institut Supérieur, 1937), pp. 41–45.

Thomas is doing a very dangerous thing in this work: he is trying to take a position somewhere between that of the Latin Averroists and the contrary view of the ultra-orthodox theologians. It is the latter group from whom he has most to fear, for they are ready at this time to condemn as heretical certain positions in philosophy and theology which they do not understand. Oddly, it is these theologians who are maintaining that philosophy can do more than Aquinas thinks it can.

Toward the end of his *De aeternitate mundi,* Thomas remarks that a person who carefully considers the view that the world could have been created from eternity should be able to see that there is no incompatibility, from the intellectual point of view, between creation and eternal duration. He claims that St. Augustine never asserted any such contradiction, though he, like Aquinas, fully believed that the world is not eternal. Thomas adds bitterly: "Yet those who do so subtly see such incompatibility are only men — but they act as though wisdom originated with them."[55] This is the most biting remark that Thomas ever wrote. It made enemies for his doctrine.

Ironically, Thomas found himself on the side of Bonaventure and John Peckham in the third area of controversy that engulfed him in the 1270's. If his adversaries in the first polemic were some radical Aristotelian philosophers, and in the second some ultra-conservative theologians, then on a third front he faced attack from a few diocesan priests who still resented the presence and activities of the religious Orders at the University of Paris.

Earlier we have seen how William of St. Amour disturbed Aquinas' first years at Paris with his jealous attacks on the university teachers who belonged to the religious Orders. William was exiled from France in 1257 and died in 1272[56] but his bitter spirit lived on at Paris. In 1269, on his return to Paris, Thomas learned that other secular priests in the theology faculty were continuing the polemic against the mendicants. A treatise called *Collations of Catholic and Canonical Scripture* was circulating, from 1267 onward. It was not the innocent tract that the title would suggest. Indeed this booklet was little more than a rewrite of William of St. Amour's

---

[55] S. Thomae, *De aeternitate mundi,* p. 320a: "Ergo illi qui tam subtiliter eam (repugnantiam) percipiunt soli sunt homines, et cum eis oritur sapientia." Eschmann ("Catalogue," p. 410) translates more freely: "they speak as though they alone were rational beings and wisdom had originated in their own brains."

[56] Cf. Van Steenberghen, *Le Mouvement,* p. 290.

condemned treatise, *On the Perils of Recent Times*.[57] The Franciscans were specifically attacked (in the person of one of their most moderate theologians, Thomas of York) by a pamphlet entitled: *Against an Adversary of Christian Perfection, the Greatest Enemy of Prelates and of the Ecclesiastical Faculty*. To this vicious work, St. Bonaventure had written, apparently in 1269, a reply: *A Defense of the Poor against Their Calumniator*. Now Thomas entered the fray, at the start of 1270, with his essay, *On the Perfection of the Spiritual Life*.[58] In this fight, at least, he was happy to be on the side of the Franciscans.

The new leader of the attack on the mendicants was Gerald (or Gerard) of Abbeville, a member of the theological faculty at Paris. He was the author of the anti-Franciscan treatise, *Against an Adversary of Christian Perfection,* though the work circulated anonymously for obvious reasons. Gerald was no callow youth; he had been teaching at Paris since 1257 and, though he had produced a *Commentary on the Sentences,* nineteen *Quodlibets,* and several *Disputed Questions,* and was not an ignorant man, he was evidently a soured and disgruntled person.[59] Like his teacher, William of St. Amour, Gerald felt that the Dominicans and Franciscans were evil influences on the whole life of the Catholic Church.

Thomas started to write *On the Perfection of the Spiritual Life* almost as soon as he reached Paris in 1269. In its first twenty chapters, he calmly and patiently describes the life of a member of a religious Order; the reason for taking vows of poverty, chastity, and obedience; the notion of the state of religious perfection; and the relation of a vowed religious to the episcopacy. He concludes Chapter Twenty with the serene statement that a secular priest is not *ex officio,* as it were, in the state of religious perfection but, when he is promoted to the episcopacy, he does assume this higher status. To some readers in the diocesan clergy, this was like waving a red flag before a bull. They took this to mean that only bishops, among the secular clergy, were on a par with the members of religious Orders.

[57] Eschmann, "Catalogue," p. 408, has an informative note on the relation between the *Collationes catholicae et canonicae Scripturae* and St. Thomas' work.

[58] *De perfectione vitae spiritualis,* ed. Parm., XV, 76–102; *Opuscula Theol.* (Turin: Marietti, 1954), II, 111. English translation in three master's theses, by G. J. Guenther, C. G. Kloster, and J. X. Schmitt (St. Louis University, 1942–1944). Cf. P. Glorieux, "Pour qu'on lise le 'De perfectione vitae spiritualis,'" *La vie spirituelle,* XXIII (1930), Suppl. 97–126.

[59] Glorieux, *Répertoire des Maîtres,* I, n. 174; Van Steenberghen, *Le Mouvement,* p. 290.

Evidently Gerald of Abbeville secured a copy of these first chapters; for, in a *Quodlibetal Question* of December, 1269, he attacked Thomas' views as expressed in Chapter Twenty. This is clear from the opening lines of Aquinas' next chapter.

> Some people who are aroused by the desire for controversy and who fail to give enough thought to what they say and what they hear are still trying to set themselves up in opposition to what is true. Their arguments have reached me, after I had written the foregoing. To refute them, it is necessary to return to the discussion of some of the points made above. First of all, they try in many ways to show that archdeacons and parish priests are in the state of perfection, and greater than the religious.[60]

Thomas now proceeds in great detail to review the arguments of the "Geraldinists" and what he considers to be the facts of the case. In effect, Gerald had argued from many texts in canon law that diocesan priests are in the state of religious perfection. Aquinas replies that such arguments are "frivolous, laughable and on many points erroneous."[61] Wherever the canons are interpreted by his opponents as speaking of the higher *status* of the secular clergy, Thomas shows that ecclesiastical law is actually speaking of something quite different, namely, *gradus*. The various levels, or degrees, of holy orders in the Church have little or nothing to do, as Thomas sees it, with personal perfection.

One of Gerald's associates in opposing the religious Orders was Nicholas of Lisieux.[62] He wrote one treatise *On the Perfection and Excellence of the Status of Clerics,* and another *Against Peckham and Thomas.* John Peckham had also defended the mendicants in some of his *Disputed Questions* and was considered a fair target by Nicholas.[63] Seeing that the debate was still continuing, Thomas Aquinas set to work and produced another treatise which reveals another facet of the attack. The title is almost long enough to tell the story: *Against the Pestiferous Teaching of Those Who Would Keep Boys from Entering the Religious Life.*[64] This work is

---

60 *De perf. vitae spirit.*, c. 21; ed. Parm., XV, 95.

61 *Op. cit.*, c. 23, *init.;* ed. Parm., XV, 97.

62 P. Glorieux, *Répertoire des Maîtres,* I, n. 172.

63 In January, 1270, Peckham discussed the admission of boys to the religious life (ed. L. Oliger in *Archivum Franciscanum Historicum,* VIII [1915], 414–439) and later in the year he disputed on the state of evangelical poverty (ed. Oliger in *Franziskanische Studien,* IV [1917], 127–176). Cf. Glorieux, *Répertoire des Maîtres,* n. 316, pp. 90–91.

64 *Contra pestiferam doctrinam retrahentium pueros a religionis ingressu,* ed. Parm., XV, 103–125; *Opus. Theol.* (Turin: Marietti, 1954), II, 159. English: J. Procter, *An Apology for the Religious Orders* (Westminster, Md.: Newman, 1950).

usually dated 1270; it would appear to have been written at the end of the year, if not later. What Thomas faced in this polemic may be gathered from a passage in his first chapter. After referring to the ancient heresies of Jovinianus (setting matrimony above virginity) and of Vigilantius (putting riches above poverty), Thomas continues.

> There have again risen up in Gaul new followers of Vigilantius who would restrain men, in manifold and astute ways, from the observance of the counsels. For they first propose that no people should take on the observance of the counsels by entering the religious life, unless they have first become practiced in the observance of the commandments. By their statement, not only children and sinners but also new converts to the faith would be precluded from embracing the way of perfection. Then too, they add that no one should assume the way of the counsels, unless he has first been judged worthy by the advice of many people. This requirement puts such an impediment before men's assumption of the life of perfection that no one of sound mind could fail to observe it. For the advice of carnal-minded men, who are in the majority, more readily restrains people from spiritual endeavors than encourages them. Moreover, they strive to hinder the obligation [by vows] of men at their entrance into religious life, whereby the mind is strengthened to take up the way of perfection. Finally, they shamelessly attack in many ways the perfection of poverty.[65]

Again in this treatise Thomas patiently discusses the charges made against his own mode of life. Texts from Scripture, passages from the Greek and Latin Fathers, and arguments from common sense, are mustered to show that people must be trained while young to practice religious perfection, just as soldiers or weavers must learn their arts before maturity. He also argues that converts and sinners may well be admitted to religious Orders, even if they have not proved their holiness before taking such a step.[66] Candidates for the religious life should not be forced into this status, Thomas insists, but should freely will to embrace the way of perfection. The charge that men should not be bound by vows is next examined and refuted. Thomas explains the various types of vows and the canonical regulations governing the minimum ages at which such solemn promises may be taken.[67] Finally, he considers the notion that poverty is not advisable for those living in a religious community but that common possessions are necessary. Thomas does not claim that mendicancy is essential for the religious life. He often refers to the Benedictine Rule (which permits common possessions) as an excellent thing. However, he argues that what

---

[65] *Contra pestiferam doctrinam*, c. 1; ed. Parm., XV, 103b.

[66] *Ibid.*, cc. 3–5.

[67] *Ibid.*, cc. 11–13.

is required is that one give up personal control and interest in wealth in order to advance in religious perfection.[68] He makes it perfectly clear that "holy poverty" does not mean that one should try to live without the bare necessities of life. The point is that, however a religious may obtain these necessities (by begging, by working for them, or by some other means), they are not to be taken as his own property but simply as things to be used humbly for his needs.

Here again Thomas closes with a challenge. There is no doubt that he is ready to continue the controversy if necessary.

> These, then, are the points that come to mind to be written against the erroneous and pestiferous teaching of those who are turning men away from entrance into the religious life. If anyone desires to contradict them, let him not gossip before boys but write something and present his writing in public, so that it may be judged by intelligent people as to what is true, and so that what is erroneous may be refuted by the authority of the truth.[69]

Aquinas also mentions these attacks on the religious Orders in his *Quodlibets* and *Sermons* from this Paris period.[70] But the men who criticized the Orders were not open to conviction by reasonable arguments. Fortunately, most of them died within a few years and much of their venom died with them.

Of course, Thomas Aquinas' regular work during the years 1269 to 1272 was teaching theology. It is difficult to determine the precise nature of his courses. The biographical sources are of little help, but some evidence of his classroom activities may be gleaned from the works of this period. Among the Scripture commentaries, one major example is the *Exposition of the Gospel of St. John.*[71] This we have in the form of a *reportatio,* made by Reginald of Piperno, which indicates that it was delivered as class lectures. As already noted, Adenolf of Anagni paid the cost of having this work copied at Paris in the 1269–1272 period. It is entered on the stationer's list as a university text.[72] Always regarded as one of Aquinas' best biblical commentaries, this exposition is the product of a mature scholar. Possibly Thomas also lectured on the Gospel of St. Matthew during these years. The *Exposition of St. Matthew* that is printed

[68] *Ibid.,* cc. 14–16.
[69] *Ibid.,* c. 16, *ad fin.;* ed. Parm., XV, 125.
[70] See *Quaest. Quodl.,* IV, qq. 23–24; for two *Sermons* related to this question (probably preached in December, 1270) see Eschmann, "Catalogue," p. 428, n. 89.
[71] *Expositio in Evangelium Joannis* (Turin: Marietti, 1952); cf. Eschmann, "Catalogue," p. 398, n. 25.
[72] See *C.U.P.,* I, 646.

among the works of Aquinas is usually attributed to his first Paris period.[73] There are references in it to France, Picardy, and Burgundy, and later on Paris is mentioned, but there are several citations of Aristotle's *Politics* which suggest a date later than 1256–1259.[74] This commentary is also a *reportatio;* its text is defective and not representative of St. Thomas at his best.

Much of Thomas' time must have been devoted to theological disputations. Of the ordinary or disputed questions, the lengthy and important *Questions on Evil* were, at least in part, works of the second Paris period. The same is true of the *Questions on the Virtues.*[75] These are very detailed considerations of the foundations of moral theology and represent a great deal of scholarly study by Aquinas. It was at this time that he was writing most of the treatises on morality in the *Summa of Theology,* for he finished the *Prima Secundae* and the *Secunda Secundae* between 1269 and 1272. These do not represent class lectures however.[76] We shall examine this *Summa* in Chapter Sixteen.

Another type of academic exercise that now occupied his time was the *Quodlibets.* In each of these years at Paris, during the Christmas and Easter seasons, Thomas engaged in these theological free-for-alls. Some of the *Quodlibets* reflect the current controversies. The printed editions of the *Quaestiones Quodlibetales*[77] contain twelve series. The dating of these is much debated but there is now rather general agreement that Quodlibets I to VI, and possibly XII, were conducted at Paris from 1269 to 1272.[78]

It does not seem likely that the many commentaries on the works of Aristotle, assigned by modern textual scholars to this period in Paris, can all represent class lectures. The explanations do suggest the classroom but probably St. Thomas was able to write in this style, even if he did not present the material orally. How a professor of theology at the University

---

[73] *Walz-Novarina (1962),* p. 221, following Mandonnet, *Des écrits authentiques de s. Thomas* (Fribourg, 1910), p. 31.

[74] For the details, see Eschmann, "Catalogue," pp. 397–398, n. 24.

[75] *Walz-Novarina (1962),* p. 223; Eschmann, "Catalogue," p. 391 (with the qualification that *De Malo,* qq. 1–5, and possibly qq. 7–15, may have been disputed earlier in Italy); cf. Grabmann, *Die Werke,* p. 306.

[76] Eschmann, "Catalogue," pp. 386–388.

[77] In ed. Parm., Vol. IX; Paris; Vivès, Vol. XV; separately printed, Paris: Lethielleux, 1926; Turin: Marietti, 1949.

[78] *Walz-Novarina (1962),* p. 223; Eschmann, "Catalogue," pp. 392–393 (with the studies of Glorieux and F. Pelster, therein cited); Grabmann, *Die Werke,* pp. 309–313.

of Paris might conduct long courses on Aristotle's philosophy is hard to imagine. In some way, he produced these detailed explanations of the *Physics, Nicomachean Ethics, On Interpretation, Posterior Analytics, Politics* (two books), and *On the Heavens and Earth* (in part). Even with secretarial assistance, the final writing of these Aristotelian studies during these three busy years at Paris is an amazing accomplishment.[79] We have already suggested that, as far as the Aristotelian commentaries are concerned, Aquinas had already done much of the detailed explanation of these in the Papal States and he supervised the editing and revision of these expositions in Paris. This is not to deny that Thomas still continued to read and study and write about philosophy, all through these later years.

The University of Paris provided Thomas Aquinas with the intellectual stimulation and opportunity to write some of his greatest works. In spite of the difficulties and criticisms encountered there, he was able to leave Paris in the spring of 1272 with the feeling that his time had not been wasted on the Rue Saint-Jacques. He was very much the university professor.

[79] *Walz-Novarina (1962)*, p. 222; Eschmann, "Catalogue," pp. 401–405.

CHAPTER FIFTEEN

Regent of Studies in Naples

A CURIOUS request came to the Dominican administration at the time of St. Thomas' appointment to take charge of the theological studies in Naples. By letter, the arts faculty at the University of Paris asked the General Chapter at Florence to send Thomas back to Paris. We have no actual copy of this petition but it is clearly mentioned in a later document from the arts teachers.[1] This request was not granted, of course, and Thomas and Reginald were soon walking south toward Naples. This was in the early summer, 1272.

One stop that they made was at the residence of Richard Cardinal Hannibaldi, near Rome. Here at Molaria they were informed that the Cardinal had died just a few weeks earlier (June 1, 1272). However, the travelers were welcomed at the estate and stayed there for some time. Bartholomew of Lucca and William of Tocco are our sources for what happened at this time. Both Thomas Aquinas and Reginald became ill at Molaria.[2] Reginald ran a continuous fever and seems to have been quite sick. Thomas took some relics of St. Agnes which he wore about his neck and placed them on Reginald's chest. His prayers for his companion's recovery were answered, for Reginald was immediately cured. It was as a consequence of this cure that Thomas resolved to celebrate the feast of St. Agnes very solemnly in each subsequent year.

Thomas and Reginald were much delayed on their journey to Naples. Apparently they also stopped at Rome and possibly at Montecassino to

[1] "Eum quem a vestro collegio in generali capitulo vestro Florentie celebrato, licet requisissemus instanter, proh dolor, non potuimus obtinere . . ." *Doc.* XXXI (*Fontes,* VI, 585).

[2] *Hist. Eccles.,* XXIII, 10; cf. Tocco, *Proc. Can. Neap.,* LX (*Fontes,* IV, 348).

see their friend, Abbot Bernard Ayglerio. On August 26, 1272, Roger of Aquila died. He was the Count of Traetto, husband of Aquinas' sister Adelasia.[3] It seems that Thomas was the only surviving male relative, for he was designated executor of the estate. This is recorded in a document from the court of King Charles of Anjou.

> For Brother Thomasius [sic] de Aquino:
> Written to the Administrator of Crown Goods of the Terra di Lavoro. . . . Since the venerable and religious man, Brother Thomas de Aquino of the Order of Preachers, stands as executor of the will of the former Roger of Aquila, we desire by prescription of your trust, having seen the will of the said Roger, in order that his will and disposition be fully carried out by the aforementioned Brother Thomasius as executor of the aforesaid will without any hindrance, we order that you secure an inventory with suitable proof of what you will receive from him and what you will give to him, observing our rights forever.
> Given at Mons Fortis, X September, in the first indiction.[4]

It was in the month of September, 1272, that Thomas arrived in Naples and took up his duties as regent of the theology course for the University of Naples. Doubtless King Charles was delighted to have such a famous teacher in the royal institution. Thomas taught at the San Domenico convent but his students now included many clerics who were not of the Order of Preachers. The *studium generale* was considered a part of the now revitalized university. In fact, Aquinas was now paid an annual salary of twelve ounces of gold from the royal treasury. This arrangement is recorded in a royal document dated October 15, 1272.

> For Brother Thomasius de Aquino:
> This is also written to the same [Administrator of the Crown Goods of the Terra de Lavoro]. Since the religious man, our beloved Thomas de Aquino, must lecture in theology at Naples, desiring to provide him with a financial stipend, we order that he be paid for this one ounce of gold of the usual weight for each month, as long as he lectures here. We order by prescription of your trust, under a penalty of twice the amount, that henceforth you arrange in each month that the aforesaid ounce of gold of the usual weight be turned over at request to the Prior of the Brothers of the same Order in Naples, as long as Brother Thomas lectures. . . .
> Given at Naples by the same [Simon de Paris, Chancellor of the Kingdom of Sicily] in the month of October XV, of the same indiction.[5]

Evidently Thomas carried out his duties as executor of his brother-in-

[3] See *Fontes,* VI, 575, note 2, citing Scandone, *Documenti sulla famiglia e sulla patria di San Tommaso d'Aquino* (Naples, 1901), p. 17, for the date of Roger's death.

[4] *Fontes,* VI, 575.

[5] *Ibid.,* 579–580.

law's estate to the satisfaction of the royal officials. He is mentioned in terms of respect and affection in several records. We have one document which inventories Roger's possessions in the castle of Traetto and its environs.[6] It lists various farm animals (with special markings or brands), clothing of different kinds, pieces of furniture, some silver cloth, and a quantity of grain. Probably these administrative details were handled by legal representatives and Thomas was only required to sign the accounts. In another legal order, Thomas was instructed to make restitution out of the proceeds of the mills at Scauri for certain lands which Roger had unjustly appropriated.[7] Even the Aquino in-laws seem to have maintained the family reputation for sharp business practice. In the year 1236, Phillip of Aquino had been reproved for trying to take away a mill from the monastery of Montecassino![8] It would be interesting to know Thomas' reactions to such chicanery but he is, as usual, completely silent about personal and family matters. At the end of September, 1272, Thomas requested the royal procurator to put the young son of Roger of Aquila under the guardianship of the Count of San Severino, another brother-in-law. This request was granted, and Thomas' career in the probate courts was brought to a successful termination.[9]

When he arrived in Naples, Aquinas was welcomed to the monastery of St. Dominic by several old friends. Bartholomew of Capua was there; or he may have accompanied Thomas on part of the trip to Naples.[10] In his canonization testimony,[11] Bartholomew mentions several other Dominicans who greeted Brother Thomas. Brother John of Caiatia had been a student under Aquinas in Paris. Eufranon da Porta had met Aquinas at various chapters and had served with him on several commissions. But doubtless the man who was happiest to see Thomas was the now elderly Brother John of San Giuliano; he had been present, almost thirty years earlier, at Thomas' reception as a novice.[12] Of course, William of Tocco

[6] *Doc.* XXVI (*Fontes,* VI, 576–578).

[7] *Ibid.,* XXVII (*Fontes,* VI, 578–579).

[8] *Ibid.,* VI (*Fontes,* VI, 538).

[9] Scandone, *La vita, la famiglia,* p. 67; cf. *Walz-Novarina* (*1962*), pp. 187–188.

[10] *Hist. Eccles.,* XXIII, 8.

[11] *Proc. Can. Neap.,* LXXVI (*Fontes,* IV, 370–371).

[12] *Ibid.:* "et frater Johannes de sancto Juliano, antiquus frater valde, homo magne vite et humilitatis, qui dicebatur notorie dictum fratrem Thomam de Aquino recepisse in ordine Praedicatorum."

was in Naples and attended the lectures in theology. He eventually devoted much time to the cause of canonization and gathered information about Aquinas' life.[13]

The Dominicans who lived to testify in 1319 at the Naples canonization investigation were young students when Thomas was regent of studies. We know the names: John of Caiatia, Peter of San Felice, Conrad of Suessa, Leonard of Gaieta, and John of Buiano.[14] One of these witnesses, Peter of San Felice, testified that he saw Thomas Aquinas frequently and described him as, "tall, a large man, balding on the forehead."[15]

Many non-Dominican clerics attended Aquinas' theology lectures and his public sermons attracted large numbers of lay people. Some of the latter also lived to give evidence for the canonization. One man was a notary, John Coppa. He said that he had visited and spoken with Thomas at the monastery of St. Dominic "continuously during one year."[16] It is possible that this man attended to some of the legal details of Thomas' executorship. John Coppa testified that he had a brother, named Bonfilio, who was in the Dominican Order and they visited Thomas when he was ill in his cell at Naples. John remembered this well, for he saw a very bright star shining through the window of Thomas' cell onto the bed where the sick man rested. According to John, this visit occurred during the year in which Aquinas died, about forty-five years prior to 1319. His testimony is important: it shows that Thomas was ill in Naples before he left for the Council of Lyons in 1274.

Another lay person, Peter Branchatius, was very young when he saw Thomas at San Domenico. Peter told under oath how Reginald of Piperno (who died in 1290) used to recount the story of Aquinas' nocturnal colloquy with SS. Peter and Paul. William of Tocco's account of this incident is thus corroborated by the testimony given by Peter.[17]

What Thomas taught in his Naples lectures on theology may be gathered from the biblical commentaries which are dated in this period. He began an exposition of the Psalms and covered the first fifty-four. We

---

[13] *Proc. Can. Neap.*, LVIII–LXV (*Fontes*, IV, 345–355).

[14] For their respective testimonies: *Proc. Can. Neap.* (*Fontes*, IV, 318–319, 322–323, 326–329, 368–370, and 393–394).

[15] *Fontes*, IV, 323: "Interrogatus cuius stature fuit dictus frater Thomas dixit (Petrus de Sancta Felice) quod fuit magne stature et fuit grossus et calvus in fronte."

[16] *Proc. Can. Neap.*, LXXXVII (*Fontes*, IV, 391).

[17] *Ibid.*, XCIII (*Fontes*, IV, 399–400).

have this commentary in the form of a *reportatio* made by Reginald of Piperno.[18] It includes many personal forms of address and informal quotations of texts which savor of classroom procedure.[19] The style used in the exposition is not technical; it is a simple meditation on the meaning, literal and allegorical, of each verse. Few references are given, either to the Fathers or to philosophical writers. At one point, Thomas takes some time to offer various theories concerning earthquakes.[20] In another place, he illustrates the meaning of "rich and poor together" with the comment that some men are wealthy in fact but not so in their sense of values (*dives in actu sed non affectu*). This kind of wealthy man can be a saint, he says, as is clear in the examples of Abraham and Louis IX of France.[21] Grabmann points out that King Louis is mentioned as if he were already dead; this indicates a late date for this commentary on the Psalms.[22]

It is also possible that Thomas lectured on the Epistles of St. Paul, in Naples. Our present editions offer a corrupted text. Part of what is now printed under the name of St. Thomas is actually an extract from a work by Peter of Tarentaise.[23] Other portions of the *Exposition of St. Paul's Epistles* represent explanations composed by Thomas at different times in his teaching career. Mandonnet conjectured that Aquinas treated the Epistles first during his residence in the Papal States and a second time in Naples.[24] These points require further investigation.

Another possibility is that Thomas returned to, and completed, his *Exposition of Isaiah* while in Naples. This commentary is notoriously difficult to date: some people think that it was produced in the first Paris professorate; others put it in the second period at Paris or in the Naples regency. Actually the commentary is in two parts which are different in style. The first eleven chapters are in a style that smacks of the academic atmosphere of the University of Paris. It is probable that this first section was done in the first teaching period at Paris. Contrasting with it is the

---

[18] *In Psalmos Davidis expositio*, ed. Parm., XIV, 148–353 (prints the commentary on the first 51 Psalms); the exposition of Ps. 52–54, was edited in: A. Uccelli, *S. Thomae Aq. in Isaiam prophetam, in tres Psalmos David* (Romae, 1880), p. 243 ff.

[19] Eschmann, "Catalogue," pp. 394–395, n. 18.

[20] *In Ps.* 17, 6 (Parm., XIV, 196–197).

[21] *In Ps.* 48, 1 (Parm., XIV, 335).

[22] Grabmann, *Die Werke*, p. 254.

[23] See the details in Eschmann, "Catalogue," p. 399.

[24] P. Mandonnet, "Chronologie des écrits scripturaires de s. Thomas d'Aquin," *Revue Thomiste*, XXXIII (1928), 222–245.

second part (Chapters Twelve to Sixty-six) which is in the form of a simple gloss. This latter section may represent Naples lectures of 1272–1273.[25]

One of the main reasons for suggesting that Thomas returned to the Isaiah commentary in Naples is the fact that Jacobinus d'Asti (a scribe who worked for Aquinas in the last years at Naples) eventually transscribed the exposition there, at Naples, after the death of St. Thomas.[26] This information comes from an explicit of one of the manuscripts of the *Exposition of Isaias.*

> Thus is brought to an end the explanation and literal exposition *On Isaiah,* according to Brother Thomas of Aquino, which Jacobinus of Asti, of the Province of Lombardy, a student at that time in the Neapolitan *studium generale,* transcribed into legible writing, along with a supplement of authoritative texts. He also edited additional notes for certain passages in some of the lectures. And he did this for the benefit of the Brothers of the Order, so that they would have a fair copy of the aforementioned writings.[27]

Recently, the suggestion has been made that Jacobinus was one of the scribes who took dictation from Thomas during these years at Naples. Several writers were kept busy at this time.[28] Besides Reginald and Jacobinus, a third secretary may have been a secular priest, Evenus Garnit, of the diocese of Tréguier in Brittany. Tocco's vague reference to "his *scriptor,* a certain Breton, Evenus Garnit," gives no indication of the dates of Evenus' work.[29] He may well have been active in Naples, since many French officials and scholars came to Naples during the reign of the French King, Charles of Anjou.

There is another story in William of Tocco which suggests that Thomas was working on the Book of Isaiah during the time when Reginald was his assistant. While it is barely possible that Reginald began to work with him during the first Paris professorate, it is much more likely that this incident refers to Thomas' later years. Indeed, the references to tears and the visit of SS. Peter and Paul seem to place it in Naples.

> When he was writing on Isaiah, throwing light in his exposition and

[25] Eschmann notes the difference between the two sections, "Catalogue," pp. 395–396.

[26] See J. Destrez, *Etudes critiques sur les oeuvres,* I, 164, 202–208.

[27] The text of this explicit is in Destrez, *op. cit.,* p. 162.

[28] Dondaine, *Secrétaires,* p. 202: "nous inclinons à l'identifier [hand A in the dictated Manuscript] soit à Jacobin d'Asti soit à Réginald de Piperno, en donnant la préférence au premier, rien de plus."

[29] Tocco, *Vita,* c. 17 (*Fontes,* II, 89).

comment on the deep mysteries of the Prophet, he came to a text of this Book, on which, since he could neither understand it nor write a satisfactory explanation of the passage, prayerfully with many days of fasting and self-imposed orations he begged for divine assistance in the resolution of his difficulty. On one of these days, having devotedly observed the fast, he was heard by his *socius* as he talked at night. It was not evident with whom he was talking. The sound of the conversation could be heard but not the actual substance of his words.

When the conversation was finished, the Doctor called out to his secretary, "Brother Reginald, get up, light a candle and get the folio on which you have been writing the exposition of Isaiah. Prepare to write again."

Then he wrote for a long time the thoughts which the Doctor easily dictated, as if reading from a book. After a time, he said to the Brother *socius,* "Go, son, and rest, for there is still much time for rest."

Now the secretary was very eager to learn what wonderful secret had been revealed in his Master's colloquy which he had heard; so he threw himself tearfully at the feet of his Master and said on his knees, "I shall not rise from this position unless you tell me to whom you were speaking at such length the other night." He continued to ask, urging him in the name of the Lord God.

After several refusals, he replied, "Son, you don't need to know this." When he was more forcefully adjured, lest he seem to contemn the name of God by which his secretary dared to beg him, the Doctor broke into tears and said, "Son, you have seen during these days the affliction I have suffered as a result of my difficulty with this text, that I have now explained. This is the information which I sought from God with many tears. As a result, God had pity on me this night and sent me the blessed Apostles, Peter and Paul. I begged Him through them and they taught me everything most fully. However, in the name of God, I command you not to dare to reveal this during my lifetime."[30]

Whether Aquinas conducted disputations at Naples is not clear. Angelus Walz has suggested that the *Disputed Question on the Incarnate Word* may belong to this period.[31] Most scholars think that it was disputed at Paris. Of course, Thomas kept on writing his *Summa of Theology.* The incomplete Third Part was written in Naples. This work, however, does not stem from class lectures. Oddly, he also appears to have continued to work on the philosophy of Aristotle. At Naples, Thomas produced the lengthy exposition of the treatise *On Heaven and Earth,* made a start on the books *On Generation and Corruption,* and may even have written his partial explanation of the *Meteorology.*[32] Whether this means that

[30] *Ibid.,* c. 31 (*Fontes,* II, 105–106). For much the same story, told under oath by Tocco, *Proc. Can. Neap.,* LIX (*Fontes,* IV, 346–347).

[31] *Thomas von Aquin* (1953), p. 103; and *Zeittafel,* which dates the *De unione Verbi Incarnati* in 1272–1273.

[32] *In libros de caelo et mundo expositio; In libros de generatione et corruptione*

Aquinas actually lectured on these works of Aristotle at Naples is uncertain. Tocco said at the canonization investigation "that he saw him writing on the book, *De generatione et corruptione,* and that he [William] believed that it was his last philosophical work."[33]

There is also a sort of note, of purely philosophical significance, *On the Combining of the Elements,* which may have been written at Naples.[34] While it bears some doctrinal resemblance to works written in the second Paris period (*Quodlibet,* I, 6, ad 3; *Q. D. de Anima,* 9, ad 10), this *opusculum* seems closely connected with the text of *De Generatione et Corruptione.* The note was, in fact, incorporated into the section of the commentary which Thomas of Sutton wrote, in order to complete Thomas' unfinished exposition.[35] Another philosophical *opusculum* which may belong to this late period is *On the Movement of the Heart.*[36] Both short works are addressed, according to some manuscripts, to a Master Phillip of Castroceli. There is much evidence, then, that Thomas Aquinas continued his interest in philosophical matters during his years at Naples.

In the Lenten period of 1273, Thomas delivered an important series of *Sermons* on various prayers. These talks were delivered in the Neapolitan vernacular but they now exist in Latin transcripts. Between Septuagesima Sunday (February 12) and Easter (April 9) of that year, St. Thomas preached fifty-seven or fifty-nine sermons in the monastery church of St. Dominic. These were explanations of the Apostles' Creed, the Our Father, the two Precepts of Love, the Ten Commandments, and possibly two sermons on the Hail Mary.[37] There is much evidence of the popularity of these sermons in the dialect of Naples. Thomas was now at the peak of his fame as a theologian; the citizens flocked to the church

---

expositio; and *In libros meteorologicorum expositio;* all three are edited in Volume III (1886) of the Leonine *Opera Omnia.* For various estimates on the dates, see Eschmann, "Catalogue," pp. 402–403.

[33] *Proc. Can. Neap.,* LVIII (*Fontes,* IV, 345).

[34] *De mixtione elementorum,* in *Opuscula,* ed. J. Perrier (Paris, 1949), I, 19; also in *Opus. Philos.* (Turin: Marietti, 1954), p. 155.

[35] See *In I de generatione,* lect. 24 (ed. Parm., XIX, 262, col. a): "Sunt enim quidam dicentes, quod qualitatibus activis et passivis" compared with *De mixtione* (ed. Parm., XVI, 553): "Videtur autem quibusdam quod qualitatibus activis et passivis. . . ."

[36] *De motu cordis,* in *Opus. Philos.* (Turin: Marietti, 1954), p. 165.

[37] *Expositio super symbolum Apostolorum; Expositio orationis dominicae; De duobus praeceptis caritatis et decem legis praeceptis;* and *Expositio super salutatione angelica.* For the Latin texts, see *Opus. Omnia,* ed. Mandonnet, Tome IV; *Opus. Theol.* (Turin: Marietti, 1954), Tome II.

to hear him. John Coppa recalled it vividly: "throughout the whole Lent of that year, he saw and heard him preaching the Lord's Prayer, that is, the Our Father, so that on each day he preached on a definite part of this prayer. . . . Practically the entire population of the City of Naples streamed in together, on each day, for this preaching."[38] Another eyewitness, John Blasio, who was a judge in Naples and a friend of Queen Mary of Sicily, testified "that he saw him preaching one whole Lent, with eyes closed and directed in contemplation toward the heavens; and his preaching in that Lent was on the Hail Mary, full of grace, the Lord is with thee."[39] Another layman, Peter Branchatius, swore that he saw and heard him preaching on these prayers.[40] A doctor of law who may also have been a banker (*zeccadenarius*), John of Caiatia, said that he saw Thomas preaching many times at the Dominican residence.[41] Of course, many elderly Dominicans testified to like effect. William of Tocco summed up the reaction of Aquinas' colleagues: "he was heard by the people with such reverence that it was as if his preaching came forth from God."[42]

Even in the present Latin transcripts (which may shorten his original text), these Lenten sermons are indeed impressive.[43] In two *Catalogues* of Aquinas' writings, Peter d'Andria is named as the man who made the Latin *reportationes* of some of these talks.[44] This Peter was a diocesan priest scholar who had come to Naples from Paris, apparently to avoid the now disturbed conditions at the French university. He was one of the many emigrés who found employment in Naples.

During 1273 a remarkable change came over Thomas Aquinas. We have already noted that he had not been well for some time; the precise nature of his illness is not recorded. One would think that he must have been in good health when he preached daily sermons in a large church. Yet he seems to have rather suddenly decided that much of his work was useless. On Passion Sunday (March 26, 1273), Thomas was celebrating Mass before a congregation that included many soldiers (*multis militibus*

[38] *Proc. Can. Neap.*, LXXXVII (*Fontes*, IV, 391).

[39] *Ibid.*, LXX (*Fontes*, IV, 362).

[40] *Ibid.*, XCIII (*Fontes*, IV, 399).

[41] *Ibid.*, LXXXVIII (*Fontes*, IV, 393).

[42] Tocco, *Vita*, c. 48 (*Fontes*, II, 122).

[43] There are several translations: L. Shapcote, *The Three Greatest Prayers* (London: Burns, Oates, 1937); J. B. Collins, *The Catechetical Instructions of St. Thomas* (New York: Wagner, 1939); two selections are in my *Pocket Aquinas* (New York: Washington Square Press, 1960), pp. 285–287, 355–358.

[44] Grabmann, *Die Werke*, pp. 92–98, prints these Prague *Catalogues*.

astantibus).[45] In the act of taking the Eucharist, he became abstracted and tearful. He remained immobile at the altar, not proceeding, as is normal, to finish the ceremony. His fellow Dominicans were astonished, but eventually they went to the altar and urged him to complete the Mass. Naturally they were curious about his behavior and asked Thomas about it. He refused to answer. At other times, they noticed similar periods of tearful abstraction during the chanting of the Lenten Office. He seems to have had some premonition of his coming death, for he wept each time that he heard the verse: "Cast me not off in the time of old age, when my strength shall fail."[46]

Strange things began to happen to Thomas. He reported that he was visited in his cell by Brother Romanus of Rome, his successor in the chair of theology at Paris in 1272. But Brother Romanus was now dead. Tocco insists that Brother Romanus appeared in the flesh and not in an imaginary vision.[47]

> In his astonishment, Brother Thomas said to him, "Welcome, when did you come?"
> He answered, "I have passed out of this life but I have been permitted to appear to you because of your merit."
> Gathering together his wits, for he was much disturbed at this sudden apparition, the Doctor replied, "Well then please God, I beg you on His behalf to answer this question. I ask you, what about myself? Do my works please God?"
> "You are in good standing and your works are pleasing to God," he answered.
> Then the Doctor continued, "What about yourself?"
> He replied, "I am in eternal life. I spent fifteen days in Purgatory, due to negligence in connection with a charge that the Bishop of Paris entrusted to me to be carried out. I delayed in doing it, through my own fault."
> Then Thomas said, "Tell me, what is the answer to the question that we frequently discussed, whether the habits of knowledge that are acquired in this life remain in Heaven?"
> But he answered, "Brother Thomas, I am seeing God; don't ask any more about this question."
> Then he asked him, "Tell me, how do you see God; do you see Him without any intermediary species, or by means of some likeness?"
> To this he replied, "Just as we are hearing, that's how we see in the City of the Lord of Powers." Then he suddenly disappeared.[48]

Each reader may judge for himself what amount of credibility this

[45] Tocco, *Vita,* c. 29 (*Fontes,* II, 103).
[46] Psalm 70:9; cited by Tocco, *ibid.*
[47] Tocco, *Vita,* c. 45 (*Fontes,* II, 118–119); Gui, *Legenda,* c. 19.
[48] Tocco, *op. cit.*

account merits. It should be noted that William of Tocco, almost fifty years later, recorded it verbatim, as if he had heard Thomas and Romanus speaking these precise words. There is no suggestion that William was present at the vision. Perhaps what is most important is the growing amount of evidence that Thomas was concerned, now, about the value of his work as a teacher and thinker.

Tocco is the source of another story of similar import.[49] A Dominican colleague, Dominic of Caserta, is said to have become curious about the time that Aquinas was spending alone in the chapel of St. Nicholas at the Naples monastery. He was watching Thomas, one day, while he stood in prayer before the altar. Suddenly he saw that Thomas was elevated about a yard from the floor! As he was listening to Aquinas weeping and praying, Brother Dominic heard a voice from the crucifix say: "Thomas, you have written well about Me. What will you receive from Me as a reward for your work?"

Thomas answered, "Lord, nothing except Thyself."

Dominican historians today do not insist on the veracity of this *"Bene scripsisti"* story.[50] Even William of Tocco (himself well endowed with a pious imagination) comments that Brother Dominic was given to miraculous visions.[51] The official canonization document makes no reference to these rumored visions at Naples but cites other evidences of Aquinas' saintliness.[52] At least the story reinforces the impression that the Dominicans at Naples were now concerned about the behavior and health of Brother Thomas of Aquino.

On the feast of St. Nicholas (December 6, 1273), Thomas decided to cease writing the Third Part of his *Summa of Theology*. For a man who had seemed to use every available moment for his scholarly work, this was a remarkable decision. It is recorded in the sworn testimony of Bartholomew of Capua.

> The same witness [Bartholomew] said that when Brother Thomas was celebrating Mass in the chapel of St. Nicholas in Naples he was struck by an astonishing change of mind. After this Mass, he neither wrote nor dictated anything more; he even stopped writing the Third Part of the *Summa*, in the midst of the treatise on Penance.
>
> When Brother Reginald saw that Brother Thomas had ceased writing,

[49] *Ibid.*, c. 30 (*Fontes*, II, 108).
[50] *San Tommaso* (1945), p. 178.
[51] "Dominicus de Caserta . . . qui alias habuit visiones mirabiles." Tocco, *loc. cit.*
[52] Cf. *Bulla canonizationis S. Thomae Aquinatis, Fontes* V, 519–530.

he said to him: "Father, why have you put aside such a great work which you began for the praise of God and the enlightenment of the world?"

Brother Thomas answered him, "Reginald, I am unable to do it."

Now Brother Reginald, fearful lest much study had caused a bit of mental distraction, kept insisting that Brother Thomas should continue his writing. But Thomas was just as persistent in his reply, "Reginald, I can't because all that I have written seems like chaff to me!"

At this, Brother Reginald was much astonished.[53]

There is an elision at this point in Bartholomew's recorded testimony, but this is not the end of the story. As Bartholomew's account is taken up again, it becomes evident that Thomas was considered ill enough to be permitted to go to visit his sister, the Countess Teodora of San Severino. The faithful Reginald accompanied him.

The said Brother Thomas went to the Countess of San Severino whom he loved in charity. With great difficulty, he made the short trip there but, when he arrived, he scarcely spoke to the Countess as she met him. Then the Countess, in great fear, said to Brother Reginald, "What is wrong with Brother Thomas? He is completely out of his senses and has scarcely spoken to me."

Brother Reginald replied, "Since about the feast of St. Nicholas, he has been in this state and from that time onward has written nothing."

Again Brother Reginald began to urge Brother Thomas to reveal why he refused to write and what was the reason for his bewilderment. After much insistent questioning by Brother Reginald, Brother Thomas said to Reginald, "I adjure you by the living and omnipotent God, by the loyalty that you have for our Order, and by the charity that binds us together, to tell nothing during my lifetime of what I reveal to you."

Then he added, "Everything that I have written seems like chaff to me, in comparison with the things that I have seen and that have been revealed to me."[54]

More than this we are never told about St. Thomas' special experience. Poor Reginald remained puzzled. The sad visit with Teodora started at the end of December and lasted into the early part of January, 1274. Something had certainly occurred to change the demeanor and scholarly habits of more than thirty years. Whether the revelation to which Thomas refers may be identified with the colloquy with SS. Peter and Paul is never made clear.

Without any effort to minimize the importance of such a striking supernatural experience, one may wonder whether St. Thomas' behavior during this year may have been due in part to physical illness. He was to die

[53] *Proc. Can. Neap.*, LXXIX (*Fontes,* IV, 376–377).

[54] Bartholomew of Capua, *ibid.*, p. 377.

within a few months. According to most estimates, Thomas was less than fifty years old. There must have been some cause of this early death, for he had been a comparatively vigorous and healthy man throughout most of his life. We shall see that the sources never give an adequate reason for his death. They speak vaguely about Thomas "striking his head on a tree!"

Amateur diagnosis of historical illnesses, after the passage of centuries, is doubtless to be avoided. However, the possibility may simply be mentioned that Thomas suffered some sort of "stroke," or aneurysm, while at Naples. His frequent tears and periods of mental abstraction may well have had some organic basis.

CHAPTER SIXTEEN

The Summation of Thomism

IF WE had to select one work which epitomizes the wisdom of St. Thomas, our choice would have to be the *Summa of Theology*.[1] As we have seen, he began to plan, and perhaps to write, this masterpiece while he was regent of studies at the Roman monastery, 1265–1267. The *First Part* was probably finished in Italy by 1268; the two divisions of the *Second Part* seem to have been written in Paris, 1269–1272; he wrote up to Question 90, Article 4, of the *Third Part* in Naples, 1273, and was unable to finish the work. The *Supplement* was compiled after Thomas' death, possibly by Reginald of Piperno, from passages selected from the fourth book of Aquinas' *Commentary on the Sentences*. Nothing is added to our knowledge of St. Thomas' thought by this *Supplement*.[2]

Early in the 1260's, Thomas began to grow dissatisfied with the way in which the subject matter of theology was treated in the standard treatises. There is a persistent rumor that he first contemplated making a revision of his own *Commentary on the Sentences*.[3] What he eventually

---

[1] *Summa Theologiae*, cura et studio Instituti Studiorum Medievalium Ottaviensis (Ottawa, Can.: Studium Generale Ord. Praed., 1941–1945), 5 vols. including the *Supplementum*. In the Leonine Edition, Vols. IV–XII (Rome, 1888–1906), in which the last five volumes are critically edited. English: *Summa Theologica*, trans. by the English Dominicans, 2 ed., 22 vols. (London: Burns, Oates, 1912–1936); a good portion of this version is revised in: A. C. Pegis, *Basic Writings of Saint Thomas Aquinas*, 2 vols. (New York: Random House, 1945). A new English version, ed. T. Gilby and P. K. Meagher (New York: McGraw-Hill; London: Eyre and Spottiswoode), in 65 vols., is announced to commence publication in 1964.

[2] The chronology is not definitive; see *Walz-Novarina (1962)*, p. 223; Eschmann, "Catalogue," pp. 386–388; Grabmann, *Die Werke*, pp. 294–301.

[3] Bartholomew of Lucca, *Hist Eccles.*, XXIII, c. 15, is the source of the story that Aquinas actually started to write a second version: "But let me add that while at

decided to do was to write a new treatise which would not be restricted by the academic *impedimenta* that theology had acquired as it moved through the schools of the twelfth century. In particular, Thomas felt that he could simplify and improve on the plan of presentation which Peter Lombard had devised. This is quite evident from the introduction that Aquinas wrote for his *Summa of Theology.*

> Since the teacher of Catholic truth ought not only to instruct advanced scholars but also has as his function to teach beginners, in accord with the Apostle's text (1 Cor 3:1), *as to little ones in Christ, I fed you with milk, not with solid food,* what we propose to do in this work is to treat those items that are pertinent to the Christian religion in a manner that is adapted to the teaching of beginners.
>
> As a matter of fact, we have thought that new students of this doctrine are held back by several features of the writings produced by different authors: partly by the multiplication of useless questions, articles and arguments; partly too, because the things that such students must know are not treated according to the order of learning but according to the order that the development of textbooks has required, or according to whatever order the occurrence of a disputation has dictated; and partly because frequent repetition of the same points has generated both boredom and confusion in the minds of their audience.
>
> So, in the effort to avoid these and other impediments, we shall try, with trust in divine assistance, to go through the pertinent points in sacred doctrine briefly and clearly, to the extent that the subject matter permits.[4]

In choosing to write in the *Summa* format, St. Thomas was not inventing something altogether new. During the twelfth century, Christian scholars had compiled *Books of Sentences,* containing the views (*sententiae*) of the Fathers and earlier teachers in the history of Christianity. We have seen how one of the most influential of these, made by Peter Lombard (A.D. 1150), became a standard textbook for part of the theology course at Paris and elsewhere. Other scholars attempted brief, concise, complete summaries of this material. Thus Hugh of Saint-Victor is sometimes given credit for a work with the title *Summa Sententiarum* which came into circulation around 1135.[5] Soon there were *Summas* of

---

Rome, and already a Master in Theology . . . he wrote a second version of the first part of his *Commentary on the Sentences:* I saw this once at Lucca but someone took it away and I never saw it again." There is no known manuscript of such a work.

[4] *Summa Theologiae,* Pars Prima, Prologo.

[5] Ueberweg-Geyer, *Die patristische und scholastische Philosophie* (Berlin: Mittler, 1928), p. 262; Chenu, *Introduction,* p. 255. It is not certain that Hugh wrote this *Summa.*

canon law, virtues, logic, grammar, and other areas of knowledge. One of the most famous and influential before St. Thomas became active was the *Summa fratris Alexandri,* compiled by several Franciscan scholars during the 1240's at Paris, in honor of one of their first great scholars, Alexander of Hales. Albert the Great had written a *Summa de Creaturis* (1236–1243) before Aquinas studied with him.[6] St. Thomas knew many of these and similar *Summas* and was doubtless influenced by them. However, his own *Summa of Theology* has become the best known and most widely read work in this genre.

For the internal style of this *Summa,* Aquinas decided to use *Questions.* Actually he employed a simplified form of the same style that is found in his *Disputed Questions.* Each of the three completed "Parts" of the *Summa of Theology* includes over a hundred questions. Each of these questions contains a number of *articles.* Each article has five *sections*: the statement of the problem under consideration, a listing of a number of objections opposed to the solution which Aquinas is going to give to the problem, a section "to the contrary" which is usually a brief quotation or reasoning opposed to the general trend of the objections, a main response (the *corpus*) in which St. Thomas gives his own answer to the problem, and numbered answers to the objections. Unlike the articles in the *Disputed Questions,* those of the *Summa of Theology* usually have fewer objections (he really tried to make this work brief), only one *Sed contra,* and no replies to the statement "to the contrary."

This style of scholarly writing is not familiar to many readers in the twentieth century and may, on first approach, seem unduly formal and cumbersome but it has its merits. For one thing, one always knows at the start what question is under discussion — this is not always apparent in the modern chapter and paragraph style. Moreover, the problem is stated as an open question and other points of view than those of the writer are immediately presented in the objections — this is very different from the "thesis" style used in later Scholasticism, in which a judgment is dogmatically stated and then "proved" by syllogistic reasoning. St. Thomas did not employ this thesis style, which only came into prominence with the Schoolmen of the Renaissance. Furthermore, one always knows where to look for the gist of Aquinas' answer: that is in the fourth section which is invariably begun by the words, "I answer that this must be

[6] For the development of the *Summa* style, see *Introd.* to Robert de Melun, *Quaestiones de divina pagina,* ed. R. M. Martin (Louvain: Univ. de Louvain, 1932).

said."[7] Finally, the question style ensures that no difficulty, or opposed view, known to the author, will remain undiscussed, for he is almost automatically forced to state what he thinks of each objection in the fifth section of the article. It goes without saying that in quoting a passage indicative of the thought of St. Thomas one does not cite the objections or even the section "to the contrary"; these represent the preliminary dialogue, as it were, not the personal views of Aquinas. Citations are made from Sections Four and Five, from the *corpus* and the replies to the objections.

Many aids to the reading and interpretation of this *Summa of Theology* are available. Of the various commentaries, the one made by Cardinal Cajetan in the early sixteenth century is considered best. It is printed along with the *Summa of Theology* in the Leonine edition.[8] The nearest approach to an English commentary is a simplified paraphrase of the main thoughts in the *Summa.*[9] Martin Grabmann, A. Legendre, and M. D. Chenu have provided informative general introductions to the work.[10] There are several useful concordances.[11] One of the best sources of help in understanding the *Summa of Theology* is found in Aquinas' other works. The *Disputed Questions,* the commentaries on Aristotle, Boethius, Dionysius and the *Book of Causes,* the expositions of the Bible, the *Summa contra Gentiles* and the *Compendium of Theology,* the various *Opuscula,* even the *Commentary on the Sentences* — all contain parallel texts which may throw light on the frequently condensed doctrines of the *Theological Summa.*[12] Most printings of the *Summa of Theology* indicate these parallels, either in footnotes or at the beginning of each article. Due attention should be paid to the chronological spread of St. Thomas' writings; his

[7] The formula, *Respondeo dicendum quod* may be an error for *Responsio. Dicendum quod.*

[8] Cajetan's *Commentary* is not translated into English.

[9] W. Farrell, O.P., *Companion to the Summa,* 4 vols. (New York: Sheed & Ward, 1939–1942).

[10] M. Grabmann, *Einführung in die Summa Theologiae* (Freiburg: Paulusverlag, 1928) (English trans. by J. S. Zybura [St. Louis: Herder, 1930]); A. Legendre, *Introduction à l'étude de la Somme Théologique* (Paris: Bloud, 1923); M. D. Chenu, "Introduction to the *Summa* of St. Thomas," *Thomist Reader,* II (Washington, D. C.: Thomist Press, 1958).

[11] R. J. Deferrari and Sr. M. Inviolata Barry, *A Lexicon of St. Thomas Aquinas based on the Summa Theologica* (Washington, D. C.: Catholic U. Press, 1948); L. Schütz, *Thomaslexikon* (Paderborn: Schöningh, 1895); *Indices* in *Editio Leonina,* t. XVI (Romae: Apud Sedem Commissionis Leoninae, 1948).

[12] Cf. J. de Guibert, *Les doublets de saint Thomas* (Paris: Beauchesne, 1926).

productive period as a writer covered twenty years and he did modify some of his views and altered certain modes of expression. Where later works consciously correct things said in earlier writings, the more mature treatments should be given precedence. However, there is a remarkable degree of consistency throughout the Thomistic corpus of writings, and a good explanation from one work may be used to clarify obscurity in another.

In thought structure the *Summa of Theology* falls into three "Parts": the First Part treats of God as Creator and Governor of all things; the Second considers God as the End to which human creatures should direct their voluntary activity; and the Third deals with Christ and the supernatural means of salvation which were made available to men through His Incarnation and Redemption. This division of material is clearly stated by Aquinas.

> And so, since the principal intent of this sacred doctrine is to convey a knowledge of God, not only as He is in Himself but also as He is the beginning of things and their end, and particularly of rational creatures. . . . with a view to the explanation of this doctrine, we shall first treat of God; second, of the movement of rational creatures to God; third, of Christ who as Man is the way for us in tending toward God.[13]

Commenting on this division, John of St. Thomas wrote at the start of the seventeenth century:

> Thus, St. Thomas divided the whole teaching of the *Summa of Theology* on the basis of a threefold consideration of God, as causing, namely, as the efficient principle, as the finalizing beatitude, and as the redemptive Saviour — as is evident at the start of question two of the First Part. So, from God in Himself and in His act of being, through God as efficient, final and salvific cause, the final glory of the Resurrection is taken back to God so that it may come to fruition in Himself. This obviously brings the golden circle of theology, around which the divine *Summa* of St. Thomas circulates, to its completion.[14]

Implicit in this triple division is the theme of the coming forth (*exitus*) of all creatures from God as their Source and the going back (*reditus*) of these creatures to God as their End. This had been enunciated by St. Thomas in his earliest years as a teacher at Paris.

> The consideration of this doctrine will be concerned with things, according as they proceed from God as from a principle, and according as they

[13] *S.T.*, I, q. 2, Prologo.

[14] Joannis a S. Thomae, *Cursus Theologicus in Summam d. Thomae* (Paris, 1883), "Introd.," Vol. I, 191.

are brought back to Him as to an end. Hence in the first part he [Peter Lombard] treats matters of divinity according to the going forth [*exitus*] from a principle; and in the second part, according to the going back [*reditus*] to an end. . . .[15]

This is a very traditional theme, that of the exit and the return of all things to their one source. It is in St. Augustine's *City of God,* in the writings of the Pseudo-Dionysius, in Erigena's *Division of Nature,* and in many Neoplatonic works. While there is some broad resemblance to the emanationism of Plotinus and Proclus, the circular theme as Aquinas develops it has nothing of the pantheistic teaching that is found in Greek Neoplatonism. How St. Thomas put the mark of his own genius on this organizing theme is well explained in the following comment.

However, this summary schematism, extremely impoverished from the point of view of the philosopher, is sharply exploited by St. Thomas, not as a commodious framework into which he will be able arrange at pleasure the immense matter of sacred doctrine but rather as an order of knowledge productive of intelligibility in the profundity of the datum of revelation. For such is precisely the really original intelligibility that the theologian seeks, and by it his science partially breaks away from the epistemology of the Greeks: he assembles and develops reasons (*"rationes necessariae"* as Saint Anselm says) in a series of contingent facts. All his edifice of demonstrations, of theological conclusions hangs on a datum in which reason can discern appropriateness but never necessity. Thus, at the head of each treatise — creation, hierarchy of beings, incarnation, redemption, sacraments — he begins by establishing an appropriateness (*convenientia*) of these "facts." Now there is a hidden relationship between this highly special type of intelligibility which provides the theologian with his argument from appropriateness (so open to scorn in Aristotelian epistemology but so essential to theological epistemology) and the pattern of emanation and return in which divine freedom, at decisive moments, prescribes the rhythm of its evolution. Sacred history and the order of learning (*ordo disciplinae*) find there precisely the right point of contact, under the guidance of a faith which leads both up to the divine Absolute, giving them at that point their definitive consistency in the order of understanding. The plan of the *Summa* is truly on a theological level, that is, a level on which God's knowledge is formally and mentally the principle of human wisdom, at once furnishing the object, the light, and the necessity.[16]

Within each part of the *Summa of Theology,* a number of distinct treatises are discernible. These are groups of questions dealing with one specific subject. We find treatises on God the Creator, on the Angels, on

---

[15] *In I Sent.,* d. 2, divisio textus; ed. Parm., VI, 20a.

[16] M. D. Chenu, *Introduction,* p. 263.

man, on the theological virtues, on law, on grace, and so on, developing in the theological literature that preceded St. Thomas.[17] He incorporated themes, divisions of the material, sets of objections, statements of various positions, even quotations of Patristic texts (*auctoritates*) from his predecessors' treatises into the various tractates of the *Theological Summa.* Some of Thomas' treatises are so newly and highly developed that they are hardly recognizable as the continuations of earlier tradition. Others show even verbal similarities to the same treatises in prior theological writings. There are long and complicated treatises which include various subtreatises. Thus, within the general tractate on the procession of creatures from God, in the First Part of the *Summa of Theology,* there is a treatise on angels, and within the latter there is a subtreatise on angelic knowledge. Again, the general treatise on the virtues (in the *Secunda Secundae*) contains subtreatises of considerable length on the theological and cardinal virtues. It is very profitable to notice the character of such treatises in reading the *Summa.* The following schematism indicates the chief ones, but does not attempt to list all the subtreatises.

Major Treatises in the Summa of Theology

I. First Part: *On God*
- A. Question 1: Nature of Sacred Doctrine
- B. Qq. 2–26: God's Existence and Essential Attributes
- C. Qq. 27–43: Trinity of Divine Persons
- D. Qq. 44–119: Procession of Creatures From God
  1. Qq. 44–46: Production of Creatures
  2. Qq. 47–102: Distinction of Creatures (General, Good and Evil, Spiritual and Corporeal)
  3. Qq. 103–119: Conservation and Governance of Creatures

I–II. First Division of Second Part: *Movement Toward God by Human Actions, in General*
- A. Qq. 1–5: Ultimate End of Human Life
- B. Qq. 6–114: Means of Attaining This End
  1. Qq. 6–48: Human Acts in Themselves
  2. Qq. 49–114: Principles of Human Acts
     - *a*) Qq. 49–89: Intrinsic Principles (Habits)
     - *b*) Qq. 90–114: Extrinsic Principles (Law and Grace)

---

[17] Cf. D. H. Pouillon, "Le premier traité des propriétés transcendentales," *Rev. Néosc. de Philos.*, XLII (1939), 58–61; D. Lottin, *Psychologie et morale aux XIIe et XIIIe siècles* (Gembloux: Duculot, 1948), Tome II, 103–235.

II–II. Second Division of Second Part: *Detailed Consideration of Human Movement Toward God*

- A. Qq. 1–170: On Virtues, Vices and Gifts
  - 1. Qq. 1–46: Theological Virtues (with Vices and Gifts)
    - *a*) Qq. 1–16: Faith
    - *b*) Qq. 17–22: Hope
    - *c*) Qq. 23–46: Charity
  - 2. Qq. 47–170: Cardinal Virtues (with Vices and Gifts)
    - *a*) Qq. 47–56: Prudence
    - *b*) Qq. 57–122: Justice
    - *c*) Qq. 123–140: Fortitude
    - *d*) Qq. 141–170: Temperance
- B. 171–189: On Specific Conditions Differentiating Men
  - 1. Qq. 171–178: Charismatic Graces (Prophecy, Tongues, Miracle Working)
  - 2. Qq. 179–182: Active and Contemplative Life
  - 3. Qq. 183–189: Diversity of Offices and States of Life

III. Third Part: *On Christ the Saviour*

- A. Qq. 1–59: The Saviour Himself
- B. Qq. 60 — Sacraments as Means of Salvation (Baptism, Confirmation, Eucharist, Penance . . . ending at q. 90, art. 4)
- C. On the End of Immortal Life as Achieved Through Resurrection (unwritten but planned by St. Thomas; see *Prologue* to Part III)

Of course it is neither advisable nor necessary to attempt to summarize the thought content of the *Summa of Theology* here. It is itself a summary made by St. Thomas and should be read as such by people who wish to understand him. The *Summa* is an encyclopedic work which gathers together the wisdom of the writers in the Christian tradition (the *Sancti*) and the wisdom of many philosophical writers who are mostly in the non-Christian tradition (the *Philosophi*). It can be disconcerting to find Aristotle quoted as much as Augustine in a work on Catholic theology. Perhaps a final word on the relations between philosophy and theology, in the *Summa of Theology,* may not be amiss.

St. Thomas Aquinas was a professional theologian: it was his job to teach and write theology. He never referred to himself as a philosopher, but he had studied the writings of the philosophers and continued to study them into his last year of life. He obviously felt that philosophy had its place in the scheme of human learning. Nor did he confuse philosophy with sacred doctrine. We have seen how Aquinas related metaphysics to sacred theology, when he commented on Boethius' work, *On the Trinity.*[18] He had found that the philosophers used the name "theology" for what we today would call metaphysics. Possibly that is one reason why Thomas usually called his own specialty sacred doctrine (*sacra doctrina*) and rarely used the word theology in that context.[19] Yet he did stress the difference between what we would call philosophical and theological work.

> So theology or divine science is of two kinds. There is one kind in which divine realities are considered not as the subject-matter of the science but as its principle: this is the kind of theology that the philosophers seek, and under another name it is called metaphysics. Then there is another kind which considers divine realities in themselves for their own sake, as the subject-matter of the science: and this is the theology that is taught in sacred Scripture. Both deal with beings that are existentially independent of matter and change — but according to two different ways in which a thing may be separate from matter and change. A first way in which a thing can be called separate stems from the fact that by virtue of its definitive character it simply cannot exist in the context of matter and change. This is the way in which God and the angels are said to exist in separation from matter and change. In a second way, a thing may not be required by its definitive character to exist in matter and change, by virtue of the fact that it is possible for it to exist apart from matter and change. This is the way that being, substance, potency and act are separate from matter and change, for they do not depend existentially on matter and change, as do the objects of mathematics which cannot be apart from matter, although they can be understood apart from sensible matter. So, philosophical theology treats of items that are separate in this second way, namely, as principles of its subject; on the other hand, the theology of sacred Scripture treats of things that are separate in the first way, as constitutives of its subject. Of course, some items are considered in it which are found in the context of matter and change, to the extent that the explanation of divine realities requires it.[20]

This famous passage establishes the charter, in Thomism, not only of metaphysics but also of sacred theology. To exist is not necessarily an act of material and mutable beings only. It is natural for men in the unreflective moments of their understanding of realities to think that all beings are bodies, that they must take up space and be subject to motion. A great effort of reflection is needed so that one may see that being and existence are not confined to the material order. Some people never achieve this judgment which separates, or frees, reality from the limitations of material existence. Yet the Thomist thinks that the making of

---

[18] *Supra,* Chapter Ten.

[19] Cf. G. F. Van Ackeren, *Sacra Doctrina* (Rome: Officium Libri Catholici, 1952).

[20] *In Boethii de Trinitate,* q. V, 4, c.

such a judgment is essential to metaphysical knowledge. It is the starting point (*principium*) for metaphysics.

But the judgment of separation is not the starting point for theology. As a theologian, St. Thomas starts at the opposite pole of reality, not with material bodies which may eventually be seen as too limited in character to constitute the whole of existing being but with the highest instance of existing immaterial reality, with God. The theologian takes this privileged and supreme beginning for his science because he *believes* in the existing God. What is first evident to the philosopher is that things on earth exist; what is first evident to the theologian is that his belief, his act of faith, is meaningless unless there be a God. Where the philosopher Descartes said, "I think, and so, *I am*," the theologian Anselm said, "I cogitate on the object of my belief, an object than which there is none greater — and so, *God exists*." St. Thomas has made this distinction with the utmost precision.

> The consideration of creatures pertains to theologians and to philosophers — but in different ways. Philosophers think of creatures as they stand in their own nature; so they investigate the proper causes and attributes of things. But the theologian considers creatures, according to their coming forth from the first principle and their being ordered to the ultimate end, who is God. Hence, divine wisdom is rightly named, for it considers the highest Cause, who is God.[21]

Where St. Thomas' wisdom extended beyond the horizons of his predecessors (and of many of his followers) is precisely in his vision of a role for philosophy in the economy of Christian intellectualism, as well as a superior role for sacred theology. There are two ways of explaining the whole of things: one may start at the bottom, with the understanding of the reality of physical beings, and eventually come to understand that there is more to existing being than these things. Eventually, too, one may dimly grasp the truth that the bodily world could not be or move unless there existed a Being of a different character, a God who caused all these limited beings to exist and to move. This is to think philosophically. The five ways of reasoning from various aspects of the physical world to the conclusion that God exists are, then, philosophical arguments.[22] Their presence in a theological work does not modify the basically natural character of such arguments. A parallel situation is found in the *Disputed Questions on the Power of God* (certainly a theological work) where

[21] *In II Sent.*, Prologo; ed. Parm., VI, 381.

[22] *S.T.*, I, 2, 3.

Thomas sketches the historical process by which philosophers came to realize that the manifold of finite beings depends on one Supreme Being. He describes one argument as that of Plato, a second as that of Aristotle, and the third as that of Avicenna.[23] The mere fact that a theologian repeats a philosophical argument in a theological work does not mean that the argument becomes theological. There are many sections in the *Summa of Theology* where the reasoning moves from an initial experience of natural things or events to certain conclusions about the life and properties of man, for instance; this is philosophy being used by Thomas Aquinas, in the service of theology. Much of the lengthy discussion of the moral virtues is of this character, for it is dependent on the Aristotelian theory of the virtues.[24]

On the other hand, St. Thomas knew the limitations of philosophy and knew that theology has different beginnings and different conclusions. The doctrine on the Gifts of the Holy Spirit, for example, is simply unknown to the philosophers. This means that wisdom itself is different in philosophy and in theology. Aquinas states this quite formally.

> Since wisdom is the knowledge of divine matters, as will be explained later, it is considered differently by us and by the philosophers. For, since our life is ordered to divine fruition and is directed by a participation in divine nature, accomplished through grace, wisdom in our view is not only considered as pertaining to the knowing of God, as with the philosophers, but also as it is directive of human life which is not only directed by human reasons but according to divine reasons, as is evident from the twelfth book of Augustine, *On the Trinity*.[25]

There is, then, a more practical character to theological wisdom than in the highly speculative wisdom of philosophy. This is particularly evident in the case of the Gift of Wisdom.[26]

If one wishes to see how Aquinas used philosophy as a springboard from which to launch his theological reasoning, a very fine example is found in the area of social virtue. The *Nicomachean Ethics* had expanded and clarified the earlier Greek notions of justice as the habit of willing to give every man his due. Aristotle had seen that there is a difference

[23] *De Potentia Dei*, III, 5 c: "ista videtur ratio Platonis . . . haec est probatio Philosophi . . . haec est ratio Avicennae."

[24] Cf. Bourke, *St. Thomas and the Greek Moralists* (Milwaukee: Marquette U. Press, 1947).

[25] *S.T.*, II–II, 19, 7 c; Ottawa ed., III, 1505b.

[26] *Ibid.*, 45, 3 c.: "Sic ergo sapientia, secundum quod est donum, non solum est speculativa, sed etiam practica."

between what is due to a person from the common good (distributive justice) and what is due from the point of view of private good (rectificatory or commutative justice).[27] A further insight in Aristotelian ethics had opened up still another social virtue, friendship. In a lengthy treatise, Aristotle showed that it is right to love another person *for his good,* as well as for one's own.[28] All of this is duly noted and assimilated by Thomas Aquinas who then proceeds to develop and broaden the altruistic and community aspects of natural and legal justice.[29] Where Greek philosophy had been able to treat justice, and friendship, as moral virtues governing the social relations among men, Aquinas brings God into the explanation and shows that, because all men are children of God, there are additional (theological) reasons for goodwill and love toward neighbor.[30] More than that, St. Thomas extends the consideration of social virtue into the domain of charity.[31] He shows how Aristotle's "love of friendship" may be elevated to a love of God for His own sake, and of other men as creatures of God. This was something that Aristotle's philosophic wisdom had never envisioned: a love of a highest Being who is in no sense an equal of the man who loves Him.

> By charity, God is loved for His own sake. Hence only one reason for loving is primarily stressed by charity, namely, the divine Goodness which is His substance, according to Psalm 105:1, "give glory to the Lord, for he is good." — For the human friendship, of which the philosopher speaks, there is a different end and a different level of intercommunication which has no place in charity.[32]

Friendship with God and His creatures goes beyond the horizons of ancient philosophy: it provides a new and Christian basis for a higher altruism. Meditation on this theme will indicate how many of our present problems (of good race relations and international peace, for instance) are not to be solved by justice alone but by the rectification of our wills in Christian charity.

Indeed, as a theologian, St. Thomas saw that there is a still higher wisdom than that of theology. There is the wisdom of God which is the source of all rightness. Even at its best, human justice is a far cry from

[27] Aristotle, *Ethica Nic.*, V, 1–7, 1129a1–1135a14.

[28] *Ibid.*, VIII–IX, 1155a1–1172a15.

[29] *In VIII et IX Ethic.*, and *S.T.*, II–II, qq. 57–80.

[30] Cf. G. B. Phelan, "Justice and Friendship," *Maritain Volume of the Thomist* (New York: Sheed & Ward, 1943), pp. 153–170.

[31] *S.T.*, II–II, qq. 23–46.

[32] *Ibid.*, q. 23, 5, ad 2 et ad 3; Ottawa ed., III, 1525.

divine justice. This relation of divine justice and wisdom is beautifully explained in the *Commentary on Job*.

> Since their legislators cannot extend them to all singular cases, human laws are concerned with universal matters and with what occurs in most cases. How general human statutes are to be applied to individual deeds must be left to the prudence of the agent. As a result, man is open to many instances in which he falls short of rectitude, even though he does not run counter to human positive law. On the other hand, divine law as contained within the wisdom of God extends to all particular cases, even the least common. So, it is impossible for a person to depart from rectitude on any point and not to run counter to divine law. Yet, since man is unable to inspect this divine law, as it is in the depths of the Wisdom of God, and consequently to know its manifold details, it does happen at times that one does not think that he is acting against the law of God, when he is indeed, or he may think that his failure is slight when, indeed, it is great.[33]

If the wisdom of the theologian, then, is higher than that of the philosopher, it is, like all human knowledges, infinitely below the wisdom of God.

---

[33] *Exp. in Job,* c. 11, lect. 1; Parm., XIV, 49; cf. Bourke, "Foundations of Justice," *Proc. Amer. Cath. Philos. Assoc.,* XXXVI (1962), 19–28.

CHAPTER SEVENTEEN

Death at Fossanova

PLANS were under way to hold a general council of the Church at Lyons, France, in 1274. Pope Gregory X wished to have the ablest theologians in attendance; as a result, both Bonaventure and Thomas Aquinas were invited to participate.

Even though Thomas was not in the best of health, he had to make an effort to assist at such an important ecclesiastical event. It must have been about the end of January or the beginning of February that he, Reginald of Piperno, and some other ecclesiastics set out for Lyons.[1] As usual, they were walking and made slow progress. Passing through the town of Teano, they were joined by a cleric named William of Teano (he later became bishop there) and his nephew, Roffridus. On the way, according to Bartholomew of Capua,[2] Thomas struck his head on a tree that had fallen across the road and he was knocked almost unconscious. Reginald asked him if he was badly hurt and Thomas said, "A little."

> Then Brother Reginald, wishing to get Thomas talking to divert his attention, said, "Master, you are on your way to the Council, where you will do many good things for the universal Church, for our Order, and for the Kingdom of Sicily."
>
> Brother Thomas then replied, "God grant that good things may be done there."
>
> Keeping up the talk, Reginald said, "You and Brother Bonaventure will be Cardinals and will bring renown to your Orders."
>
> At this Brother Thomas replied, "Reginald, in no status can I be as useful to our Order as in my present one."

[1] Mandonnet, "Le carême de s. Thomas à Naples," in *S. Tommaso d'Aquino. Miscellanea* (Rome, 1924), p. 202, places their departure in January.

[2] *Proc. Can. Neap.*, LXXVIII (*Fontes*, IV, 375), records the conversation.

To which Brother Reginald retorted, "Father, I'm not saying this for your sake but for the common good."

Immediately, Brother Thomas cut off his words and said, "Reginald, rest assured that I shall never at any time change my status."

It is impossible to say what connection this alleged head injury had with the final illness of Aquinas. The whole account may have been modified in later oral tradition. One may point out that at the time of this incident, Bonaventure was already a cardinal, having been raised to the purple on June 3, 1273.[3] Though the conversation is recorded in the sworn testimony of Bartholomew of Capua, he does not claim to have been present but states that he heard about the incident from Roffridus and his servant.

There is some difficulty in tracing the route followed by the travelers to the Council. One biographer has even suggested that they decided to go by way of Aquino, Roccasecca, and Montecassino, so that Thomas could revisit the haunts of his childhood![4] They were at Aquino when a letter reached Thomas from the Abbot Bernard of Montecassino. We have the reply which Aquinas wrote to his friend. It is without doubt the last thing that Thomas wrote. The opening lines are strikingly personal:

> To the Reverend Father in Christ, Lord Bernard, through the grace of God venerable Abbot of Cassino, Brother Thomas of Aquino, his devoted son ever and everywhere ready in obedience.
>
> You have requested, venerable Father, that I give an answer orally to the assembled Brothers who are taking a false impression from the text of the celebrated Doctor Gregory — but this the extent of the divine office and the length of the fast prevent. Perhaps it will be fruitful for this answer to be given in writing so that it may benefit not only those in the present time but also those in the future. Nor can I think that it has happened apart from divine providence, that your letter has caught me at Aquino on my way to Gaul. For it was here that the Blessed Maurus, the disciple of our most holy Father Benedict was favored to receive the letter and sacred gifts of such a Father, when he was sent by him to Gaul.[5]

---

[3] G. Abate, *Per la Storia e la Cronologia di S. Bonaventura* (Roma: Editrice 'Miscellanea Francescana,' 1950), p. 130.

[4] Toso, *Tommaso d'Aquino,* p. 124.

[5] *Epistola S. Thomae Aq. ad Bernardum, Abbatem Casinensem,* opera et studio monachorum O.S.B. (Montecassino, 1875), pp. XXIV, with folded reproduction of the manuscript. This unique text is from the margin of a manuscript of St. Gregory's *Moralia* (*Cod.* 82, *Bibliot. Casin.,* pag. 320–322) in the library of the monastery of Montecassino. Some scholars have thought that the marginal text is an autograph of Thomas Aquinas (see Grabmann, *Die Werke,* pp. 377–378) but Dondaine (*Secrétaires,* p. 20, note 18) rejects the view that it is in the hand of Aquinas.

The *Letter* then proceeds to deal with the problem which worried the monks at Montecassino. Like many men before and after them, they could not understand how God's foreknowledge did not wholly necessitate the occurrence of all future events. Aquinas explains how God may foreknow from all eternity that a certain man will die at a definite time, because all events of past and future are known to Him in an eternal present. Yet, he adds, this does not mean that, from an earthly and temporal viewpoint, this man's death may not freely occur at any time.[6]

The *Letter to Bernard* closes with the words: "May Your Paternity enjoy many more years. Brother Reginald commends himself to you."[7] Of course the letter raises some problems. There is no mention of the fact that Brother Thomas belongs to the Order of Preachers. Instead, Aquinas' opening lines almost suggest that he is a Benedictine. Moreover, the phrase "to the assembled Brothers" (*convocatis Fratribus*) strikes a discordant note: one would not expect an alumnus of Montecassino to speak of the monks as friars. Nor does the reference to the Office and Lenten fasting suggest that a sick traveler is writing. Most Thomistic scholars, however, accept this letter as authentic.[8]

The party of travelers stopped later with Thomas' niece, Francesca, at the castle of Maenza. Bartholomew reports that Aquinas was there attacked by the illness from which he eventually died.[9] No indication of the nature of this sickness is given. Another witness named Peter of Montesangiovanni helps to fill in some details on this part of the journey.

> He [Peter] said that while the said Brother Thomas was going to the Council of Lyons, called by the Lord Pope Gregory X of happy memory, he passed by the castle of Maenza in the diocese of Terracina and stayed there for some days because he was a little indisposed (*aliquantulum discrasiatus*). Brother James de Florentino, at that time Prior of the [Cistercian] monastery at Fossanova, along with the present witness [Peter], Brother John of Piedmont and Brother Fidelis, a monk of the same monastery, went to visit Brother Thomas at the castle of Maenza, where he, the Prior and the monk stayed with him [Thomas] for four or five days. During this period he saw him celebrating [Mass] with great devotion and shedding of tears, as he had mentioned before. . . .

---

[6] See a similar, briefer, explanation, *Exp. in Evang. Math.*, c. 1, ed. Parm., X, 18: "Se numquid prophetia imponit necessitatem praescientiae? . . ."

[7] For this explicit, not printed by Mandonnet, see Grabmann, *Die Werke*, p. 378.

[8] Cf. Eschmann, "Catalogue," n. 62, p. 418. Scandone, *La vita, la famiglia*, p. 31, rejected the authenticity of this letter.

[9] *Proc. Can. Neap.*, LXXIX (*Fontes*, IV, 377): "Et in itinere invasit ipsum infirmitas in castro Magentie de Campania, de qua postmodum decessit."

While the said Brother Thomas was living and staying at the said castle of Maenza, and had begun to grow somewhat ill because of weakness, he was asked by his companion [Reginald] to take some food, Brother Thomas said to the same companion, "I think that some fresh herrings might be found."

His companion replied, "I think that they are found in the regions beyond the Alps, in the English and French districts."

Now, while they were conversing with each other, a certain fishmonger, called Bordonarius, came as was his custom from Terracina to Maenza with some little fish. The companion of Brother Thomas who was called Brother Reginald of Piperno asked this fish peddler what fish he had. He said sardines. When he had uncovered the boxes in which he carried the said fish, he found one box full of fresh herrings! When they saw this, they were all overjoyed and astonished, because fresh herrings were never found in these parts of Italy. The said fish merchant became more vehement in his astonishment and protested violently that he sold sardines and not herrings.

Hurrying to Brother Thomas, Reginald said to him, "God has fulfilled your request and you have what you desired, for the herrings that you mentioned have been found."

He [Thomas] said, "Where did they come from; who brought them here?"

And he replied, "God sent them to you."[10]

This minor miracle of the fishes suggests that Thomas was hardly aware that he was in the throes of a fatal illness. We are told that Peter of Montesangiovanni saw Thomas eat some of the fish and that, in fact, Peter and the other religious and seculars all enjoyed the herrings. Even the Lady Francesca had some, as Peter assured the interrogators at the canonization proceedings. These learned clerics then asked at what time the herrings were eaten. Peter said he could not remember the month or day (after all, this questioning was more than forty years after the event) but it was in Lent. Then they quizzed Peter on his knowledge of herrings. He replied that he had seen salted herrings at the Roman *Curia* at Viterbo. Moreover, he reminded them that Brother Reginald, a more cosmopolitan traveler, had seen and eaten fresh herrings in the ultramontane regions and he had said they were herrings. Then the interrogators asked the most amazing question of all — how were the herrings cooked? Peter solemnly replied that they were simmered in broth and then sautéed![11]

Thomas' illness grew worse and the kindly Prior James invited him

[10] *Ibid.*, L (*Fontes,* IV, 333).

[11] *Ibid.*, "dixit quod elissitas in brodio et etiam assatas." The Abbot of Fossanova, Brother Nicholas, also an eyewitness of the last days of Thomas, testified that Thomas did not eat the herrings (*ibid.*, IV, 279).

to the Cistercian monastery at nearby Fossanova. It was but six miles away. Here again the testimony of Brother Peter of Montesangiovanni takes up the account:

> After the passage of four days, the aforementioned Brother Thomas rode on horseback [no longer able to walk, it would seem] with the said Prior and monks and other companions away from the castle of Maenza to the said monastery of Fossanova. When he [Thomas] entered the monastery, he uttered these words in the guest room, "This is my rest for ever and ever . . ." [Ps 131:14]. While staying in this monastery his illness began to grow worse. Yet he suffered this illness with great patience, reverently and devotedly received the sacraments of the Church, in particular receiving the Body of Christ with many tears and great devotion.
>
> Before receiving the Body of Christ, he spoke many fitting words concerning the Body of Christ in the presence of the whole congregation of monks of the said monastery and of many from the Order of Preachers and of Minors [Franciscans]. In the midst of this discourse, he uttered these words, "I have taught and written a great deal about this most holy Body and the other sacraments, in the faith of Christ and the holy Roman Church, to whose correction I submit and leave it all."
>
> Then, having received this Body, he lived for three days and on the third day he slept in the Lord.[12]

William of Tocco rather formally records the chronological details, as he knew them, of Aquinas' death.

> The aforementioned Doctor died in the year of Our Lord 1274, in the fourth year of the papacy of Gregory X [his pontificate ran from 1271 to 1276], in the forty-ninth year of his own life, during the second [imperial] indiction, on the seventh of March, in the morning.[13]

On the other hand, Bernard Gui says that death occurred on March 9, 1274, and that Thomas was starting on his fiftieth year.[14] We shall see that, when the investigation for the canonization was held some forty-five years later, several men who knew Thomas Aquinas personally were still alive and a few of them testified concerning his age at death. Brother Octavian [Cistercian] said that Thomas looked about fifty years of age.[15] Brother James de Caiatia, O.P., testified that he met Thomas at Naples and Capua and when he first saw him he could have been about forty-six.[16] Bartholomew of Capua reported that Thomas died in his forty-eighth

[12] *Proc. Can. Neap.*, XLIX (*Fontes*, IV, 332). Tocco, *Vita*, cc. 56–58 (*Fontes*, II, 129–132), gives substantially the same account.

[13] Tocco, *Vita*, c. 65 (*Fontes*, II, 138).

[14] Gui, *Legenda*, c. 39 (in Foster, *Life*, p. 56).

[15] *Fontes*, IV, 286.

[16] *Ibid.*, 318.

year.[17] Brother Nicholas of Piperno [Cistercian] witnessed the death and burial, and he could only say that Thomas appeared to be "fiftyish or sixtyish."[18] So, the general consensus is that Thomas Aquinas lived to be almost fifty years old. His old master, Albert the Great, died in Cologne in 1280. Bonaventure did reach the Council of Lyons, preached a famous sermon on reunion with the Eastern Churches, but died on July 15 in the same year, 1274. Reginald of Piperno lived for fifteen years or so after Thomas Aquinas, dying around 1290.[19]

St. Thomas' funeral was held (we do not know on what day) in the Cistercian church which still stands at Fossanova. Consecrated in 1208, the building is one of the finest examples of Italian Gothic architecture.[20] Many Dominican friars, particularly from the monasteries of Gaeta and Anagni, had come to be with Thomas in his final illness and they stayed for the solemn rites. Bishop Francis of nearby Terracina (a Franciscan) attended with several Friars Minor. Of course, the Cistercians were well aware of the fame and importance of Thomas Aquinas; their abbot and prior saw to it that the ceremonies were conducted with all proper solemnity. Lay people, relatives, and friends of the Aquino family were there in goodly number, for Fossanova is not far distant from Roccasecca. Lady Francesca, Countess of Ceccano, came from Maenza, to attend the last rites for her uncle. She was not permitted to enter the monastery gates, because of the rule of cloister, but the body was carried to the gates so that she might see it. This was the occasion for loud demonstrations of grief. We are told by the early biographers that the mule on which the sick Thomas had been carried from Maenza to Fossanova broke its tether in the stables, ran up to the bier, and fell dead. It was a scene of intense emotion.[21] The body was interred in front of the high altar in the abbey church.[22] The liturgical ceremony of the funeral was that used in Benedictine monasteries.[23]

---

[17] *Ibid.*, 384.

[18] *Ibid.*, 290: "videbatur sibi quod fuerit quinquegenarius vel sexagenarius."

[19] Taurisano, "Discepoli e Biografi di S. Tommaso," *Miscellanea Storico-artistica* (Roma, 1924), p. 121.

[20] For a description and photograph of the nave and choir, with a plan of the whole church building, see H. W. Janson, *History of Art* (Englewood Cliffs, N. J.: Prentice-Hall, 1962), pp. 244–245.

[21] Much the same account is in: Gui, c. 40; Tocco, c. 62; and Peter Calo, c. 30.

[22] *Proc. Can. Neap., Fontes,* IV: for the testimony of Abbot Nicholas, p. 278; of Brother Nicholas de Fresolino, p. 280. Cf. B. Gui, *Legenda,* c. 40 (in Foster, *Life,* p. 56).

[23] See note (a) in *Proc. Can. Neap.,* LI (*Fontes,* IV, 335).

However, Thomas' body was not permitted to rest in peace. Its mutations and pious mutilations make an almost incredible story. The subprior at Fossanova was partially blind, and when he touched the body before it was washed for burial, his sight was fully restored.[24] This was but one of many miraculous cures described in the investigation for the canonization. Now, shortly after the original burial, the body was removed from before the main altar. This is the sworn testimony of the Abbot Nicholas:

> After his death, while the body of Brother Thomas was buried before the altar of the monastery [church], the monks of the monastery began to worry that the corpse might be stolen, so they secretly transferred the body from this sepulcher to a chapel, called the chapel of St. Stephen, within the same monastery. Then, after the passage of about seven months, Brother Thomas appeared in a dream to Brother James [of Ferentino], Prior of the monastery . . . and said to him: "Return me to the original place." This return was accomplished with due solemnity by the monks of the monastery. . . . When the sepulcher was opened, such a fragrance came forth that the chapel and cloister of the monastery was filled with the sweetest odor. With all the monks assembled, he [the Prior] then celebrated Mass for Brother Thomas, as for a holy confessor, chanting the *Os justi,* etc. They felt that it was not fitting to sing the [ordinary] Mass for the Dead, since they regarded him as a saintly man.[25]

Less than two years later, in 1276, the Dominican Peter of Tarentaise (one of Aquinas' colleagues in his first Paris professorate) became Pope Innocent V. The Cistercians at Fossanova now feared that steps would be taken to remove the body to some Dominican center, so they again uncovered it. Here we may take up the events as found in the testimony of Bartholomew of Capua:

> When about eight months had elapsed, the rumor circulated that Brother Peter of Tarentaise, O.P., was to become Pope and that he wished the corpse of Brother Thomas to be transferred to some more worthy location belonging to the Friars Preachers; for this reason, the monks of the monastery of Fossanova grew fearful that they would lose the body of Brother Thomas. So, they selected three representatives and one night they exhumed the corpse of Brother Thomas from its resting place. They cut off the head and placed it in a hiding place in a corner of the chapel which lies behind the Choir (which the present witness has seen several times). Their thinking was that, if the said body were lost, at least the head would remain with them. The same witness heard from Brother Peter of Montesangiovanni and another Brother Siculus,

[24] Testimony of Brother Peter de Montesangiovanni (Cist.) who was an eyewitness. *Proc. Can. Neap.*, LI (*Fontes,* IV, 335).

[25] *Ibid.*, VIII (*Fontes,* IV, 278).

> subprior at the time, that it was said that the whole body was uncorrupted and had suffered no diminution or change, nor had the hair fallen from the head. Of course, one had to except the hand which his sister, the Countess of San Severino had taken, and a certain indentation at the point of the nose much like a mouse bite. . . .[26]

By this time the saintly body was rather badly mutilated. Another witness, John of Buiano, O.P., swore that Reginald of Piperno removed a thumb from the hand which was taken by Teodora. This thumb was given by Reginald to Bishop Hugh of Ostia.[27] The same witness testified that Teodora acquired her brother's hand almost fifteen years after Thomas' death. This is explained more fully by Nicholas of Piperno (Cistercian):

> Again, about fourteen years after his [Thomas'] demise, at the urging of his sister, Lady Teodora, the Countess, his sepulcher was opened. Since the Lady had asked to have some relics of her brother Thomas, he [Peter of Montesangiovanni] gave her a hand from the corpse of Brother Thomas. . . .[28]

Teodora's son, Count Thomas of Marsico, later gave this hand to the Dominicans at Salerno.[29]

In 1303, another Dominican became pope (Benedict XI) and the Cistercians again became apprehensive, so they moved the body still another time. This was by no means the end of ghoulish activities. At some time before the first canonization investigation (A.D. 1319) the corpse was boiled until only the bones remained![30] William of Tocco testified under oath that he saw the bones in a casket which was now kept by a lay sacristan in the sacristy of the monastery at Fossanova.[31] There is later testimony concerning this mutilation of the corpse. Pope Urban V, in 1368, after much legal maneuvering on the part of the Dominicans and the Cistercians, finally ordered that the corpse (such as it was) be turned over to the Order of Preachers. According to an old French life of St. Thomas,[32] the Count of Fondi (apparently a descendant

---

[26] *Ibid.*, LXXX (*Fontes*, IV, 380).

[27] *Ibid.*, LXXXIX (*Fontes*, IV, 394).

[28] *Ibid.*, XX (*Fontes*, IV, 291–292). William of Tocco, *Vita*, c. 68 (*Fontes*, II, 141) says that the right hand was given to Teodora.

[29] *Proc. Can. Neap.*, XCV (*Fontes*, IV, 402).

[30] Cf. Foster, *Life*, p. 81.

[31] *Proc. Can. Neap.*, LXV (*Fontes*, IV, 354).

[32] A. Touron, *La vie de saint Thomas* (Paris, 1740), pp. 287–297; Touron claims to base his account on a manuscript (not otherwise identified) in the Vatican Library.

of Roger d'Aquila and Thomas' sister, Adelasia) gained possession of the remains of the torso in the year 1349. The Bishop of Lucca, at the order of Pope Urban V, in 1368, claimed the head from the monastery at Fossanova and returned it to the care of the Dominican Master General.[33] During the same year, 1368, the bones were sent to the Dominican monastery at Toulouse, France. A witness who viewed the bones at this time said that they were, "of a reddish color, looking as if by boiling, or some other change effected by heat, they had been violently detached from the flesh."[34]

These bones remained at the Dominican monastery, Toulouse, until the French Revolution required their removal to the Church of St. Sernin, Toulouse, where they are kept today. A bone from the left arm is said to be in the Naples cathedral and the right arm is claimed by the Church of the Minerva in Rome.[35] Thus ends the gloomy story of the mortal remains of St. Thomas Aquinas.

That some sort of mystery attended the premature death of Thomas Aquinas is clear from later legends which are found in fourteenth-century writings. The poet, Dante, knew a great deal about the life and thought of Thomas Aquinas and frequently mentioned him in the *Divine Comedy* which was written within a quarter century of the saint's death. In one place,[36] Dante has Thomas clearly identify himself as the pupil of Albert the Great.

> He who is nearest me on my right was my brother and master; he is Albert of Cologne, and I am Thomas of Aquino.

Now, in another section of the *Divine Comedy,* we find three enigmatic lines:[37]

> Charles (of Anjou) came to Italy, and
> He made a victim of Conradin; and then
> He sent Thomas to heaven,

A few years after the death of Dante (1321) a commentary on the *Divine Comedy* written by Jacopo della Lana offers the following explanation of the lines just quoted:

---

[33] *Ibid.,* p. 295.

[34] English version from Foster, *Life,* p. 81, citing C. Douais, *Les reliques de saint Thomas d'Aquin,* p. 84. Cf. Mandonnet, "La canonisation de s. Thomas d'Aquin," *Mélanges Thomistes* (Le Saulchoir, 1923), p. 18.

[35] Foster, *Life,* p. 81.

[36] *Paradiso,* X, lines 97–99.

[37] *Purgatorio,* XX, lines 67–69.

It should be understood that St. Thomas Aquinas of the Order of Preachers, after being a Master at Paris, lived at Naples where the aforesaid Charles [II, King of Naples] had wished to have him near at hand to take counsel with him, which he did many times. In the course of time his Excellency the Pope ordered a Council at Lyons, on the Rhone river in Provence. Invitations were issued and calls went forth quickly to all the noted clerics; among the others, the aforesaid Thomas was ordered to attend. When the day arrived for the departure of St. Thomas from Naples, he went to take his leave of Charles and to find out whether Charles had any message which he wished to give him.

The King said to him: "Brother Thomas, if the Pope inquires about me, what answer will you give?"

And St. Thomas replied: "I'll simply tell him the truth." [*Io dirò pure la verità.*]

Now St. Thomas left to go to Lyons and the King thought over Thomas' words. He grew afraid that if the truth were known about his activities, it would displease everyone and cause much bad feeling. The physician who had charge of the King's person came to him and asked what was wrong. The King told him and the physician said: "Sire, if you wish, the remedy has been found."

The King said: "I do wish something done." The aforesaid physician got on a horse and with some attendants who suited him rode night and day until he caught up with him.

Then he said to Brother Thomas: "His Excellency the King is much disturbed at your leaving without a physician who would take care of your person on this trip and so he has commanded me to come and care for you."

The Friar thanked him for what he had done and said: "May the will of the Lord be done."

Two days later the physician used what was necessary of a poison, through which the aforesaid Brother went to another life.[38]

The same story, that Thomas Aquinas was poisoned at the order of the Emperor Charles of Anjou, is repeated in many Dante commentaries.[39] In a shorter Latin account, Peter Allighieri bluntly states another reason for the Emperor's action: "Then Charles . . . had Thomas of Aquino put to death while he was going to the Roman Curia, suspecting as it was thought that he might become Pope, and on the way he had him killed by means of poison."[40]

[38] The Old Italian text is printed in *Doc.* LVI (*Fontes,* VI, 669–671); the rough translation is my own.

[39] For further details, see the notes by M. H. Laurent, O.P., in *Fontes,* VI, 670–671.

[40] "Inde Karolus . . . occidi fecit Thomam de Aquino dum iret in curiam Romanam, suspicatus ne papa fieret, ut credebatur, et in itinere fecit veneno extingui." Cited in *Fontes,* VI, 671, note 1, from *Petri Allegherii super Dantis ipsius genitoris Comoediam commentarium* (Firenze, 1845), p. 436.

This grotesque legend is doubtless the fabrication of overactive Italian imaginations. Yet it indicates one interesting point: not only do we not know what illness brought about St. Thomas' early demise, literate men in Italy within a generation or two of his death were ignorant of the details of the last days of one of their best known scholars.

Within two months of Thomas' death the news had reached the University of Paris. It elicited a quick response from the arts faculty. They wrote a letter, dated May 2, 1274, which is important enough to be quoted here almost in its entirety.[41]

> To the venerable Fathers in Christ, the Master-General and Provincials of the Order of Friars Preacher and to all brethren assembled at the general chapter meeting at Lyons — the Rector of the University of Paris, the Procurators [of the four national groups of students, French, Normans, Picards, and English] and the rest of the professors in Arts at Paris send greetings, in Him who doth savingly dispose of all things and careth wisely for the whole universe. . . .
>
> [There follows a florid rhetorical peroration to the effect that the world has come on bad times.]
>
> News has been received, which brings sorrow and a wail of lamentation, which transports the mind of each of us to unaccustomed and unheard of feelings, causing inestimable astonishment — news which, at long last, has transfixed our innermost parts, which in a sense has penetrated to our hearts' depths with deadly effect. We confess that we can hardly express ourselves; love restrains us indeed, but sorrow and vehement anguish compel us to speak out; we have learned the definite news that Brother Thomas of Aquino has been called from this world. Who could have thought that divine Providence would permit the morning star which shines over the world, the beacon and light of this world, yea, to speak more truthfully, a greater light than that which heralds the day, to withdraw his rays of light? . . .
>
> And why do we now vainly dwell upon such words? He [Thomas] whom we, alas, could not obtain from your assembly at the Chapter meeting at Florence [1272] but to whose memory we remain grateful — such a great cleric, such a priest, such a teacher — he whom we could not regain while he was alive in spite of our dedicated affection, we now at his death humbly beg of you, that his bones may be given the utmost care — for it is quite unfitting and inappropriate that an alien earth or another place than the City of Paris, the noblest center of all studies, *which first educated, nourished and cherished him* and later received ineffable nourishment and education from him, should keep his bones buried and entombed. For, if the Church properly honors the bones and relics of the saints, it seems that we, not without reason, should be ever established in the hearts of our successors by virtue of his burial here.

[41] Latin text in *Fontes,* VI, 583–586; a full English version is in Foster, *Life,* pp. 153–155.

In the hope that you will accede to this, our pious petition, we further humbly beg that your kindness will procure and send quickly to us certain writings of philosophical importance which were begun by him at Paris but left unfinished at his departure, yet which we believe he completed in that place to which he was transferred. In particular: The *Commentary* of Simplicius on the treatise *De Coelo et mundo,* and the *Exposition of Plato's Timaeus,* and the book on the *Transportation of Water and the Erection of Engineering Works,* are works which he especially promised to have sent to us. If he composed likewise, any works pertaining to logic (such as we humbly requested of him when he left us), may your kindness deign to share them with our Faculty. . . .

We order this Letter to be sealed with the seal of our Rector and Procurators. Given at Paris in the year of Our Lord MCCLXXIV, on the Wednesday preceding the Feast of the Finding of the Holy Cross [May 3, 1274].

In spite of its flowery rhetoric, this is a very touching document. We may note the extraordinary tone of affection on the part of professors in the faculty of arts for a man who had neither taught nor studied in their division of the University of Paris. Whatever the role of Thomas Aquinas in the controversies of 1269–1272 at Paris, we can be sure that he never alienated the majority of the arts teachers. It is to be emphasized that this letter is not some document from a later century but was written within two years of his departure from Paris by men who knew him well. The unusual request, that the Dominican Order send back Thomas' body for burial in Paris, was never granted, of course. But it shows the affection that they felt for Aquinas as their academic colleague.

Second, we should notice that the letter is the first document to recognize the personal saintliness of Thomas Aquinas. They quite clearly indicate the parallel between the relics of the saints and the "worthy and saintly body" (*honestum et sanctum tanti doctoris corpus*) of their friend. This was written forty-nine years before the official canonization of St. Thomas. Remember, too, that this official document was written by scholars who were themselves Catholic priests. In his comment on this letter, Kenelm Foster, makes the point that "the students in Arts were boys in their teens."[42] However, this should not mislead us as to the status of the writers of this letter. It was written by masters of arts, marked with the seal of the university rector (probably Master Albericus of Rheims),[43] and issued as an official university document.

---

[42] *Life,* p. 155, note 1.

[43] Cf. Mandonnet, *Siger de Brabant,* I, 198–208. Peter of Auvergne was designated rector in the early months of 1275; it is even possible that Siger of Brabant had something to do with the writing of this letter.

CHAPTER EIGHTEEN

The Golden Wisdom

"WE EARNESTLY exhort you, venerable brethren, to restore the golden wisdom of St. Thomas," wrote Pope Leo XIII in 1879.[1] This is one of the best known quotations from the famous letter which touched off the modern revival of interest in Aquinas' personality and thought. Pope Leo reviewed the repeated approvals of Thomism that are found in the words of nearly all the Roman pontiffs in the years since his canonization.[2] He also spoke with sorrow of the neglect into which the golden wisdom had fallen in Christian schools. The encyclical *Aeterni Patris* ended with a challenge to modern Catholic scholarship to adopt and carry on the spirit of St. Thomas' scholarship in the present day.

We do not propose to investigate here this story of the modern Thomistic revival. Instead, we shall look in this final chapter at what happened to the reputation and thought of Thomas Aquinas during the fifty years that followed his death. Many of his contemporaries and immediate successors felt that his wisdom was anything but golden. Still, there were always some who appreciated, at least in part, the heritage of Aquinas.

One way of judging the ability of a teacher is to examine the record of his students. If we applied this test to Thomas, we would have to conclude that he was not a successful teacher; for it is very difficult to find an outstanding thinker among the members of his immediate school. Certain men, like Giles of Rome and Henry of Ghent, are still remembered

[1] *Aeterni Patris*, in *The Church Speaks to Modern World*, ed. E. Gilson (New York: Doubleday, 1954), pp. 31–51; the quotation is from p. 50.

[2] For details of these encomia by many popes, see: J. Maritain, *The Angelic Doctor: the Life and Thought of St. Thomas Aquinas*, trans. J. W. Evans and P. O'Reilly (New York: Meridian Books, 1958).

in the history of scholasticism but they are no longer regarded as Thomists. They thoroughly misunderstood Aquinas and, in fact, opposed him on many basic issues. Even within the Dominican Order, no scholar was found with the ability to carry on his work. Various people collected and edited his works. Several men wrote completions for the unfinished writings. Generally speaking, these jobs were done badly. Much of our present difficulty with the text and chronology of the Thomistic writings could have been obviated by Reginald of Piperno, if he had seen fit to write down what he knew about Thomas Aquinas. To this date, no one has been able to find anything that Reginald surely wrote.

Peter of Auvergne may be taken as typical of these first-generation "Thomists." He has been pictured as a devoted follower of Aquinas.[3] Peter did write some of the complements that are now printed at the end of Thomas' unfinished commentaries on Aristotle, notably for the *Politics, On Generation and Corruption,* and *On the Heavens.* He had been designated rector of the university of Paris in 1275, and was doubtless one of those who admired Thomas in the arts faculty. Peter taught liberal arts at the University of Paris until the 1290's and served as professor of theology there from 1296 to 1302.[4] It has long been known that he differed from Thomas on important theological questions;[5] now we know that he disagreed on fundamental philosophical issues.[6] This was not a matter of being an independent-minded student; Peter's tendency was toward a strict Aristotelianism similar to that of Siger of Brabant.

Not only did St. Thomas' students fail to understand him; there is much evidence of open antagonism to the whole thrust of Thomism during the 1270's. At Paris, Bishop Etienne Tempier (a former professor himself) was still worried by the prevalence of erroneous teachings at the university. We have seen how he condemned thirteen propositions in 1270. Apparently this preliminary act of censorship was ineffective. Bishop Tempier

[3] M. Grabmann, *Die Werke,* p. 297, cites a fourteenth-fifteenth-century note from a Toledo manuscript of the *Summa Theologiae,* concerning the *Supplement:* "Similiter magister Petrus de Alvernia complevit omnes libros, quos beatus Thomas dimisit incompletos, videlicet istam ultimam partem, libros meteorum, de generatione et corruptione, celi et mundi et alios; et iste doctor fuit sectator doctrine sancti Thome."

[4] Van Steenberghen, *Le Mouvement,* p. 313.

[5] E. Hocedez, "La théologie de Pierre d'Auvergne," *Gregorianum,* XI (1930), 526–552.

[6] A. P. Monahan, "The Subject of Metaphysics for Peter of Auvergne," *Med. Studies,* XVI (1954), 118–130. Monahan notes (p. 130) "the singular lack of favour St. Thomas' doctrine held among his immediate successors."

next called upon a commission of sixteen theologians (including Henry of Ghent) to prepare a more complete list of errors. They must have worked diligently: on March 7, 1277, Tempier issued a resounding condemnation of two hundred and nineteen theses which were now forbidden to be taught in the diocese of Paris.[7] Approximately twenty of these "erroneous" propositions partially represent teachings of Thomas Aquinas. Without naming Aquinas, the Bishop forbade teaching such views as these: that a separate substance which moves nothing is not part of the universe; that individuals differ only by virtue of their matter; that separated substances exist in no place; that all intellects are basically possessed of the same power and that differences of actual intelligence stem from the body; that the will is determined by intellectual cognition.[8] In effect, many basic themes in Thomism were now called errors at Paris.[9] While Thomas was not formally named by Tempier, it was soon generally recognized that certain of his views were included in this condemnation.[10] Not until February 14, 1325 (after the canonization of St. Thomas), did Bishop Etienne Bourret of Paris remove this censorship, insofar as it applied to Thomas.[11]

Within ten days of Tempier's action, Robert Kilwardby (now Archbishop of Canterbury) moved to condemn thirty "erroneous" teachings in his diocese.[12] These were points in grammar, logic, and natural philosophy that were not to the liking of the former Dominican. Seven of the propositions in natural philosophy (Numbers 17, 21, 24, 26, 27, 28, and

---

[7] The text of Tempier's famous condemnation of 1277 is printed in *C.U.P.*, I, 543–558; reprinted with some corrections in *Fontes,* VI, 596–614; with a different numbering, in Mandonnet, *Siger de Brabant,* 2me éd., II, 175–191.

[8] For a detailed list of the propositions that approximate the thought of Thomas Aquinas, Gilson, *Hist. of Christ Philos.,* p. 728.

[9] For a historical study of this and associated acts of ecclesiastical censorship in the period: J. Koch, "Philosophische und theologische Irrtumslisten von 1270–1329. Ein Beitrag zur Entwickelung der theologischen zensuren," in *Mélanges Mandonnet,* II, 305–329.

[10] Koch, *art. cit.,* p. 307, lists *Quodlibets* by Godfrey of Fontaine, Gervais de Mont Saint-Eloi, and John of Naples which make this clear. John's *Quodl.,* VI, q. 2, is: Utrum doctrina fratris Thomae quantum ad omnes conclusiones possit licite doceri Parisius. (John lists, by number, various Thomistic theses in Tempier's condemnation.)

[11] *Doc.* LV (*Fontes,* VI, 666–669). The operative phrase in the lengthy episcopal letter is: "supradictam articulorum condemnationem et excommunicationis sententiam, quantum tangunt vel tangere asseruntur doctrinam beati Thome predicti, ex certa scientia tenore presentium totaliter annullamus. . . ."

[12] *Ibid.,* XXXIX (*Fontes,* VI, 615–617); dated March 18, 1277.

30) are obviously Thomistic in character. They are principally views concerning the passivity of prime matter, the type of distinction that obtains between matter and form, and, of course, the unity of the substantial form in one material substance. Kilwardby never liked Thomism and he wasted no time in showing his dislike. To put teeth into his disapproval, he ended his edict with these words:

> He who supports, teaches or defends any of the aforementioned theses, as a result of his own intention, if he is a master he may be deposed by common counsel from the office of master, if he is a bachelor he may not be promoted to the magistrate but may be expelled from the University [Oxford].[13]

Ten years later (April 30, 1286), another man whose name we know, John Peckham, had become Archbishop of Canterbury. Acting as Primate of England, with the concurrence of three other English bishops and of several British theologians, Peckham formally renewed Kilwardby's edict.[14] John Peckham was, of course, the Franciscan theologian who had come into open conflict with Aquinas around 1270. He particularly condemned the "presumptuous opinion" that there is but one substantial form in a composite.

Thus, within fifteen years of his death, a portion of Thomas Aquinas' doctrine was under condemnation by three bishops—one a former diocesan professor of theology, the second a fellow Dominican, the third a noted Franciscan scholar. By 1277, under serious ecclesiastical penalties, Thomistic views were forbidden to be taught at the two greatest universities in Christendom, Paris and Oxford.[15] It was not a propitious start for a future Doctor of the Church.

For the next forty years or so (1280–1320), continual bickering occurred between the supporters and the opponents of Thomism. It was the period of the so-called "Correctorial" literature.[16] Stimulated in part by the widespread criticism of Thomas, but also moved by a growing realization of the significance of his thought, the Dominican officials began to rally to the support of Thomism. The General Chapter

---

13 *Ibid.*, 617.

14 *Ibid.*, XLVI (*Fontes*, VI, 647–648).

15 Cf. D. Callus, *The Condemnation of St. Thomas at Oxford* (Westminster, Md.: Newman Press, 1946).

16 Cf. A. Maurer, *Medieval Philosophy* (New York: Random House, 1962), pp. 208–219; for more complete bibliography on the Correctorial writings and studies of them, see E. Gilson, *Hist. of Christ. Philos.*, pp. 410–427, 730–735.

at Milan (June, 1278) ordered two lectors from France (Raymond de Mévouillon and Jean Vigouroux) to make a hurried trip to England, there to inquire into the "scandalous detractions" of some of the British Friars Preacher against the writings of "the venerable Father, Brother Thomas de Aquino."[17] A year later (June, 1279), the General Chapter at Paris ordered Dominican superiors in all provinces to punish severely any irreverent or unfitting talk about the person or writings of Thomas Aquinas.[18] That these formal efforts to defend Thomas within the Dominican Order were deemed necessary is itself a good indication of the contemporary state of affairs.

Yet his writings were being read — and not only by Dominicans. About the year 1280, an English Franciscan scholar, William de la Mare, prepared a sort of commentary on selected portions of Aquinas' major writings (sixty-three articles from the *Summa of Theology,* twenty-four from the *Disputed Questions,* nine from the *Quodlibets,* and another nine questions from the *Commentary on Book I of the Sentences*). William's purpose was to "correct" the doctrine of these passages, so that his fellow Franciscans would be able to detect the errors when reading Thomas. At their general chapter in Strasbourg (1282), the Franciscan authorities ordered their provincial ministers to require that all copies of Aquinas' *Summa of Theology,* in the use of Franciscan lectors in theology, be accompanied in the text by the "Declarations" of Brother William de la Mare.[19] Soon an English Dominican (either Thomas of Sutton or Richard Clapwell) wrote a set of "corrections" of William's "corruptions"! The text of this amazing contribution to the literature of Catholic intellectualism was widely circulated in manuscript and has received a modern edition.[20] There is a sort of comic-opera quality about these attacks and counterattacks, but the situation was not amusing to those immediately involved.

More and more Dominicans, from various provinces, now rose to the defense of Thomas Aquinas. John of Paris, O.P., produced his *Correctorium Corruptorii "Circa";* Robert of Orford, O.P., issued his *Correctorium "Sciendum";* another Englishman, William of Macclesfield, O.P., wrote a *Correctorium "Quaestione."* By 1290, an Italian, Rambert of

[17] *Doc.* XLI (*Fontes,* VI, 621).

[18] *Ibid.,* 622.

[19] *Ibid.,* XLIII (*Fontes,* VI, 624–625).

[20] P. Glorieux has edited the work of William de la Mare, plus the Dominican response, in: *Les premiers polémiques thomistes. I. Le "Correctorium Corruptorii QUARE* (Kain: Bibliothèque Thomiste, 1927).

Bologna, O.P., had entered the fray with a new title: *Apologeticum veritatis contra Corruptorium*. Most of these controversial writings have only been discovered, in manuscript, comparatively recently and are not yet in print. Probably other items in the Correctorial literature remain to be identified.

About the year 1282, Roger Marston, O.F.M., circulated the rumor that an opinion of Thomas Aquinas (concerning the type of distinction that obtains among the Persons of the divine Trinity) was "excommunicated" at Paris back in 1270.[21] Between 1284 and 1287, John Peckham, as Archbishop of Canterbury, sent a series of letters to various officials of Oxford University and to other ecclesiastical personages. These letters emphasized the doctrinal differences that had arisen between the Dominican and Franciscan Orders, frequently mentioned the unfortunate errors that Aquinas had introduced into Christian learning, and expressed the wish that the Pope would soon act to separate the wheat from the chaff.[22] Peckham's disagreement with Aquinas mainly concerned philosophical questions, but this Archbishop would have been shocked at the suggestion that there was anything "golden" about the wisdom of Thomas.

At the same time (1286–1324), various chapter meetings in the Order of Preachers (Paris, Cologne, Metz, London, Bologna, Rouen, Vienne, and Bordeaux) forcefully enjoined the study of Thomas Aquinas' writings and general respect for his doctrine. By 1313, the chapter of Metz was ordering: "No one may be sent to the Paris *studium*, unless he has diligently studied the doctrine of Brother Thomas for at least three years."[23] Much of the internal Dominican opposition to Thomism was a phenomenon of the English Province, possibly due to the influence of Robert Kilwardby. However, anti-Thomism was not confined to England. In Italy, a young Florentine, named Uberto Guidi, O.P., openly attacked some features of Thomism. The provincial chapter at Arezzo in 1315 castigated his disrespect, suspended all his scholarly functions for two years, removed him from the Florence to the Pistoria monastery, and assigned him to a ten-day fast on bread and water as a punishment![24]

By the beginning of the fourteenth century, the Dominicans of the new

---

[21] R. Marston, *Quaestiones disputatae de Emanatione aeterna* (Bibliotheca Franciscana, VII) (Quaracchi, 1932), pp. 116–117.

[22] Peckham's letters on this matter are reprinted in *Fontes,* VI, 627–648.

[23] "Nullus etiam ad studium Parisiense mittatur, nisi in doctrina fratris Thome saltem tribus annis studuerit diligenter." *Fontes,* VI, 656.

[24] *Ibid.,* 661–662.

Neapolitan Province began to hope that Brother Thomas of Aquino might be formally recognized as a saint.[25] The Provincial, Nicholas Brunacci, had known Brother Thomas from the time of the second Paris professorate and much favored the idea of canonization. Of course, William of Tocco was eager to promote the cause, and he began to assemble information on the life and works of the prospective saint. William had been with Thomas at Naples and was acquainted with many relatives and friends of the Aquino family. Tocco was himself a distinguished figure in the province, having been made a preacher general in 1288.[26] John XXII became pope in 1316, during the period when the papal residence was at Avignon, France. He proved to be very favorable to the movement for canonization. The provincial chapter in 1317 met at Gaeta (not far from the birthplace of Aquinas, Gaeta was the town from which the great Thomist, Cardinal Cajetan, took his name in the Renaissance) and directed two Brothers, William of Tocco and Robert of San Valentino, to prepare and present the required documents at the papal court.[27] After gathering what material he could in support of the petition, Tocco (now in his seventies) made the trip to Avignon and was cordially received by Pope John. In fact, the Pope assured the elderly Dominican: "We believe that Brother Thomas is a glorious saint in Heaven, for his life was saintly and his teaching was not possible without a miracle."[28] Probably no promoter of a cause has ever had a better reception at the papal court. Pope John was much impressed by letters of approval from the dowager Queen Mary of Sicily and other officials in the Sicilian government. A papal commission of non-Dominican cardinals was appointed to examine the documentation supplied by William of Tocco. Of course, the *Life of St. Thomas Aquinas* by Tocco, which is the source of much of our present information, was a part of this dossier submitted at Avignon.

William found two men already at Avignon who gave added support to his efforts, if anything more was needed. Bartholomew of Lucca, the Dominican author of the *Ecclesiastical History* in which Thomas Aquinas

---

[25] The Sicilian Province (including Naples and south Italy) was formed by partition of the Roman Province in 1294. A. Walz, *Compendium Historiae Ordinis Praedicatorum*, ed. 2a (Roma: Angelicum, 1948), pp. 123, 142.

[26] Cf. Foster, *Life*, pp. 6–7.

[27] A. Walz, "Historia canonizationis S. Thomae de Aquino," in *Xenia Thomistica*, III (Rome, 1925), 105–172.

[28] Tocco, *Vita*, Suppl. 12 (*Fontes*, II, 148).

had already figured, was there and eager to help. So was another prominent Dominican, Bernard Gui, now the procurator general of the Order. Doubtless these influential friars (Bartholomew had been raised to the episcopacy) compared information on Thomas Aquinas. One of the earliest Latin biographies was written by Gui.[29] There is, however, little information in it that was not in Tocco's *Life,* which appears to be the first.

Pope John appointed the Archbishop of Naples, the Bishop of Viterbo, and a notary (Pandolfo de Sabbello) to conduct a formal investigation at Naples into the life and works of Thomas Aquinas.[30] The canonization proceedings at Naples were duly held at the Archbishop's residence, from July 21 to September 18, 1319. Many Dominicans, several Cistercians from Fossanova, and some lay people were interviewed and asked to tell, under oath, what they knew about Thomas and his reputation. Ten of the witnesses were people who had been personally acquainted with Aquinas, or had heard him preaching, during the last years in Naples and, of course, at Fossanova. Some of the testimony was from witnesses who had simply heard of his reputation for holiness. Many told of apparently miraculous cures effected during Thomas' lifetime and after his death.[31] Today St. Thomas is remembered chiefly as a great theologian; to many of these witnesses he was, rather, a holy man whose powers of intercession were remarkable.

William of Tocco and two notaries who substituted for the absent Pandolfo de Sabbello brought the records of the Naples investigation to Avignon in the winter of 1319–1320. After more than a year had elapsed, in June of 1321, Pope John directed William to return to Italy and gather more complete information about miracles that had occurred after Thomas' death. Many witnesses from the region about Fossanova and the countryside of Aquino had been unable to go to Naples for the first proceedings. Thus the indefatigable old Brother William went back and arranged for a second investigation at the Cistercian monastery of Fossanova. Appointed by the Pope to take charge of these proceedings

---

[29] Edited by D. Prümmer in *Fontes,* III, 168–263; translated in Foster, *Life,* pp. 25–58.

[30] The papal letter is in *Fontes,* IV, 269–271; it is dated at Avignon, September 13, 1318.

[31] Some sample passages from this Naples testimony have been translated in Foster, *Life,* pp. 82–119; the original Latin transcript is in *Fontes,* IV, 273–407. We have used much of this material earlier.

were the Bishops of Anagni and Terracina, together with the notary, Pandolfo. Testimony was taken at Fossanova from November 10 to 20, 1321.[32] Again Pandolfo was absent.

At this investigation many more Cistercians were heard and the details of Thomas' last days and death were well covered. Also, about one hundred lay people (men and women) from the Terra di Lavoro were heard. They made it very clear that a local cult of the saintly Tommaso d'Aquino had spontaneously developed in southern Italy. Many of these simple country people did not know their own ages (which they were invariably asked when being sworn in), but they were quite sure that Brother Thomas was indeed a saint. They told of dozens of wonderful cures that had come about through his intercession. To determine the precise nature of their manifold ailments is not easy (the proceedings were conducted in the vernacular and then translated into Latin for the official record) but at least one striking fact comes to light from a careful reading of the record. Sufferers from arthritis and rheumatism might do well to take Thomas Aquinas as their patron and intercessor.

In due time the Fossanova proceedings were brought to Avignon — but not by William of Tocco. He died before the final decision was made to canonize Thomas. Papal approval was now given the cause and the canonization was formally proclaimed at Avignon on July 18, 1323.[33]

From two complementary accounts by eyewitnesses (one anonymous and the other by a Brother Bentius, O.P., from Bologna) we have a rather full description of the ceremonies and festivities in Avignon. At the public consistory, Pope John XXII preached first on the holiness of Thomas' life and the eminence of his teaching. This papal discourse ended with the announcement that Thomas Aquinas was worthy of being inscribed in the catalogue of the saints.[34] Then Brother Peter Canterius, O.P., representing the ailing John of Naples, replied as promoter of the cause. After that, King Robert of Sicily (who was there with the Queen) spoke on the text: "He was the lamp, burning and shining" (Jn 5:35). A series of bishops then added their encomia: the Dominican Patriarch of Alexandria, the Archbishop of Capua, the Bishop of Winchester in England, and the Archbishop of Arles. As a crowning gesture of goodwill, the final speaker on this first day was Bishop Jean de Tixanderie, a

---

[32] *Proc. Can. Fossae-novae, Fontes,* V, 417–510.

[33] The date is given in an anonymous record, *Fontes,* V, 513.

[34] *Ibid.,* 514.

Franciscan, who added his voice to the general acclaim. The anonymous account adds: "Nor were there then heard so many commendations of St. Thomas, as from this man."[35]

Three days later, in the Church of Notre-Dame des Doms in Avignon, Pope John celebrated the Mass of St. Thomas and preached on the text: "For thou art great and dost wonderful things" (Ps 85:10). Before the King and Queen and a great crowd of notable ecclesiastics, Thomas Aquinas was now declared a saint. The King proclaimed to the whole city of Avignon that festivities were to be held on a par with those of Christmas! The Dominicans of the monastery of Avignon offered a reception which was attended by King Robert and his Queen. For two more days, special Masses were celebrated. On one of these days, Thomas' nephew, Count Thomas of San Severino, provided a sumptuous banquet.[36] As the wide-eyed Brother Bentius concluded his report to his superiors in Bologna, "The actual occurrence of the solemnity exceeds my words."[37]

There will always be accountants. We even have four carefully preserved documents which record the expenses for the various banquets given at the time of the canonization. Many gold florins were paid out for soup, fowl, eggs, beef carcasses, and fish. There was even a special account for the dishwashers. On the margin of one of these accounts, some diligent clerk noted: "It was the canonization of St. Thomas of Aquino; the King and seven Lord Cardinals ate."[38]

In the *Bull of Canonization,* Pope John briefly reviewed the highlights of St. Thomas' life and character. He listed a few of the many miracles that had been attributed to him. Just before describing these ten miracles, the Pope made a very penetrating remark: "His life was attested to by miracles, yet this man's miracles simply carry forward the testimony of his own life."[39] Pope John saw that Thomas' life and teaching were at least as much a miracle as the great things that were later done in his name.

What made St. Thomas' wisdom golden was not the philosophical, or even the theological, detail of his thought. He left an example of what can be done by a Christian scholar who is willing and able to learn from any source of information. His mind was open to the insights of pagan philosophers, of Mohammedan and Jewish sages, of the long tradition of

---

[35] *Ibid.,* 515.
[36] *Ibid.,* 518.
[37] "Solemnitatis veritas superat verba mea." *Ibid.,* 518.
[38] *Ibid.,* 531–532.
[39] *Ibid.,* 524.

Greek and Latin Christian Fathers. Thomas was able to admit his own limitations: there were things that he never understood; there were times when he could only resort to prayer. The myth of an Aquinas who knew all the answers is a false construction of overzealous followers. Yet Thomas was always optimistic and hopeful in his quest for truth: with God's help, he approached every problem in a spirit of confidence. Neither pessimism nor skepticism held any virtue for him. He did not pretend that he had solved all the riddles of reality and life; he kept looking for ever better answers; and he enjoyed the challenge of his search.

This spirit of his life cries out in one of the most memorable sentences in all his writings.[40]

> Of all the pursuits open to men, the search for wisdom is more perfect, more sublime, more profitable, and more full of joy.

[40] "Inter omnia vero hominum studia sapientiae studium est perfectius, sublimius, utilius et iucundius." *Summa contra Gentiles,* I, 2.

Index